AFTER SAID

By the time of his death in 2003, Edward Said was one of the most famous literary critics of the twentieth century. Said's work has been hugely influential far beyond academia. As a prominent advocate for the Palestinian cause and noted cultural critic, Said redefined the role of the public intellectual. This volume explores the problems and opportunities afforded by Said's work: its productive and generative capacities as well as its inbuilt limitations. *After Said* captures the essence of Said's intellectual and political contribution and his extensive impact on postcolonial studies. It examines his legacy by critically elaborating his core concepts and arguments. Among the issues it tackles are humanism, Orientalism, culture and imperialism, exile and the contrapuntal, realism and postcolonial modernism, world literature, Islamophobia, and capitalism and the political economy of empire. It is an excellent resource for students, graduates, and instructors studying postcolonial literary theory and the works of Said.

BASHIR ABU-MANNEH is Reader in Postcolonial Literature and Director of the Centre for Postcolonial Studies at the University of Kent, and author of *The Palestinian Novel: From 1948 to the Present* (2016) and *Fiction of the* New Statesman, *1913–1939* (2011).

AFTER SERIES

This series focuses on the legacy of several iconic figures, and key themes, in the origins and development of literary theory. Each book in the series attempts to isolate the influence, legacy and the impact of thinkers. Each figure addressed not only bequeathed specific concepts and doctrines to literary study, but they effectively opened up new critical landscapes for research. It is this legacy that this series tries to capture, with every book being designed specifically for use in literature departments. Throughout each book the concept of 'After' is used in 3 ways: After in the sense of trying to define what is quintessential about each figure: 'What has each figure introduced into the world of literary studies, criticism and interpretation?' After in a purely chronological sense: 'What comes after each figure?', 'What has his/her influence and legacy been?' and 'How have they changed the landscape of literary studies?' Lastly, After in a practical sense: 'How have their respective critical legacies impacted on an understanding of literary texts?' Each book is a collaborative volume with an international cast of critics and their level is suited for recommended reading on courses.

Published Titles

After Foucault: Culture, Theory and Criticism in the 21st Century
Edited by LISA DOWNING, University of Birmingham

After Derrida: Literature, Theory and Criticism in the 21st Century
Edited by JEAN-MICHEL RABATÉ, University of Pennsylvania

After Lacan: Literature, Theory, and Psychoanalysis in the Twenty-First Century
Edited by ANKHI MUKHERJEE, University of Oxford

After Said: Postcolonial Literary Studies in the Twenty-First Century
Edited by BASHIR ABU-MANNEH, University of Kent

AFTER SAID

*Postcolonial Literary Studies in the
Twenty-First Century*

EDITED BY

BASHIR ABU-MANNEH

University of Kent

CAMBRIDGE
UNIVERSITY PRESS

CAMBRIDGE
UNIVERSITY PRESS

University Printing House, Cambridge CB2 8BS, United Kingdom

One Liberty Plaza, 20th Floor, New York, NY 10006, USA

477 Williamstown Road, Port Melbourne, VIC 3207, Australia

314–321, 3rd Floor, Plot 3, Splendor Forum, Jasola District Centre, New Delhi – 110025, India

79 Anson Road, #06–04/06, Singapore 079906

Cambridge University Press is part of the University of Cambridge.

It furthers the University's mission by disseminating knowledge in the pursuit of education, learning, and research at the highest international levels of excellence.

www.cambridge.org
Information on this title: www.cambridge.org/9781108429177
DOI: 10.1017/9781108554251

First published 2019

Printed in the United Kingdom by TJ International Ltd. Padstow Cornwall

A catalogue record for this publication is available from the British Library.

Library of Congress Cataloging-in-Publication Data
NAMES: Abu-Manneh, Bashir, 1972– editor.
TITLE: After Said : postcolonial literary studies in the 21st century / edited by Bashir Abu-Manneh.
DESCRIPTION: Cambridge, United Kingdom ; New York, NY : Cambridge University Press, 2018. | Series: After series
IDENTIFIERS: LCCN 2018029281 | ISBN 9781108429177 (hardback) | ISBN 9781108453219 (pbk.)
SUBJECTS: LCSH: Said, Edward W.–Influence. | Literature–History and criticism. | Critical theory. | Postcolonialism. | Postcolonialism in literature. | Orientalism.
CLASSIFICATION: LCC PN75.S25 A48 2018 | DDC 801/.95092–dc23
LC record available at https://lccn.loc.gov/2018029281

ISBN 978-1-108-42917-7 Hardback
ISBN 978-1-108-45321-9 Paperback

In memory of the late Raymond Williams
and Edward Said

Contents

Contributors

BASHIR ABU-MANNEH is Reader in Postcolonial Literature and Director of the Centre for Colonial and Postcolonial Studies at the University of Kent, and author of *The Palestinian Novel: From 1948 to the Present* (2016) and *Fiction of the* New Statesman, *1913–1939* (2011).

VIVEK CHIBBER is Professor of Sociology at New York University and author of *Postcolonial Theory and the Specter of Capital* (2013) and *Locked in Place: State-Building and Late Industrialization in India* (2003).

JOE CLEARY is Professor of English at Yale University and author of *Literature, Partition and the Nation-State: Culture and Conflict in Ireland, Israel and Palestine* (2002) and *Outrageous Fortune: Capital and Culture in Modern Ireland* (2007).

JOAN COCKS is Professor of Politics at Mount Holyoke College and author of *On Sovereignty and Other Political Delusions* (2014) and *Passion and Paradox: Intellectuals Confront the National Question* (2002).

SEAMUS DEANE is Professor of English and Irish Studies Emeritus at the University of Notre Dame and author of *Strange Country: Modernity and Nationhood in Irish Writing Since 1790* (1999), *Reading in the Dark* (1996), and *Celtic Revivals: Essays in Modern Irish Literature, 1880–1980* (1987).

KEYA GANGULY is Professor of Cultural Studies and Comparative Literature at the University of Minnesota and author of *Cinema, Emergence, and the Films of Satyajit Ray* (2010) and *States of Exception: Everyday Life and Postcolonial Identity* (2001).

LAUREN M. E. GOODLAD is Professor of English and Comparative Literature at Rutgers University and author of *The Victorian Geopolitical Aesthetic: Realism, Sovereignty and Transnational Experience* (2015) and *Victorian Literature and the Victorian State: Character and Governance in a Liberal Society* (2003).

SAREE MAKDISI is Professor of English and Comparative Literature at the University of California, Los Angeles and author of *Reading William Blake* (2015), *Making England Western: Occidentalism, Race, and Imperial Culture* (2014), *Palestine Inside Out: An Everyday Occupation* (2010), *William Blake and the Impossible History of the 1790s* (2003), and *Romantic Imperialism* (1998).

CONOR MCCARTHY is Lecturer in English at the National University of Ireland Maynooth and author of *The Cambridge Introduction to Edward Said* (2010) and *Modernisation, Crisis and Culture in Ireland, 1969–1992* (2000).

DOUGAL MCNEILL is Senior Lecturer in the School of English, Film, Theatre and Media Studies at Victoria University of Wellington and author of *Forecasts of the Past: Globalisation, History, Realism, Utopia* (2012) and coauthor of *Writing the 1926 General Strike: Literature, Culture, Politics* (2015).

JEANNE MOREFIELD is Professor of Politics at Whitman College and author of *Empires without Imperialism: Anglo-American Decline and the Politics of Deflection* (2014) and *Covenants without Swords: Idealist Liberalism and the Spirit of Empire* (2004).

ROBERT SPENCER is Senior Lecturer in Postcolonial Literature and Culture at the University of Manchester and author of *Cosmopolitan Criticism and Postcolonial Literature* (2010) and coeditor of *For Humanism: Explorations in Theory and Politics* (2017).

Acknowledgments

I would like to gratefully acknowledge the following institutions and individuals in the creation of this volume: the School of English and the Centre for Postcolonial Studies at the University of Kent, Nadia Abu El-Haj, Gilbert Achcar, Vivek Chibber, Alison Donnell, Abdulrazak Gurnah, Ross Hamilton, Nancy Henry, David Herd, Rashid Khalidi, Nivedita Majumdar, and Mariam Said (who generously provided the volume's cover photo).

I owe a warm thank you to the volume's dedicated contributors for their openness and productive engagement. Thanks are also due to Cambridge University Press's commissioning editor Ray Ryan for his encouragement and support, and to his production team.

CHAPTER I

Said's Political Humanism
An Introduction

Bashir Abu-Manneh

In 1967, politics burst into Edward Said's life and changed him instantly and permanently. From a conventional liberal humanist literary critic, ruminating on the relationships between individual author and human existence, Said became a political critic and public intellectual committed to Arab and Palestinian freedom and self-determination. What triggered this transformation was Israel's decisive victory in the June 1967 war in which, in a mere six days, Israel occupied the remainder of Palestine, Syria's Golan Heights, and Egypt's Sinai. The abject defeat of Nasser's Arab nationalism left Arabs reeling in yet another historical crisis of self-examination, less than two decades after the loss of Palestine in 1948. With further domination came new resistance, and Palestinians rose to challenge the new Arab status quo.[1]

In one of his first political essays after 1967, Said would dub this new alternative "Palestinianism." The shift was distinct: "from *being* in exile to *becoming* a Palestinian once again"; from "a political living death" to "vitality" and "a revitalization of thought." For Said, "[A] void, felt by every Palestinian, has been altered by an event into a discontinuity . . . One is inert absence, the other is disconnection that requires reconnection." To describe this new reality a "whole range of Palestinian speech has erupted," including Said's own. A political baptism of a whole people is being announced here: "Previously a classless 'refugee,' since 1967 he [the Palestinian] has become a politicized consciousness with nothing to lose but his refugeedom." Note the language. It echoes Marx and Engels's famous phrase from *The Communist Manifesto*: "The proletarians have nothing to lose but their chains." But Said substitutes a class of workers with a nation of refugees that is coming into political consciousness and determining their own fate. The "new Palestinian ideology," he proudly proclaims, "owes next to nothing to the Western Left," which he saw as either complicit with Israel (like official communism) or contributing nothing to Palestinians.[2] Substituting nation for class and distancing himself from the socialist left are early indications of Said's emerging political orientation: nationalist but neither communist, Marxist, nor internationalist. Said's challenge was now clear: how to contest Israel's occupations and Western empire using the ideological tools and instruments he selected.

The impact of 1967 goes much deeper than Said writing political tracts and analyses of the question of Palestine. Its effect was structural and marked everything Said did afterward. The year 1967 meant a long-lasting intellectual orientation that focused Said's critical faculties on the nexus of colonialism and imperialism in the region and motivated him to locate empire's cultural and political forms within the West's own national cultures. Said's own process of becoming was thus triggered: From being a mainstream literary academic, he would become his generation's most influential cultural critic of empire. To understand the nature and contours of this change is to understand Edward Said: his varied intellectual and cultural investments; his distinct methodological combinations, ambivalences, and anxieties; and his firm anti-imperial principles. During the period of the defeat of the grand narratives of global emancipation (including decolonization and socialism), Said emerges as a defender of the colonized and oppressed. First, as a new species of radical intellectual: anti-imperialist but not socialist; materialist but oblivious to political economy; political but inflating culture in human affairs. Second, as embodying anxious critical energy: in search of anchoring foundations yet profoundly skeptical about their permanence and value. Third, as an endlessly curious mind: engaging with intellectual and political questions beyond the narrow confines of his academic discipline.

How can one characterize the nature of Said's thought and capture the range of his contributions? For someone as prolific and erudite as Said, whose work ranges widely from British fiction, Oriental studies, Middle East politics to music and cultural theory, this is no easy feat. No one volume is adequate for the task, and it is not the aim of this one to be either exhaustive or complete. Before I delineate the specific contribution that this volume aims to make to scholarship on Said and postcolonial studies, I propose to focus on some core features of Said's thought. These may help orient the reader to Said's *oeuvre*. Exactly because Said's work ranges across disciplines and themes, it is essential to identify his core intellectual features to understand what is distinctive about Said as critic and theorist. The features I examine speak to his method and style as well as to his intellectual tendencies and critical dispositions. I have clustered them into three categories: his political humanism, commitment to modernism, and antisystemic theory. I will spend most of my time defining his distinctive humanism and elaborating on why it is so consequential in his work. I will then briefly link it to the two other features of his thought.

Why is Said a political humanist? *Humanism* is hard to define and its multiple forms range across civilizations and traditions. To specify Said's own sense and usage is to say that Said saw himself as both a cultural and secular humanist, cultural because "secular humanism" encapsulates the idea that the humanities are worth studying because they foster valuable features of human life and celebrate valuable qualities of human beings, and secular because secular humanism involves "the positive affirmation that human beings can find from within themselves the resources to live a good life without religion."[3] Said believed in the humanities as an intellectual vocation and thought that it should return to its "rightful concern with the critical investigations of values, history, and freedom." He also thought that the questioning of certainties entailed by humanism should be turned against the artistic and literary products of the humanities "to challenge and defeat both an imposed silence and the normalized quiet of unseen power wherever and whenever possible."[4] What makes Said's humanism political is his preoccupation with uncovering culture's complicities in injustice and power and exposing its role in historical injury. What if the culture Said revered and admired so much did play a role in the political oppression and domination he despised? That is Edward Said's defining problem. In *Culture and Imperialism*, he defines it as follows: how to connect "the prolonged and sordid cruelty of such practices as slavery, colonialist and racial, and imperial subjection" with "the poetry, fiction, and philosophy of the society that engages in these practices."[5]

Said had a lifelong commitment to the philological tradition epitomized by Erich Auerbach's *Mimesis: The Representation of Reality in Western Literature* (1953). What struck him most about Auerbach's project is that it affirmed the redeeming value of a sympathetic imagination able to capture and affirm the particularity of individual authors at a time of devastating European interwar conflict and antagonism. To see beyond national divisions and codify a common human heritage was key. What captivated Said about Auerbach's humanism was "its emphasis on the unity of human history, the possibility of understanding inimical and perhaps even hostile others despite the bellicosity of modern cultures and nationalisms, and the optimism with which one could enter into the inner life of a distant author or historical epoch even with a healthy awareness of one's limitations of perspective and insufficiency of knowledge."[6] Said defended the universal kernel of this vision – even when he came to worry about its purely European register. He also cotranslated Auerbach's powerful defense of the concept of world literature "Philology and *Weltliteratur*." In the face of emerging Cold War divisions and the pressures of cultural standardization, Auerbach sought to renew humanism. He did so by extending his literary brief to the whole globe and gesturing toward a conception that seeks "a spiritual exchange between peoples," "the reconciliation of peoples," and an exchange "between partners" that "hastens mutual understanding and serves common purpose." As he concludes: "our philological home is the earth: it can no longer be the nation."[7] These are constitutive motifs for Said: culture as a precarious repository of human value in a world debased by power and national antagonism.

But what if, again, culture is not only involved in worldly politics but, through its own workings, contributes to conflict and dehumanization? What if humanism and the humanities are as much a part of the problem as the solution? More. What if culture leads to political domination? As when Said says: "I very much doubt that England would have occupied Egypt in so long and massively institutionalized a way had it not been for the durable investment in Oriental learning first cultivated by scholars like Edward William Lane and William Jones."[8] Said's answer to this possibility is "secular criticism," an ideological house clearing of sorts. Rather than isolating both text and critic from historical circumstances, contemporary criticism needs, he posits, to re-engage with the world, actively interfere in it, and undermine the unjust status quo created by "a new cold war, increased militarism and defense spending, and a massive turn to the right on matters touching the economy, social services, and organized labor." Simply put, Said argues that: "The realities of power and authority – as well as the resistances offered by men, women, and social movements to institutions, authorities, and orthodoxies – are the realities that make texts possible, that deliver them to their readers, that solicit the attention of critics. I propose that these realities are what should be taken account of by criticism and the critical consciousness."[9]

Imperialism was the one reality that exercised Said most. After 1967, it hit home. As he clearly states in his massively influential *Orientalism* (1978): "The web of racism, cultural stereotypes, political imperialism, dehumanizing ideology holding in the Arab or the Muslim is very strong indeed, and it is this web which every Palestinian has come to feel as his uniquely punishing destiny."[10] *Orientalism*'s theoretical contradictions, between an Auerbachian humanism and a Foucauldian antihumanism, have been widely discussed. What I want to do here is look at the problems of knowledge and imperial power that *Orientalism* raises in its sequel *Culture and Imperialism* (1993). Because it examines both domination and resistance, domestically and in the outlays of empire, *Culture and Imperialism* is a more complete theorization of that nexus. It also allows Said to anchor his political humanism in Fanon's emancipatory "new humanism."

The basic claim Said makes in *Culture and Imperialism* is that national cultures in the West are imperial. This is not a new claim. *Orientalism* advanced it in a more ontological manner: that anyone who speaks about the Orient is subject to the constitutive pressures and enunciative powers of Orientalist knowledge. For example: "So far as anyone wishing to make a statement of any consequence about the Orient was concerned, latent Orientalism supplied him with an enunciative capacity that could be used, or rather mobilized, and turned into sensible discourse for the concrete occasion at hand."[11] In *Culture and Imperialism*, this notion is generalized. The book is not only about how the West narcissistically develops self-constituting and self-generating (Oriental) knowledge about others but also about how active resistance in the colonies breaks that generative power and makes new knowledge in the center possible.[12] Until the consequential moment of decolonization, empire and culture can, for Said, be spoken about as practically the same.

To convey the sweep and permeation of imperial culture, two examples from the text will suffice. First: "The great cultural archive, I argue, is where the intellectual and aesthetic investments in overseas dominion are made. If you were British or French in the 1860s you saw, and you felt, India and North Africa with a combination of familiarity and distance, but never with a sense of their separate sovereignty." Second: "With few exceptions, the women's as well as the working-class movement was pro-empire. And, while one must always be at great pains to show that different imaginations, sensibilities, ideas, and philosophies were at work, and that each work of literature or art is special, there was virtual unity of purpose on this score: the empire must be maintained, and it *was* maintained."[13] Imperialist assumptions and imperatives affected the realistic novel, fiction narratives, philosophers, deconstruction, Marxism, opera, and so forth. In short: "Modern imperialism was so global and all-encompassing that virtually nothing escaped it" (81). I shall show in the following text why modernism for Said disrupts this total imperial hegemony. But what I want to emphasize now is that the reason why Said views Western culture as inescapably imperial is clear: because he regards silence or indifference to empire as consent.

What the decolonization generation taught him was "that in so global-izing a world-view as that of imperialism, there could be *no neutrality: one either was on the side of empire or against it*, and, since they themselves had lived the empire (as native or as white), there was no getting away from it" (337, emphasis added). These may well have been the political terms of the decolonization struggle *in* the colonies: If you are not with us, then you are with the colonists. Said, however, assumes that metropolitan culture was as contentious and affected by imperial struggle as colonized society, and that not taking a position about empire in the imperial metropolis is the same as not taking one in the colonies. This equation, however, makes no historical sense, not only because it is, in fact, the structural privilege of national societies that had overseas empires (like Britain) to be able to ignore empire – unless one was part of the small elite minority actively involved in running it – but also because attitudes to empire varied across classes and were strongly impacted by purely domestic concerns. Only exceptionally was the choice either *for* or *against*. The Boer War is a good example, when British elite interests in South Africa required public support and involvement. Mostly, though, empire was beyond the realm of everyday concern for the majority of Britons, and the imperial elite wanted to keep it that way.

This is the argument that Bernard Porter makes in *The Absent-Minded Imperialists* (2004). Indifference to empire and a lack of commitment to it were widespread in British society. Britain, obviously, benefitted from empire, and its material impact was widespread (sugar, profits, trade, etc.). Porter recognizes this, and puts it in no uncertain terms when he says:

> The empire probably affected nearly everyone materially . . . They [effects] include Britain's participation in two world wars, her economic rise and decline, the perpetuation of her class structure, and the state of her people's teeth. In all of these ways the empire impacted hugely on her culture and society. That should be enough material repercussions for anyone. But they were all indirect.

After reviewing hundreds of tracts and diaries, he does find, though, that empire's attitudinal and cultural effects were far less evident and that, crucially, when they did exist they were determined by class. Porter does affirm that the British elite (especially its aristocracy) was profoundly imperialist and believed in its mission of ruling over others (as it did throughout the British empire). But what he finds no evidence for is that the majority class in Britain had any interest in empire or actively supported it. The reason for this, he argues, lay in the nature of Britain's *two-nations* class structure, which was premised on the "principle of complementarity, rather than community or commonality."[14] Porter also shows that even the middle class was more ambivalent about imperialism than some presume: They were not demonstratively imperialist, were more interested in settlement colonies than in others, and had no distinctively imperial ideas of their own (unlike the upper classes). His conclusion is therefore clear. Contra Said: "[T]here can be no *presumption* that Britain – the Britain that stayed at home – was an essentially 'imperialist' nation in the nineteenth and twentieth centuries."[15]

Said, in fact, never examines either the working class or women's movements. Yet he tars them both with imperial sympathies. And he even concedes that there is a long lull in representing empire in the British novel (which he, nonetheless, regards as born imperial): "But most of the great nineteenth-century realistic novelists are less assertive about colonial rule and possession than either Defoe or late writers like Conrad and Kipling" (75). There is no question that imperial presence is registered in the British novel: mentions of colonies, characters being shipped off to British dominions or shipped back, colonial inheritances, and even colonial dispossession as structuring of novelistic plot lines and as shaping fictive events (as in Wilkie Collins's *The Moonstone* [1868] – strangely ignored by Said). There is also no question that a whole genre of colonial travel and adventure writing arose to account for actual imperial encounter, especially when imperial ideology was at its strongest and most widespread in the late nineteenth century (Conrad is its high literary incarnation).[16] But that hardly makes the British novel as a category imperial, or makes empire (more sweepingly) its main condition of possibility, as when Said says: "Without empire, I would go so far as saying, there is no European novel as we know it" (82). The picture is more complicated and nuanced than Said posits. Purely by virtue of representing history and capturing various historical processes, British novels could have, of course, responded to colonialism and empire. But that is not what is at stake here. The argument with Said is not *whether* the British novel contains invocations, traces, or registers of empire. These are undeniable. The argument is about what those mean and whether the whole trajectory of the British novel can be explained by empire.[17]

A famous case in which Said deploys this reading mode is Jane Austen's *Mansfield Park* (1814). If Raymond Williams, in his pioneering reading in *The Country and The City* (1977), saw Sir Thomas Bertram as *both* domestic capitalist owner (improver) and imperial plantation exploiter (a "great West Indian" and "a colonial proprietor in the sugar island of

Antigua") at the same time, Said radically revises this assessment.[18] He insists that slavery is the silenced core of the novel – even though that is a flawed claim because Austen was an abolitionist and her main protagonist in the novel actively raises the topic of slavery with the master of the house. Said also argues that slavery alone *makes possible* Mansfield Park both as a country house and as a novel. I will later on examine what this tells us about Said's understanding of the relationship between capitalism and imperialism. What, though, does it tell us about Said's critical reading practices? That empire for Said is the *primary* if not the *singular* determiner of meaning in the novel; that this is why he rejects Williams's account of empire as playing only a part in a wider integrated capitalist accumulation process; and that this is why it is not enough for him to argue, as Williams does, that *Mansfield Park* is at the cutting edge of the moral and ideological negotiation between different fractions of the British elite. For Said, the novel has to be actively structured by the decisive and generative power of empire, which trumps all else in explaining the novel. Austen thus exemplifies a core notion for Said: that British domestic culture is simply imperialist and that all novels and intellectual tracts published in the last 300 years identify with an imperial identity.

This far is clear. But what has not been explored before is why Said believes that British domestic culture is imperial. I want to argue that he does so because of his particular conception of empire and its relationship to metropolitan capitalism. Said believes that empire as a category is equivalent to British "servants in grand households and in novels" and "transient workers": "profitable without being fully there" (75). But to make that assumption is to make a category mistake. Workers have a different relationship to Britain than the colonized, and the British working class is much more centrally located within the British polity than the imperialized living in the outlays of empire. By putting them on a par with the domestically exploited and seeing both servants and colonized as subjects suffering from invisibility and silence, Said devises his job as literary critic: to counter their exclusion and register their (overlooked) voice and presence in text.

This equivalence and lack of clear distinction between different social categories suggests that Said has a very specific understanding of empire. And this is my point. Simply put: Said assumes that the imperialism he refers to is of the settler-colonial variety – a distinct version of empire. He thus regards empire *as a way of life*, exactly as it is for America in relation to Native Americans and for Israel in relation to Palestinians.[19] In such settlement societies, the frontier is close to home and the struggle for territory and sovereignty shapes all aspects of life: Empire is a constitutive part of everyday politics, society, and culture. The colonized native is not *out there*, to be ignored or forgotten by most, but *in here*, seen as either an immediate threat to colonial security and survival and requiring exclusion (as dispensable) or controlled as exploited labor.[20] Whatever the case, settler colonies are different from purely imperial societies. William Appleman Williams emphasizes their distinctive nature when he says: "We Americans, let alone our English [colonist] forefathers, have produced very, very few anti-imperialists. Our idiom has been empire, and so the primary division was and remains between the soft and the hard [imperialists]." In settler colonies, empire permeates all core aspects of life and the anti-imperialism (of settlers) is a far more restricted activity.[21]

Said transposes this understanding of settler colonialism to empire in general. Rather than focus on the specific structures and histories of different imperialisms and their commensurate political and cultural forms, Said posits one category that fits all: control of land. As when he says, "The actual geographical possession of land is what empire in the final analysis is all about . . . Imperialism and the culture associated with it affirm both the primacy of geography and an ideology about control of territory" (93). The focus on land, he argues, is how a "spatial moral order" is sanctioned "even where colonies are not insistently or even perceptibly in evidence" (94). Spatiality aids the imperial process by "validati[ng] its own preferences while also advocating those preferences in conjunction with distant imperial rule" (96) and by "devalu[ing] other worlds" (97). In other words, empire as control of land gives you a culture spatially structured by imperialism. But this is only true for settler colonies that require possession of land. Said presumes that the effects that are distinct to settler colonialism are general to all forms of empire. And that is the profoundly consequential slippage that lies at the heart of *Culture and Imperialism* and mars it.

Said gives empire such extensive domestic influence for another reason. Because he believes with Fanon that "Europe is literally the creation of the Third World. The wealth which smothers her is that which was stolen from the underdeveloped peoples."[22] This statement, too, is not without its problems. That Britain and France impoverished the Third World and ravaged its independent modes of existence is without doubt. But does this mean that Europe's overall economic and material self-making can be extrapolated from this fact? Not really. There is a whole tradition of radical critique in Britain that shows that: "Not only were the costs of imperialism higher than the benefits: the benefits went to the few, the nation paid the costs." A host of contemporary economic historians have also argued that the benefits of empire were, in fact, underwhelming. Peter Cain summarizes these findings when he states that "[key] calculations probably indicate the upper bounds of possible gains from trading with empire before 1914 and that, if underconsumption is taken seriously, the empire may even have had a negative impact on British growth." Indeed "the whole imperial exercise was actually a burden on the economy even if it was beneficial to some sectional interests such as traditional elites." Cain's conclusion goes against Fanon's blanket generalization that Said shares: Empire "probably slowed down the development of industry in Britain" and "undoubtedly slowed down the rate of social and political change."[23] Individual imperialists and some elite sectors did benefit from empire, but probably at the cost of everyone else. These economic findings thus undermine the notion that modern Britain was economically made by its empire.

The same conclusion can be reached about the profits coming specific-ally from slavery. In his symptomatic reading of *Mansfield Park*, Said relies on Eric Williams's *Capitalism and Slavery* (1944) to show how central plantation profits were to the development of industrial Britain. That too, however, cannot be empirically sustained. After reviewing the economic record, Kenneth Morgan concludes: "Slavery and Atlantic trade made an important, though not decisive, impact on Britain's long-term economic development between the late Stuart era and the early Victorian age, playing their part in enabling Britain to become the workshop of the world." But that, "Despite the lucrative returns arising from these [slave plantation] investments, however, the various arguments for slavery and sugar's role in metropolitan capital accumulation have not proven that the direct connection between the two was substantial." Individual plantation owners may well have used their profits in "conspicuous consumption" back in the metropolis to build country houses, "but it is doubtful whether the impetus [to 'British economic development'] was on a sufficient financial scale to have had a major impact."[24]

What this research shows is clear: Empire did contribute to metropol-itan economy and society and it did shape some of its elite forms in decisive ways. What it did not do is make the overall basis of British economy possible. Capitalism did that – as Raymond Williams had originally suggested. As Marx's analysis in *Capital* shows, a whole world of colonial loot came with the "primitive accumulation" that announced the emergence of capital in Europe:

> The discovery of gold and silver in America, the extirpation, enslavement and entombment in mines of the aboriginal population, the beginning of the conquest and looting of the East Indies, the turning of Africa into a warren for the commercial hunting of black-skins, signalised the rosy dawn of the era of capitalist production. These idyllic proceedings are the chief momenta of primitive accumulation.

What Marx's materialist conception shows is that it is capitalist production that fueled colonial exploitation, not the other way around.[25]

To summarize my argument: Because Said ignores capitalism and class as determinate and structuring processes, he overestimates the significance of empire in domestic metropolitan affairs. By replacing political economy with geography and by spatializing empire, distinct causalities and determinations are ignored. Imperial center and periphery become mutually constitutive. What Said risks here is positing that domestic society in imperial nations is as determined by empire as colonized society: a negation of imperial inequality if ever there was.[26] To avoid such distortions, Said's two core presumptions need to be rejected: that imperial practices have wall-to-wall domestic effects and that domestic culture is *carte blanche* imperial. The historical record is far more uneven than he presumes, and far more determined by class than he wishes to acknowledge. Rather than assuming that every worker and humanist was an imperialist, the work of pinpointing the influence of empire should be a more determinate question.[27]

Said is on firmer ground when he argues that a new form of humanism was generated by the decolonization struggle. As he argues, the struggle against imperialism was not just nationalist but had a universal emancipatory core as well. It shunned the "national bourgeoisie and their specialized elites, of which Fanon speaks so ominously, [that] in effect tended to replace the colonial force with a new class-based and ultimately exploitative one, which replicated the old colonial structures in new terms" (269). Fanon epitomizes this anticolonial culture for Said: a universalist who struggles against chauvinist nativism and colonial mimicry and formulates an alternative politics of liberation instead. Said describes Fanon's position as real humanism: "more generous human realities of community *among* cultures, peoples, societies. This community is the real human liberation portended by the resistance to imperialism" (262). If Said simply ignores Fanon's clear socialist worldview and commitments, he does anchor his own humanism in Fanon. He also contrasts it with "an astonishing sense of weightlessness with regard to the gravity of history" (366–367) that postmodernism represents for him. With Césaire (another socialist from Martinique), Said affirms that "no race has a / monopoly on beauty, on intelligence, on strength" and that "there is room for everyone at the convocation of conquest" [or: "rendezvous of victory"] (279). He also shows that such grand narratives of emancipation had global effects. They helped spur internal "humanist opposition to colonial practices like torture and deportation" (292) in the metropolis. These came not only from colonial émigrés like George Padmore, C. L. R. James, and Kwame Nkrumah, but from prominent European intellectuals like Jean-Paul Sartre and Jean Genet as well.

What Said takes from this decolonizing generation is the insistence on resistance. To register both humanism's participation in domination and in resistance Said formulates a new construct: contrapuntal. This epitomizes his method in *Culture and Imperialism*: to unpack the complexities of the "intertwined and overlapping histories" (19) of empire while emphasizing its conflictual nature. As he clearly states: "But this global, contrapuntal analysis should be modelled not (as earlier notions of comparative literature were) on a symphony but rather on an atonal ensemble; we must take into account all sorts of spatial or geographical and rhetorical practices – inflections, limits, constraints, intrusions, inclusions, prohibitions – all of them tending to elucidate a complex and uneven topography" (386). With that, Said revises Auerbach's cultural humanism and turns it into a global critique of imperialism.

Said's humanist commitment is also entangled with aesthetic and non-systematizing preferences: modernism and eclecticism. Let me comment on both briefly. Modernism provides Said with an atonal ensemble. He relies on it to critique the imperial real. If Orientalism is philosophically seen as "a radical realism," as a language that "is considered to have acquired, or more simply to be, reality," then what disrupts realism's seamless connection to empire is the antirepresentational energies of modernism.[28] The form's ironic resistances to the imperium are advanced in "A Note on Modernism" in *Culture and Imperialism*. And modernism's core features are posited as a critical response to empire: "Conrad, Forster, Malraux, T. E. Lawrence take narrative from the triumphalist experience of imperialism into the extremes of self-consciousness, discontinuity, self-referentiality, and corrosive irony, whose formal patterns we have come to recognize as the hallmarks of modernist culture, a culture that also embraces the major work of Joyce, T. S. Eliot, Proust, Mann, and Yeats" (227).

Said favored modernism over realism. Though his first two books had absolutely nothing to do with empire and had conventional titles like

Joseph Conrad and the Fiction of Autobiography (1966) and *Beginnings: Intention and Method* (1975), they conveyed Said's modernist investments and his methodological tendencies.²⁹ Conrad was regarded as an individual mind grappling with the problems of objective chaos and egoistic order. And *Beginnings* were conceptualized as a source of potential freedom – as departures, discontinuities, divergences, displacements, and modes of complementarity and adjacency. These were contrasted with forms of restriction that for him are linearity, succession, mimesis, dynasty, and theology. Said believed that a (molestive) affiliation is superior to bounded filiation. What *Beginnings* ultimately articulates is Said's own sense of critical self-invention and political rebirth after 1967, but at this stage in a literary-philosophical register and not yet in the language of political humanism that would define his books from *Orientalism* onward.

There are lines of continuity here, especially with modernism. Said's modernist investments, evident in his early work, are transposed onto the relationship between empire and culture. Against the authority of imperial rule, the full exilic force of modernist anxiety and ambivalence are unleashed. Realism becomes part of imperial representation while modernism stands in the vanguard of resistance to it. The problem with that is that such a binary cannot be historically sustained, and a literary mode by itself is no indication of orientation toward political power. Both modernism and realism could justify empire. If modernism can give you a communist Bertolt Brecht or a Fascist Ezra Pound, realism can give you an anti-imperialist George Orwell or an imperialist Kipling. Said ignores the ramifications of this point. Embedded in his analysis is the notion that, because modernism is ambivalent and ironic, it is a historically progressive literary mode. But that is a context-specific question and depends on many other variables. It is impossible to read into a representational crisis like modernism one kind of political attitude or another. If Said seems aware of this when he suggests that Conrad is both imperialist and anti-imperialist, he does not change his overall conception of modernism as simply an anti-empire mode.

The emphasis on discontinuities is a key element in Said's theoretical toolkit. Discontinuities disrupt authorities, solidarities, and systems – which Said tends to regard as oppressive. That is why Said advances the notion of "never solidarity before criticism." Criticism stands over solidarity. It is also elevated over method. The "dangers of method and system" is of becoming "sovereign" and having "their practitioners lose touch with the resistance and heterogeneity of civil society." To avoid this eventuality is to embrace eclecticism. As Said put it in an illuminating interview in

1995: "[O]ne is moved in ways that are mysterious, and that is better for me than trying to find some system to contain them [interests] all. I am invariably criticised by younger postcolonialists (Ahmad, etc.) for being inconsistent and untheoretical, and I find that I like that, who wants to be consistent?"[30] If system is external and imposing, what is needed is something closer to the modernist sensibility he held so dear: atonal rupture. "Criticism in short is always situated; it is sceptical, secular, reflectively open to its own failings."[31]

Whether one agrees with Said's methodological preferences, they were guided by one political constant: his commitment to truth and justice.[32] This comes across most powerfully in his work on Palestine. Whether as a Palestinian nationalist in the 1970s and 1980s or as both a critical nationalist and binationalist after the capitulation of the Palestinian Liberation Organization (PLO) in the Oslo Peace Accords of 1993, Said actively participated in the struggle for Palestinian justice and liberation. In his most radical work, Said articulated the urgent necessity of both Palestinian self-criticism and the critique of Israeli power. For the first time since the rise of "Palestinianism," Said developed an internal critique of Palestinian elite nationalism that mirrors Fanon on the social betrayals of the "national bourgeoisie." Said's anti-PLO *Peace and Its Discontents* thus performs a similar task to Fanon's *The Wretched of the Earth*. By holding out for the justice embodied in the popular self-organized mobilizations of the first intifada, Said affirms the potentialities of mass politics against a defeatist Palestinian elite. He also exposes a whole imperial morality when he argues that: "Peace really means peace between equals; it means freedom and equality for both peoples, not just one, nor peace for one as a lesser appendage to the other, who has full rights and security. Above all it means understanding the coherence and integrity of our own history as Palestinians and Arabs."[33] Such judgments exemplify Said's political humanism. As Noam Chomsky acknowledged, Said's life project sought to undermine both the dominant principles of empire and the culture of imperialism.[34] Herein lies his real political legacy.

This volume ruminates on the problems and opportunities afforded by Said's work: its productive and generative capacities as well as its inbuilt limitations. *After Said* aims to capture the essence of Said's intellectual and political contribution and his extensive impact on postcolonial studies; it also reflects on what comes *after* Said. How have literary criticism and literary and political theory changed in the light of Said's field shaping and multifaceted interventions? The main objective of this volume is to examine Said's legacy both intensively and extensively: by critically elaborating his core concepts and arguments and by tracing some of their significant afterlives.

By moving simultaneously inward into Said's *oeuvre* and outward to his growing legacy, this volume reframes and refashions key areas in the postcolonial literary field, especially the relationship between imperialism and culture. Critical thought *after* Said requires radical reorientations. Does the contemporary political moment, marked by imperial war, disorder, and neoliberal economic crisis, usher in the return of politics and political economy in postcolonial studies? What happens to postcolonial studies with capital (rather than just culture) as a core analytic category? A *materialist* Said is here excavated to fortify a materialist critique of historical and contemporary imperialism.

The volume is divided into three interconnected clusters.

First: clarifying Said's key concepts, interpretations, and critical contributions from his earliest book on Conrad to his Adornian ruminations on exile. Examined here are Said's formative humanism, critique of Orientalism, own distinction as postcolonial theorist, and rich response to exile as a mode of critical affiliation. Conor McCarthy captures Said's birth as a critic and his early intellectual investments in modernist exile and philological humanism that shape his life project. Vivek Chibber zooms in on the dual legacy of *Orientalism* as both razor-sharp critique of imperial ideology and theoretically contradictory and shows how through its culturalism the book risks disabling its own resources of political critique. Seamus Deane revisits *Culture and Imperialism* and Said's project of moving American criticism to a critique empire, and he too thinks about the costs of dismissing Marxism and turning imperial violence into a question of culture. Keya Ganguly identifies the contours of Said's exilic standpoint and its political determination by Palestinian dispossession, and shows how concepts like the contrapuntal and the paratactic express real-world irreconcilabilities and historical irresolution.

Second: charting Said's transformation of key intellectual fields and his generative intellectual legacy. Examined here are Said's seminal reinterpretation and reframing of the British literary canon from the perspective of empire, his emerging impact on the political theory of empire, the struggles between postcolonialism and theories of world literature, and the inflations of postcolonial modernism as an anticolonial transnational mode. Lauren M. E. Goodlad reads nineteenth-century British literature contrapuntally *after* Said as "a world-system in motion," remobilizes existing links between capitalism and colony and reformulates Jane Austen's *Mansfield Park* as "a groundbreaking novel of geopolitical consciousness" – productively engaging Raymond Williams in the process. Jeanne Morefield identifies the value of Said's contrapuntal disposition for the "turn to empire" in political theory and posits its importance for analyzing contemporary American imperial power. Joe Cleary shows how postcolonial criticism ran up against its own culturalist limitations and neglected the crucial resources of a sociology of culture, thus allowing world-system theory to step in and challenge its global ambition – where should radical theory go from here? Dougal McNeill shows how the Saidian inflation of modernism has contributed to the distortions of transnational modernism, obscuring the key role that realism and the universalization of capitalism play in contemporary culture.

Third: focusing on key areas of Said's afterlives. Examined here are theoretical and political issues crucial to postcolonial studies today, such as migration and exile; the resurgence of orientalism and Islamophobia; and the crucial significance of political economy to the analysis of imperialism after the Iraq War. Joan Cocks critically engages with Said and Freud on exile to advance a politics of possibility for both strangers and natives in our turbulent present, connecting immigration with alleviating the domestic problems of class inequality. Saree Makdisi renews the ideological critique of orientalism today in order to counter an America-led global demonization of Islam after 9/11 that dovetails with America's resurgent imperial policy. Robert Spencer calls on the resources of political economy (ignored by Said) to reveal the role of American imperialism in the organization of the global economy and in the neoliberal resurgence of capitalism and shows how it is simply impossible to understand the Iraq War without them.

The combined effect of *After Said* is clear: a materialist postcolonial study that takes both capitalism and imperialism seriously as core and connected categories of analysis, and that critiques the forms of culture they both generate to justify their dominations. Only then can the field join with Raymond Williams and say: "I believe that the system of meanings and values which a capitalist society has generated has to be defeated in general and in detail by the most sustained kinds of intellectual and educational work."[35] For Williams, the Welsh European, that meant defeating capitalism on an imperial scale: an objective worth upholding both in theory and in practice.

Notes

1 Looking back on this period in his *Out of Place: A Memoir* (London: Granta, 1999), Said explained: "I was no longer the same person after 1967; the shock of that war drove me back to where it had all started, the struggle over Palestine" (p. 293).
2 Edward W. Said, "The Palestinian Experience," in *The Politics of Dispossession: The Struggle for Palestinian Self-Determination 1969–1994* (New York: Vintage, 1995 [1968–1969]), pp. 3–23, p. 4, p. 18, p. 9, p. 19.
3 Richard Norman's definitions are concise and clarifying: *On Humanism* (London: Routledge, 2004), p. 14, p. 18.
4 Edward W. Said, *Humanism and Democratic Criticism* (Basingstoke: Palgrave Macmillan, 2004), p. 14, p. 135.
5 Edward W. Said, *Culture and Imperialism* (London: Vintage, 1994 [1993]), p. xiv.
6 Edward W. Said, "Introduction to the Fiftieth-Anniversary Edition," in Erich Auerbach, *Mimesis: The Representations of Reality in Western Literature*, trans. by Willard R. Trask (Princeton, NJ: Princeton University Press, 2003), pp. ix–xxxii, p. xvi.
7 Erich Auerbach, "Philology and *Weltliteratur*," trans. by Maire and Edward Said, *The Central Review* XII. (Winter 1969), 1–17 (6–7, 17).
8 Edward W. Said, *Covering Islam: How the Media and the Experts Determine How We See the Rest of the World* (New York: Vintage, 1997 [1981]), p. 26.
9 Edward W. Said, *The World, the Text, and the Critic* (New York: Vintage, 1991 [1983]), p. 4, p. 5.
10 Edward W. Said, *Orientalism: Western Conceptions of the Orient* (London: Penguin, 1995 [1978]), p. 27.
11 Said, *Orientalism*, pp. 221–222. Aijaz Ahmad rightly describes this as Said seeing "that Europeans were ontologically incapable of producing any true knowledge about non-Europe": In *Theory: Classes, Nations, Literatures* (London: Verso, 1992), p. 178.
12 For an excellent reading of *Orientalism*, see Timothy Brennan, "The Illusion of a Future: *Orientalism* as Travelling Theory," *Critical Inquiry* 26 (Spring 2000), 558–583.
13 Said, *Culture and Imperialism*, p. xxiii, p. 62. Page numbers follow future quotations in the body of the text.
14 Bernard Porter, "'Empire, What Empire?' Or, Why 80% of Early-and Mid-Victorians Were Deliberately Kept in Ignorance of It," *Victorian Studies* 46.2 (Winter 2004), 256–263 (260).
15 Bernard Porter, *The Absent-Minded Imperialists: Empire, Society, and Culture in Britain* (Oxford: Oxford University Press, 2004), p. xv, p. 24. There is now a voluminous body of historical writing around these issues. For a similar perspective to Porter, see Andrew Thompson, *The Empire Strike Back? The Impact of Imperialism on Britain from the Mid-Nineteenth Century* (Harlow: Pearson, 2005). For a range of historical work from the opposite (though

non-Saidian) perspective, see John M. Mackenzie, "Empire and Metropolitan Cultures," in *The Oxford History of the British Empire: Volume III: The Nineteenth Century*, ed. by Andrew Porter (Oxford: Oxford University Press, 1999), pp. 270–293.

16 Patrick Brantlinger's most recent book provides a good introduction to this genre: *Victorian Literature and Postcolonial Studies* (Edinburgh: Edinburgh University Press, 2009).

17 For an excellent refutation of Said on the Victorian novel, see Nancy Henry, *George Eliot and the British Empire* (Cambridge: Cambridge University Press, 2002). Henry shows that by searching for a nonexistent imperial ideology in Eliot, critics like Said have been "blinded to the visible": Her actual material links to empire (p. 113). Another important materialist reading of the Victorian novel is Lauren M. E. Goodlad, *The Victorian Geopolitical Aesthetic: Realism, Sovereignty, and Transnational Experience* (Oxford: Oxford University Press, 2015). Goodlad anchors her study in the geopolitics of transnational capital but without assuming that "Victorian culture was built around a coherent idea of Britain as an imperial nation-state" (p. 6).

18 Raymond Williams, *The Country and the City* (London: Hogarth Press, 1973), p. 114.

19 I take that evocative phrase from a book Said quotes: William Appleman Williams, *Empire as a Way of Life* (New York: Ig Publishing, 2007 [1980]). Williams shows how America's vast and expansive imperial worldview begins as colonial at home. Next quotation is from page 34.

20 Said elaborates on Zionism's exclusionary settler colonial dynamics in *The Question of Palestine* (New York: Vintage, 1992 [1979]), pp. 56–114. For an examination of the colonization model in Israeli sociology, see my "Israel in US Empire," *New Formations* 59 (Autumn 2006), pp. 34–51.

21 Said does refer to the British anti-imperial tradition and to Bernard Porter's *Critics of Empire: British Radicals and the Imperial Challenge.* He concludes that anti-imperialists like Wilfrid Scawen and William Morris "were far from influential" and that "there was no overall condemnation of imperialism until – and this is my point – *after* native uprisings were too far gone to be ignored or defeated" (291). But this is factually incorrect. For example, Marx in 1869 conditioned the success of the working-class revolution in Britain on anticolonialism in Ireland and thought that Ireland is closer to revolution than Britain because the Irish question combined economic exploitation with national oppression (his and Engels's anticolonialism was evident from the late 1850s, with both supporting the Indian Rebellion of 1857). Marx's anticolonial views on Ireland are well known. Lenin utilizes them to formulate his principles of self-determination and socialist strategy. See Kevin B. Anderson, *Marx at the Margins: On Nationalism, Ethnicity, and Non-Western Societies* (Chicago: University of Chicago Press, 2010), pp. 115–153. Said ignores all this (including the fact that all the major socialist revolutions happened in the Third World) because he wrongly believed that Marx was both Orientalist and Eurocentric, and that the tradition he spawned, therefore, was implicated

in empire. For a recent review of Said's "fundamentally flawed and unsound" views on Marx, see Gilbert Achcar, *Marxism, Orientalism, Cosmopolitanism* (London: Saqi, 2013), pp. 68–102, p. 90.

22 Frantz Fanon, *The Wretched of the Earth*, trans. by Constance Farrington (London: Penguin, 2001 [1961]), p. 81.

23 Peter Cain, "Was It Worth Having? The British Empire 1850–1950," *Revista de Historia Económica* 16.1 (March 1998), 351–376. Quotations, in order, are from pages 352, 356, 359, 367, and 371.

24 Kenneth Morgan, *Slavery, Atlantic Trade and the British Economic, 1660–1800* (Cambridge: Cambridge University Press, 2000). Quotations from pages 97 and 95. For the most extensive analysis of country houses and empire, see Stephanie Barczewski, *Country Houses and the British Empire, 1700–1930* (Manchester: Manchester University Press, 2014).

25 Ellen Meiksins Wood has argued that we cannot attribute to empire "any decisive role in the *origin* of capitalism": *The Origin of Capitalism: A Longer View* (London: Verso, 2002), p. 148.

26 For an example of such conceptual obfuscation, see Gauri Viswanathan, "Raymond Williams and British Colonialism: The Limits of Metropolitan Cultural Theory," in *Views beyond the Border Country: Raymond Williams and Cultural Politics*, ed. by Dennis L. Dworkin and Leslie G. Roman (New York: Routledge, 1993), pp. 217–230.

27 An illuminating example from political theory is Jennifer Pitts, *A Turn to Empire: The Rise of Imperial Liberalism in Britain and France* (Princeton: Princeton University Press, 2005). For an excellent materialist critique of postcolonial theory's flaws and blind spots, see Vivek Chibber, *Postcolonial Theory and the Specter of Capital* (London: Verso, 2013).

28 The phrase comes from *Orientalism*, p. 72.

29 For Said's partiality to modernism as a critical mode of interrogating modernity and later empire, see Abdirahman A. Hussein, *Edward Said: Criticism and Society* (London: Verso, 2002), p. 111, p. 119.

30 *Interviews with Edward W. Said*, ed. by Amritjit Singh and Bruce G. Johnson (Jackson: University Press of Mississippi, 2004), p. 90.

31 Said, *The World, the Text, and the Critic*, pp. 25–26.

32 Jan Selby thinks that Said's "concern with narrative is epistemologically and politically subordinate to a concern with justice and truth": "Edward W. Said: Truth, Justice and Nationalism," *Interventions: International Journal of Postcolonial Studies* 8.1 (2006), 40–55 (51).

33 Edward W. Said, *Peace and Its Discontents* (London: Vintage, 1996 [1993]), p. 25.

34 Noam Chomsky, "The Unipolar Moment and the Culture of Imperialism," Edward Said Memorial Lecture at Columbia University, December 3, 2009: https://chomsky.info/20091203-2/.

35 Raymond Williams, *Resources of Hope: Culture, Democracy, Socialism* (London: Verso, 1989), p. 76.

CHAPTER 2

Said: Birth of the Critic

Conor McCarthy

Edward Said was preeminently a *critic*, as against a scholar or theorist. This is not to say, of course, that he was unscholarly, or that he was uninterested in theory. His latter gruff impatience with "theory" as it developed in the American academy was less a hostility to theoretical discourse than a view of it that was entirely continuous with his lifelong skepticism about the institutional fate of radical ideas generally.

Said is best described, in the end, as a radicalized *humanist*, a description for which he felt, he said in 1982, "contradictory feelings of affection and revulsion."[1] Or, as Seamus Deane has put it, Said should be seen as having practised "a late style of humanism" – that is, Said embodies a European humanism that is alienated both temporally and spatially and that is belated or asynchronous with its context; which is brought to productive crisis by his analysis of its inner contradictions; by its being transplanted (by Said) to the non-European world; by the revelation of its complicity in its own Eurocentrism, masculinism, class prejudice; and by its acceptance of its location in "humane marginality" when put there by modern institutions of political and economic power.[2] The most interesting work Said did arose from the ways he brought various critical or hermeneutic traditions together, or the ways he put such theories or methods to work in unexpected or hitherto unprecedented places or situations. This was a matter and a practice Said raised to a self-conscious principle: In *Beginnings*, he quotes Gaston Bachelard as suggesting that a theoretical rationality worthy of the name must push itself up to its own limits: "If during an experiment one does not risk one's reason, then that experiment is not worth the attempt."[3] It was in this sense that Said was a "humanist." Toward the end of his life, discussing James Clifford's brilliant early critique of *Orientalism*, Said pointed out that despite that critique's intelligence and sympathy, it could see only contradiction in Said's simultaneous investment in humanism and his critical willingness to wager humanism on its own future.[4] As Isaac Deutscher called himself a "non-Jewish Jew," so Said saw himself as an antihumanist humanist.[5] A profound investment in humanism – the humanism of Auerbach or Spitzer, the humanist Marxism of the early Lukács or of Gramsci, running right up to the critique of the limits of humanism in Foucault and Derrida, the Third Worldist existential humanism of Fanon, the late humanism of Adorno – runs through his entire career from beginning to end. I will argue here that his work on Conrad, the early encounter with Vico, and his 1969 cotranslation of a major late essay of the great Romance philologist Erich Auerbach provide the coordinates within which Said's later career can be triangulated.

Joseph Conrad and the Fiction of Autobiography, based on Said's doctoral thesis, sets out a phenomenologically inflected interest in the "mind" of its subject, as that mind can be accessed in Conrad's letters and short fiction. The mind of Conrad is interesting to Said, however, precisely because it was unsettled, agonized, contradictory, exiled, and riven. Conrad's mental world is a strikingly dramatic and alienated place. Proceeding from this example, Said would go on to focus on intellectual or writerly drama in a great many of the figures about whom he chose to write. As Abdirahman Hussein so cogently pointed out, we must attend to such early work carefully to understand Said's origins as a critic, and where he thought he was going in his overall career.[6] Equally, Timothy Brennan long ago and very cogently pointed out how *Beginnings* sets up a group of issues or problematics that would preoccupy Said for the rest of his career.[7]

Said published his Conrad book in 1966. Immediately following it came essays on Swift, Vico, and the French structuralists. Many of these essays would feed into *Beginnings*, but some stand alone or somewhat apart and can be shown to have foundational importance for him. Specifically, "Vico: Autodidact and Humanist" (1967) and the translation (with Maire Said) of Erich Auerbach's "Philology and *Weltliteratur*" (1969) are crucial to an understanding of Said's "beginning," and to his whole career that would follow. From Conrad, Vico, and Auerbach, we can say, Said derived a model of the writerly subject, a set of methodological guidelines, and a program. Furthermore, on closer examination, the work on Conrad and the interest in Vico and Auerbach are not simply separate channels or themes of interest. Though it may not be obvious on the surface of his texts, there are various points of convergence and cross-fertilization.

Conrad, as was always clear, was an unusual "English" writer – a displaced and exiled Pole, working in what was only his third language after Polish and French, who both felt and dramatized in his fiction a powerful sense of dislocation and alienation and a strong, if pessimistic, sense of the globalized and imperial world. The similarities with Said are clear enough, and he was well aware of them, even if he only alluded explicitly to this later in his life: "I have found myself over the years reading and writing about Conrad like a *cantus firmus*, a steady groundbass to much that I have experienced." And further, "[T]he moment one enters his writing the aura of dislocation, instability and strangeness is unmistakeable. No-one could represent the fate of lostness and disorientation better than he did, and no-one was more ironic about the effort of trying to replace that condition with new arrangements and accommodations – which invariably lured one into further traps."[8] In *Joseph Conrad and the Fiction of Autobiography*, Said mined the Polish writer's short fiction and letters to offer a phenomenological portrait of his "mind," as it struggled with problems of exile, self-division, depression, artistic doubt, and political pessimism. But more than this, Said, equipped with ideas from Husserl and Schopenhauer, takes from Conrad a "theory" of intellection both artistic and critical. This model of reflexive intellectual work would remain with Said from the start to the finish of his career.

For Said, Conrad was an author for whom the making of fictions was both an element of the making of the self – through the making of what Wayne Booth would call an "implied author" – and a way of grasping and comprehending the world.[9] These two processes interact in powerful and significant ways in the Conradian self. So, early in his career, Said is as interested in what a text – a novel, a critical essay – tells us about an author, by its mode of somehow hinting at or dramatizing his presence, as he is in that text's relationship with the social and historical world. Furthermore, under the influence of the will philosophy of first Schopenhauer and then (more clearly in *Beginnings*) Nietzsche, Said sees texts as willed intentional acts. Conrad, he notes, sees books as "deeds": "[A] good book is a good action," he suggested in a letter to E. V. Lucas. Not merely this, but in an essay of 1904, "A Glance at Two Books," published posthumously, Conrad argues that "the national English novelist ... seldom regards his work ... as an achievement of active life by which he will produce certain definite effects upon the emotions of his readers ... It never occurs to him that a book is a deed, that the writing of it is an enterprise as much as the conquest of a colony."[10] The comparison of writing to conquest is striking, but one that hints at the approach to empire and culture much later in Said's career.

Said's project, in *Joseph Conrad and the Fiction of Autobiography*, is to study the development and mutation of Conrad's writerly self through at least three stages of his career. Sifting the letters and short stories, Said finds Conrad's consciousness wrestling with limits and strains, on the road to eventual mastery. This trajectory of mind is set against the background of a period of great turbulence in European history – the race toward high imperialism, the "scramble for Africa," the Great Power rivalry that would eventually issue in World War I, and, along with these global changes, radical alterations in European societies, with mass industrialization, urbanization, and the massification of politics and culture. But at this early stage of Said's career, the stress is less on the "worldly" politics of empire and revolution, than on Conrad's own extraordinary struggles with himself, as he aspires to become, and then fights to remain, a writer. Said draws on (though he does not explicitly refer to) Husserl's negotiation between philosophical idealism and philosophical realism, to map and to synthesize Conrad's development, both personal and artistic. But out of this, Said shapes certain problematics that will occupy him for much of the rest of his career: intellectual performance and reflexivity; the pain and torsions, as well as the exhilarating liberatory potential, of modernity; and the capacity or the failures of language's capacity to grasp empirical reality.

Said finds in Conrad a writer with a radically alienated relationship with language and its purchase on truth and reality. As he would say of Conrad later,

> Both in his fiction and in his autobiographical writing, Conrad was trying to do something that his experience as a writer everywhere revealed to be impossible ... He was misled by language even as he led language into a dramatisation no other author really approached. For what Conrad discovered was that the chasm between words saying and words meaning was widened, not lessened, by a talent for words written.[11]

Conrad thus offered Said a writer with a powerful modernist doubt and skepticism about language and representation. But Conrad also revealed to Said that alongside that doubt as to the efficacy of language went a recurrent human will to create verbal representations as a way of laying hold of the world, and further that this discursive purchase on the world served human collectivities as well as individuals.

The foundation, as we've seen, is always a subject that is the fount of discourse. In creating verbal representations, that subject is engaged in internal and external development at the same time and in ways that interact with each other:

> We have a sense of ourselves within us (intelligible); when put into practice (empirical), this sense is modified; and when put within the framework of the society in which we live, it becomes further modified (acquired). As a

result of the interplay between the individual and the world, we endow
ourselves with a sense of ethical and psychological self-location ... which in
most cases stays with us all our lives.[12]

In Conrad's case, and in that of many of his fictional characters, this sense
and process of self-location is often shattered or damaged. When this
happens, the self's understanding is likewise damaged, resulting in an
overwhelming sense of defeat and confusion. At such a point, knowledge
of the world, of truth, is both dark and enigmatic.

As a way of trying to deal with this, Said sees Conrad, and his characters,
in distinctly Schopenhauerean terms, as selves trying to impose a structure
on the world external to them, as part of their self-creation. This will
produce a model that we will see repeated at various points of Said's career:
not only in the early work but also in *Orientalism* and *Culture and
Imperialism* – an image of a self-authorizing, self-aggrandizing, tautologic-
ally self-engendering mechanism that for Said may describe the ego and
the work of the writer, the intellectual, the scholar, or indeed the "mind"
of the institutions or departments of empire. For Said, this self is intimately involved with a conception of truth – an anthropomorphic but also
egoistic conception of truth, as Nietzsche would have suggested. This inter-
locking of subjectivity and truth finds both resistance in the empirically
experienced world and, through consequent self-adjustment, a renewed
affirmation. This model subtends nearly all of Said's writing – not only
about literary authors but also about intellectuals and their projects, their
writing, and their writings relation to the world and to its objects.

A brief but famous example: Conrad's Marlow, in *Heart of Darkness*:

> Now when I was a little chap I had a passion for maps. I would look for
> hours at South America, or Africa, or Australia, and lose myself in all the
> glories of exploration. At that time there were many blank spaces on the
> earth, and when I saw one that looked particularly inviting on a map (but
> they all look that), I would put my finger on it and say, When I grow up
> I will go there.

And Said reading Conrad through Schopenhauer:

> The trouble with unrestrained egoism as Conrad saw it was that it becomes
> an imperialism of ideas, which easily converts itself into the imperialism of
> nations. In spite of the obvious injustice done to those upon whom one's
> idea can be imposed, it is important to understand that the reason an
> individual imposes his idea is that he believes he is serving the truth.[13]

The parallels are powerful and important. The upshot of Said's understanding of Schopenhauer is that any kind of intellectual work involves

both illusion and coercion. All knowledge is the product of a version of "will," where will is either an individual or collective subject that intends sense and meaning, which acts, overcomes, makes distinctions, and is driven to this activity not by normativity beyond itself (ideological or institutional) but in accordance with its own inner logic. At this early stage of his career, Said's thinking in this regard is inflected through Schopenhauer, as I say; later, it is to be found working through Vico, Nietzsche, and Foucault.

In *The World as Will and Representation*, Schopenhauer suggests that man subsists in a gray world of pure will. Once thought begins, man becomes "objectified will." Civilized man, with the greatest sharpening of his mental powers, attains the highest form of objectified will. The end product of this process is an overweening sense where "the world is my idea." The self possessing the "truth" produces an *idea* of itself to vindicate itself. It goes on then to produce an image of itself possessing the truth. A good example of this arises in Said's discussion of Lord Cromer in *Orientalism*. Cromer writes, in his essay on "The Government of Subject Races," on the relationship between the local agent of empire, on the ground, and a central authority in London, which is able to obviate any local or specific solecisms perpetrated by the agent.

> Cromer envisions a seat of power in the West, and radiating out from it towards the East a great embracing machine, sustaining the central authority yet commanded by it. What the machine's branches feed into it in the East – human material, material wealth, knowledge, what have you – is processed by the machine, then converted into more power. The specialist does the immediate translation of mere Oriental matter into useful substance: the Oriental becomes, for example, a subject race, an example of an "Oriental mentality," all for the enhancement of the "authority" at home. "Local interests" are Orientalist special interests, the "central authority" is the general interest of the imperial society as a whole.[14]

Therefore, one hears echoes of much later work, in *Orientalism* and *Culture and Imperialism*, in the transition from "unrestrained egoism" through the "imperialism of ideas" to the "imperialism of nations." Hence, too, Said's point in the latter book that "Kurtz's great looting adventure, Marlow's journey up the river, and the narrative itself all share a common theme: Europeans performing acts of imperial mastery and will in (or about) Africa."[15]

The most profound model for Said of historicizing the insights he derives from Conrad and Schopenhauer was the work of Giambattista Vico, the eighteenth-century Neapolitan philosopher. Vico is important to

Said in various ways. Most simply, perhaps, Vico stands arguably as the inventor of historicist humanism in the European intellectual tradition. He sets out his theory of history in *The New Science* (1744), and Said is plainly drawn to it for reasons both explicit and unspoken. Vico shows none of the cultural nationalism or Eurocentrism that mar the German historicist tradition from Herder onward, and he also predicates much of his understanding on a resolute historicization of himself – he locates himself explicitly in his work, in a move that Said would repeat at the start of all his major books.

Therefore, in the essay "Vico: Autodidact and Humanist," which was published in journal form in 1967, and then as the last chapter of *Beginnings* in 1975, Said offers a reading of the *New Science* alongside Vico's *Autobiography*, which meshes in important ways with his Husserlian-Schopenhaurean reading of Conrad. Said recognizes in Vico's autodidactic approach to intellectual activity a version and a model of his own. Incorporated as the coda to *Beginnings*, Said's discussion of Vico becomes an essential manifesto of his work to come. The self-declaration comes in two forms: the first, entirely explicit; the second, worked out over the course of the essay. Section II of the essay baldly sets out seven Vichian themes crucial to *Beginnings*, and therefore crucial to Said. These include the distinction between origins and beginnings; the combination of intellectual work and a commitment to collectivity; an interest in lateral or adjacent (affiliative) relationships in cultural and intellectual work as much as linear (filiative) ones; and beginning in writing as inaugurating a new order.

Said's substantive discussion of Vico then notes how he takes his own life and his own intellectual leanings, as the root of his project:

> For he was pre-eminently an autodidact (*autodidascolo*) . . . Everything he learned, he learned for and by himself; he seems to have been convinced of his individuality and strength of mind from his earliest days, and most of the time, his *Autobiography* is an account of this self-learning.[16]

Looking at Vico's *Autobiography*, in the earlier version of this essay, Said notes that "the anchoring centre of Vico's work . . . is a paradigm of the disengaged, neutralised mind that is locked in a conflict with itself. The mind's role as an infinite series of modifications on the one hand is opposed by its role on the other as total structure."[17] This is an image of the writerly or intellectual mind of a piece with the earlier Schopenhauerian-Conradian model. Through the influence of Vico, Said generalizes his ideas taken from Conrad outward toward at least two major terrains or themes – the "world of nations," as Vico often called the secular historical and geographical world, and the historical discipline of philology.

Vico, Said tells us

> undertook to demonstrate that in certain provinces of thought or writing, a theory and an actual experience are interchangeable because directly adjacent. The notion of man, as the humanist conceives it, and the experience that man actually undergoes, in all its untidy diversity, are for Vico two sides of the same coin. To ascertain an actual point of historical departure, and to speculate on the nature of things in terms of an abstract origin not renderable accurately in language; these are the extreme opposites that Vico, as philologist and student of language, is able to think and maintain.[18]

Reading this, one sees a version of the Conradian-Husserlian model of the intellectual or writerly subject, which, at times painfully self-divided, forms itself in dialectical contact with and reaction to the external world. But what Vico offers is an historicization of that process, an historical or "worldly" location of that subject. And that historical status is one that is mediated in language. Calling himself an *autodidact*, Vico makes a connection to *authority*, which for the Italian thinker is a product of the human will. To learn something is to exert one's will. But more flows from this: One cannot learn without being conscious of that process. This then can be seen as a principle, and so one arrives at the relationship between *scienza* and *conscienza* – the mind in action and the mind observing itself in action. Hence, to Said (but following Benedetto Croce and Erich Auerbach), the value of reading the *Autobiography* and the *New Science* together:

> the *Autobiography* is Vico's history of himself viewed temporally as a series of successive episodes in the life of a thinker, and the *New Science* is a history of the modifications of man's mind viewed in their eternal aspect – as an enduring thought.[19]

In exactly this vein, Auerbach suggests that "the simple fact [is] that a man's work stems from his existence and that consequently everything that we can find out about his life serves to interpret the work."[20]

Said then sums up this paired reading of Vico's texts. Confronted with the objective presence of nature, and the subjective character of thought, man must seek ways to bring these two elements together in a meaningful way. The mind is most clear in its knowledge of itself, and then only on condition of observation – observation implies the will:

> But will is practically appetitive, and it is soon discovered that intellectual will has little real effect on nature. Human will has . . . a real effect on what

is intellectual and human; yet the substance of thought is sense perception, which is recorded in the mind as imagery . . . Men, however, are gifted with language; and language, because it is associated with the mind, expresses the result of sense perception.[21]

For Vico, language, as expressed in written records, is significantly historical. Philosophy and philology are aspects of each other, as they later would be for Herder, Nietzsche, and indeed for the structuralists and poststructuralists. And indeed, Said compares Vico's self-historicizing view of language to that of Levi-Strauss and Foucault and Derrida, concluding that Vichian humanism "thus engenders its own opposite": One has returned to Said's self-understanding as an antihumanist humanist.[22]

What Vico allows Said is a model of mind and thought that stresses both intellectual activity and language as its tool, and the imbrication of that activity and that instrument in the very history they seek to confront. But Vico, with his stress on *secular* humanism, and on the need to understand human activity in terms of its *beginnings* (which are man-made) rather than "origins" (which may be divine), also underpins Said's sense of criticism as a worldly everyday activity and as what he would later call "an unstoppable predilection for alternatives."[23]

It is not surprising, then, that Said should also find in the work of Erich Auerbach an exceptional model and example for his own beginning. Auerbach was Vico's most important literary reader in the twentieth century, the translator into German of *The New Science*, and Said's own predecessor in the field of comparative literature. Said's translation (along with M. Said) of Auerbach's autumnal essay "Philology and *Weltliteratur*" was published, along with an introductory commentary, in the *Centennial Review* in 1969. In executing this translation at this moment, Said declared his affiliation to the great *philolog* and implicitly situated himself as Auerbach's successor. This essay reveals itself not only as Auerbach taking a position, but also as a program for Said, worked out in the great career-making books of the 1970s.

Said's passionate (but romanticized) account of Auerbach's exile in Istanbul during World War II is well-known, but his affiliation with Auerbach runs much deeper. In both Auerbach and Said, their positions are founded in a sense of civilizational crisis. The crises are significantly different, but that does not prevent Said from creating a powerful and legitimating precursor for himself and his own project. Both Auerbach and Said display a deep unease at the repercussions of modernity. Auerbach, a Jewish exile from the Nazi regime, was writing when the flood of fascism had receded to reveal a shattered and exhausted Europe. Said writes at the end of the long cycle of European imperial retreat that was brought on in part by World War II, and as an intellectual laureate of that decolonization. Auerbach wrote his masterpiece outside of Europe and held his last academic positions in the heart of the new empire; Said's whole career was forged in that same American intellectual-metropolitan core, but this was a position and a tradition from which he felt a powerful alienation due to his Palestinian Arab (or "Oriental") provenance. Both figures hold out some kind of hope for the mission of Romance philology and Goethean *Weltliteratur*, even as they realize that it can never be accomplished as Goethe had once imagined it.

Auerbach's ultimate concern is his sense of philology as an *historical* discipline. His quandary is his acute sense that the general crisis of Western culture in modernity and in the wake of the war is in particular a crisis of historical consciousness. Seeking to revivify historicist scholarship, Auerbach firmly chooses Vico as his model, significantly for himself and for Said. He criticizes Herder's stress on individuality and his failure to analyze the relations of language and power. Noting Herder's interest in the Romantic notion of "folk genius," Auerbach sees that this origin story for historicism turned out to be vulnerable to appropriation by cultural nationalism. But Vico offered Auerbach a nonélitist model of culture and a nonnationalist structure of cultural history – indeed an anti-Utopian model of history.

Auerbach's ultimate statement of historicism or, as he called it, "historism" is *Mimesis*. As Paul Bové shows, this book is a distinctly Vichian work, in its highly engaged sense of its own historicity and indeed of its author's own historical location. Auerbach locates himself in his own text and produces "an engaged history of the present meant to intervene authoritatively in modernity," which accomplishes a number of goals: It shows that in the impoverished conditions of modernity, historical and cultural synthesis can be made; offers an alternative to the overspecialized scholarship of the present; and authorizes Auerbach's own work and project. All these possibilities will later be attributes of Said's own *Orientalism*.

"Philology and *Weltliteratur*" recalibrates Auerbach's position from that of *Mimesis* a little. In this meditative and speculative essay, Auerbach reflects on the state of Romance philology and comparative literature in the early 1950s. In it he sets forth his view of the need for a revitalization of philology, the tasks that face the discipline, and the formidable and alarming new conditions in which this work is to be undertaken: conditions of massification, homogenization, the dwindling of historical consciousness, and what today we'd call globalization. For Auerbach (and later for Said), one of philology's greatest aims is to preserve the humanistic tradition. In the ever-spreading and ramifying conditions of capitalist modernity, this aim is now increasingly difficult to realize. It is and has been the duty of philological humanism to hand on this tradition, and this duty must now be carried out in the teeth of modernity.

The task is one of what Said would later call "civilisational survival," and it is one that he would draw his readers back to in the posthumously published manifesto, *Humanism and Democratic Criticism*, where he explicitly calls for a return to philology and its humanistic values.[24] Auerbach, showing his Vichian inheritance, believes that "humanity" is made by humanistic historical intellectual and cultural activity. Humanity, in other words, is no essence, but the result of human labor. Man makes humanity, makes the conditions for it, has been recording it in written records since the high Middle Ages, and interprets it publicly. "The inner history of the last thousand years is the history of mankind achieving self-expression: this is what philology, an historicist discipline, treats."[25] This has developed in a profound European context:

> It is approximately five hundred years since the national European literatures won their self-consciousness from and their superiority over Latin civilization; scarcely two hundred years have passed since the awakening of our sense of historicism, and a sense that permitted the formation of *Weltliteratur* . . . And already in our own time a world is emerging for which this sense no longer has much practical significance.[26]

The drama of Auerbach's position, and self-positioning, is clear. He feels himself possibly to be writing at the "end of history" or at the "end of the human" (conceived of in terms of the historicist tradition that he traces from Vico, Goethe, and Herder), the end of that tradition, and the end of *Weltliteratur*. But, even more, this is Said's position. Where Auerbach found himself in a temporally disjunctive position vis-à-vis the European tradition, Said is, additionally, profoundly geographically and *spatially* at odds with it, as an exiled intellectual born into a community ruptured and scattered, though now working in the heart of the metropolis.

Bové describes the idea of historicism as historical self-consciousness in Auerbach very well. "'Historism' is an awakening created by and reflecting the process of humanization," he tells us, "that is, of the unfolding of human development resulting from social intercourse among different figures":

> As humanity comes to self-consciousness, historism makes possible the discovery of a new reality and the writing of its history; that is, it makes

possible the writing of a new kind of history that is itself in turn enabled by the humanizing process resulting from the common humanity, the "unity" achieved in diversity, which it records and dramatizes. Auerbach believes that reality can be found in the sense of history that "guides" the humanizing process over the course of its development. He speaks of the "inner bases of national experience" and an "inner history of mankind." Historism is not just a product of the process of this "inner history"; rather, once it emerges as its fulfilment, it is an agent, too, in the humanizing process. So much is humanity dependent on historism that its threatened end in modernity's amnesia also threatens the long-term process of mankind humanizing itself.[27]

Now we can see that the stakes involved in this nexus of humanism, historical consciousness, modernity, and philological practice are tremendously high for Auerbach. If modernity erodes the conditions for the ongoing creation and re-creation of "humanity," then the destruction of historicism will bring the dissolution of *memory* of humanity. More particularly, if modernity, with its leveling and homogenizing tendencies, destroys the possibility of cultural diversity, then the only place where such diversity may exist is in historical memory – that is, in historicist philological memory. For Auerbach, the mission of philology is to be the preservation of that memory, as a possibility, a "message in a bottle" for the humanizing process in the future. In Bové's words, "[T]he preservation of history so that it may in turn be our preserver, is essential."[28]

For Said, the stakes are at least as high, and it is this sense that accounts for the scorching tone of the famous Gramscian account of the *askesis* and work to be performed by the Oriental intellectual within and against Orientalism, in the book of that name.[29] Furthermore, the task of *Orientalism* is to draw the attention of the humanistic and philological tradition to its own involvement in the *dehumanization* of human beings outside of Europe.

Modernity threatens humanity in two particular ways: the decline of education and the subsuming of culture to nationalism. Nationalist chauvinism often stakes its claim on the basis of national cultural exclusivity, but Auerbach, writing at the height of the Cold War, recognizes the remorseless flattening of cultural difference operative in the modern world. He is not interested in national culture as seen in hierarchical or competitive terms: National cultures have their significance only as part of a wider overall ensemble, in which they participate equally. Education, Auerbach reckons, is unhistorical and so fails to engender the historical consciousness that is the core element of humanism and the making of humanity:

> History is the science of reality that affects us most immediately, stirs us
> most deeply and compels us most forcibly to a consciousness of ourselves. It
> is the only science in which human beings step before us in their totality.
> Under the rubric of history one is to understand not only the past but the
> progression of events in general; history, therefore, includes the present.[30]

Auerbach fears that modern cultural education in the West has become
functionalist and self-referential – that is, that it has become a kind of
machine predicated on reified critical concepts or "methods" that turn
every interpretation into an instance and confirmation of themselves.
Writing under the hegemony in the United States of the ahistorical
formalism of the New Criticism, Auerbach seeks to reactivate the historical
contextualization of texts.

Auerbach's negative view of national culture also allows him to see that
while a Goethean idea of *Weltliteratur* may now be apparently realizable –
in the globalized conditions of modernity – this can only take place in the
form of a unity of objectification, exchangeability, and formlessness.

Auerbach's primary mode of dealing with these conditions is through
the idea of exile. This condition, as experienced by Dante (the central
writer for Auerbach, across his career), and indeed by Auerbach, spatializes
the kind of alienation that permits a rational philological vision in and
of the cultural conditions of modernity. "Our philological home is the
earth," he declares; "it can no longer be the nation."[31] Only by way of an
alienation from one's national cultural heritage can one attain the position
worthy of real philological historical consciousness today. To be a humanist in exile is self-consciously to come to grips with the globalizing conditions that harshly cut across humanity and humanism in modern times.
Yet Auerbach does not advocate a direct engagement by the historicist
humanist intellectual with the forces that make the philological mission so
necessary; rather he seems to feel that the task is one of transcendence.

Methodologically, Auerbach offers two techniques for scholarship of the
kind he anticipates. The first of these is the idea of the *Ansatzpunkt* or
starting point; the second is the idea that such work should be accessible –
it must have some public effect. Auerbach is fully convinced that under
the reifying conditions of modernity, specialism in the university and in
knowledge generally is destructive and antihumanistic.

Therefore, the humanist scholar has a twofold duty. She must try to
reach beyond his specialization to grasp, study, and account for the full
range of new knowledge, and she must try to understand the new and
complex experiences of which they are the evidence to understand the

historicity of the present moment. These duties are both the subject matter and the training of the humanist.

The approach to be taken by the humanistic scholar is that of "synthesis." At its simplest, this is Auerbach's mode of scholarly resistance to modern specialization and professionalism. But for Auerbach, the synthetic approach to philological material is inevitably individual and intuitive, and it is also a *performance*: "Should it succeed perfectly we would be given a scholarly achievement and a work of art at the same time. Even the discovery of a point of departure [*Ansatzpunkt*] . . . is a matter of intuition: the performance of a synthesis is a form which must be unified and suggestive if it is to fulfil its potential."[32] Such work has no aspiration to "objectivity": the scholar-critic is always already present in his work from beginning to end. Bové rightly points out that, in the context of German idealism and the hermeneutic tradition, "intuition" suggests an intention on the part of the scholar to move in a certain direction through a mass of mastered textual material.[33] The *Ansatzpunkt* from which this process begins is to be less an imposition of the will of the critic but rather some intuited issue, theme, or problematic that emerges from within that mass of material, which then gives it its coherence and structure in the scholar's study. As such, it is the modern philologist's mode of initiating scholarly work amidst the political and institutional, even moral and epistemological, chaos and variety of modernity.

Returning briefly to Said's major texts, we see this Auerbachian program being critiqued, reanimated, and reinflected in new ways. It is *never* abandoned or swept away – Brennan (again) noted in 1992 how eagerly Said wished to articulate the legacy of Romance philology with the new critical methods emerging in the 1960s.[34] Historically, Said began his career in the high Cold War, but he also wrote in dynamic relation with the period of decolonization. He attributed the energy required to write *Beginnings* to the crisis brought on for the Arab world generally, the doctrine of pan-Arabism, and the Palestinians, specifically, by the June 1967 War. His disjunct sense of the Palestinian dilemma – ongoing conquest and colonization, where the other territories of the former empires were gaining independence – fed into his early sympathy with the structuralist and poststructuralist swing away from Western Marxism. Said, in other words, found himself writing at a hinge moment in the relations between the former "imperial" world, and the emerging new Western order of reassertive capital, information technology, and consumer culture. In this quandary, his identification with Auerbach writing in 1952 is intense. As with Auerbach in the early 1950s, Said in the late 1960s considers himself to be writing at a crucial moment of transition, culturally and politically, and he situates himself, quite deliberately, both to inherit Auerbach's mantle and to adjust it. The notion of the *ansatz-punkt* is clearly fundamental to Said's *Beginnings*, but it is present in all the major books, each of which start with disquisitions on initiating an intellectual project.[35] In the Vichian spirit, the personal note is added – most clearly and dramatically in the model of the Gramscian inventory of the critical self that opens *Orientalism*.

Said's text where the Auerbachian program is spelled out most directly is perhaps *Culture and Imperialism*. In this book, Said invokes the historicist and comparativist tradition going back to Herder and Goethe, while noting that in the postcolonial world it needs to be both critiqued and renewed. The historical situation no longer permits the overall concert of cultures on which the German tradition was predicated. Said's alternative approach is to draw on Gramsci's essay "On the Southern Question," in such a way as to suggest a dynamic interplay, both historical and geographical, between the "canon" of Western literature and cultural history, and the fragmentary, dissonant, and resistant spirit of decolonizing writers and intellectuals. It is in this sense that Herbert Lindenberger can legitimately compare *Culture and Imperialism* to *Mimesis*. The point is not that Said's book aspires to the grand narrative of Auerbach's masterpiece, but rather that Said is moved by a comparable sense of cultural-intellectual crisis and of mission. Where Auerbach saw himself as writing at the end of the concept of *Weltliteratur*, at the end of a grand conception of unitary high literary culture, and therefore (in *Mimesis*) providing a last grand image of that culture at its meridian – a vision of totality – Said writes at a time when the crowding voices of "Third World" writers and intellectuals (of which he is one) can no longer be gainsaid, and when some new model of a world literary system must be advanced.[36]

That model will necessarily, in Said's hands, be of its moment: It will both focus on and bring into being the present cultural and critical moment. Many critics have noted the unevenness of *Culture and Imperialism* – in tone, pattern, content – and concluded that this was due simply to a falling off of Said's critical focus. But W. J. T. Mitchell's view is more accurate: *Culture and Imperialism* is a "great and flawed book," whose flaws are due in part precisely to its Vichian and Auerbachian self-positioning in the historical processes of which it is a "vulnerable" account.[37] For Mitchell, implicitly, *Culture and Imperialism* is a vulnerable and necessarily rifted and fractured version of Auerbach's goal of "synthesis." A totalizing literary history is no longer possible, but this does not mean that the effort toward bringing to performance such unity in diversity cannot be made. This view argues that *Culture and Imperialism* has taken the Auerbachian gesture of *Mimesis* and pressed it into even more dramatic service than that of the philolog in Istanbul, writing his great book without German scholarly resources. Said, too, writes as a kind of critical and philological "memory," after the great period of decolonization, after the Cold War, after the triumph of Zionism, as "the last Jewish intellectual."[38] He writes from what is the ultimate position of "exile" – physically located within the very heart of the metropolis of the last "empire," but ideologically marginal to it, possessed of and embodying a relentless sense of the problematic of the classical humanist tradition but unwilling to cease drawing out its own resources of self-critique; the very self-consciousness of humanism turned against itself; alienated from many of the most obvious cultural and intellectual movements of his own time, a self-conscious autodidact who embodies secular and worldly criticism in himself.

Notes

1 Edward Said, "Opponents, Audiences, Constituencies and Community," in *Postmodern Culture*, ed. by Hal Foster (London: Pluto, 1985), pp. 135–159 (p. 135).

2 Ibid., p. 157; see Seamus Deane, "Edward Said: A Late Style of Humanism," *Field Day Review* 1 (2005), pp. 188–202.

3 Gaston Bachelard, *L'engagement rationaliste* (Paris: Presses Universitaires de France, 1972), p. 7; quoted in Said, *Beginnings: Intention and Method* (New York: Columbia University Press, 1985 [1975], p. 40.

4 See James Clifford, "Review of *Orientalism*," *History and Theory* 19.2 (February 1980), 204–223.

5 Isaac Deutscher, *The Non-Jewish Jew* (London: Merlin, 1981 [1968]), pp. 25–41; see Said, *Humanism and Democratic Criticism* (New York: Columbia University Press, 2004), pp. 76–77.

6 Abdirahman A. Hussein, *Edward Said: Criticism and Society* (London: Verso, 2002).

7 Timothy Brennan, "Places of Mind, Occupied Lands: Edward Said and Philology," in *Edward Said: A Critical Reader*, ed. by Michael Sprinker (Oxford: Blackwell, 1991), pp. 74–95 (pp. 75–77).

8 Said, *Reflections on Exile and Other Essays* (Cambridge, MA: Harvard University Press, 2000), pp. 554–555.

9 Wayne C. Booth, *The Rhetoric of Fiction* (Chicago: University of Chicago Press, 1961).

10 Joseph Conrad, *Last Essays* (Garden City, NY: Doubleday, Page and Company, 1926), p. 197.

11 Said, *The World, the Text, and the Critic*, p. 90.

12 Said, *Joseph Conrad and the Fiction of Autobiography* (New York: Columbia University Press, 2008 [1966]), pp. 108–109.

13 Ibid., p. 140.

14 Said, *Orientalism*, p. 44.

15 Said, *Culture and Imperialism* (London: Chatto and Windus, 1993), p. 25.

16 Said, *Beginnings*, p. 358.

17 Said, "Vico: Autodidact and Humanist," *Centennial Review* 11 (Summer 1967), 336–352 (340).

18 Said, *Beginnings*, p. 350.

19 Ibid., p. 363.

20 Auerbach, *Literary Language and Its Public in Late Latin Antiquity and in the Middle Ages*, trans. by Ralph Mannheim (Princeton, NJ: Princeton University Press, 1965), p. 12.

21 Said, *Beginnings*, p. 364.

22 Ibid., p. 373. Hayden White has suggested that analogies between structuralist and poststructuralist thought and that of Vico are mistaken; see his "Vico and the Radical Wing of Structuralist/Poststructuralist Thought Today," *New Vico Studies I* (1983), 63–68.

23 Said, *The World, the Text, and the Critic*, p. 247.

24 Ibid., p. 6.

25 Erich Auerbach, "Philology and *Weltliteratur*," in *The Princeton Sourcebook in Comparative Literature: From the European Enlightenment to the Global Present*, ed. by David Damrosch, Natalie Melas, and Mbongiseni Buthelezi (Princeton, NJ: Princeton University Press, 2009), pp. 125–138 (p. 128).

26 Ibid., p. 127.

27 Paul A. Bové, *Intellectuals in Power: A Genealogy of Critical Humanism* (New York: Columbia University Press, 1986), pp. 164–165.

28 Ibid., p. 165.

29 Said, *Orientalism* (New York: Pantheon, 1978), pp. 25–27.

30 Auerbach, p. 128.

31 Ibid., p. 137.

32 Ibid., p. 133.

33 Bové, Intellectuals in Power, p. 187.

34 Brennan, "Places of Mind, Occupied Lands," p. 77.

35 See Conor McCarthy, "Said, Lukács and Gramsci: Beginnings, Geography and Insurrection," *College Literature* 40.4 (Fall 2013), 74–104.

36 Herbert Lindenberger, "On the Reception of *Mimesis*," in *Literary History and the Challenge of Philology: The Legacy of Erich Auerbach*, ed. by Seth Lerner (Stanford, CA: Stanford University Press, 1996), pp. 195–211 (pp. 207–210).

37 W. J. T. Mitchell, "In the Wilderness," *London Review of Books* 15.7 (April 8, 1993), 11–12.

38 Said, *Power, Politics and Culture: Interviews with Edward W. Said*, ed. by Gauri Viswanathan (New York: Pantheon, 2001), p. 458.

CHAPTER 3

The Dual Legacy of Orientalism

Vivek Chibber

There is little doubt that Edward Said's *Orientalism* is one of the most influential scholarly works of the past few decades. While it was initially presented by its author as a study of how a particular body of knowledge contributed to the spread of European colonial rule, its influence has extended to just about every domain connected with imperialism, colonial history, race, and political identity. Owing to the very scope of the work that either builds directly on Said's argument or is inspired by it, it is not a simple task to assess his legacy. Perhaps the most contentious issue is its impact on the study of the Global South and, more specifically, on the field that developed rapidly after *Orientalism*'s publication, postcolonial studies. In many ways, it is hard to imagine that there could be a direct connection between Said's profound commitment to humanism, universal rights, secularism, and liberalism, on the one hand, and postcolonial theory's quite explicit disavowal of, or at least its skepticism toward, those very tropes on the other hand. And indeed, his most able interpreters have made a powerful case that the connection is, at best, tenuous. In this essay I will suggest that whatever his own commitments, *Orientalism* prefigured, and hence encouraged, some of the central dogmas of postcolonial studies – indeed, the very ones that cannot withstand scrutiny. And despite its very many strengths, its legacy is therefore a dual one – propelling the critique of imperialism into the very heart of the mainstream, on the one hand, but also giving strength to intellectual fashions that have undermined the possibility of that very critique on the other hand.

Orientalism as Cause and Effect

There are two arguments in *Orientalism* about the relation between Western imperialism and its accompanying discourse. The first, and the one that has emerged as a kind of folk conception of the phenomenon, describes Orientalism as a *rationalization* for colonial rule. Said dates this

Orientalism to the eighteenth century, with the rise of what is now called
the Second British Empire, and Orientalism continued into the Cold War
when the United States displaced Britain as the global hegemon.[1] It was
during these centuries that Orientalism flourished as a body of knowledge
that not only described and systematized how the East was understood but
also did so in a fashion that justified its domination by the West. Hence,
if nationalists demanded the right to self-governance by Asians, or criticized the racism of colonial regimes, defenders schooled in Orientalism
could retort:

> That Orientals have never understood the meaning of self-government the
> way "we" do. When Orientals oppose racial discrimination while others
> practice it, you say "they're all Orientals at bottom", and class interest,
> political circumstances and economic factors are totally irrelevant ... His-
> tory, politics, and economics do not matter. Islam is Islam, the Orient is the
> Orient, and please take all your ideas about a left and a right wing,
> revolutions, and change back to Disneyland.[2]

In other words, the normal grounds of political judgment did not apply to
colonial settings, because, in relying on them, colonial critics presumed
that Eastern peoples were motivated by the same needs and goals as those
of the West. But this, Orientalism advised, was a fallacy. Asians did not
think in terms of self-determination, class, their economic interests, and so
forth. To object to colonialism claiming it rode roughshod over these
needs, or, more ambitiously, to generate a system of rights based on the
presumptive universality of those needs, was to ignore the distinctiveness of
Eastern culture. It was based on a category mistake and, indeed, could even
be criticized as an insensitivity to their cultural specificity. In so conceptualizing the colonial subject as the quintessential Other, Orientalism
absolved imperialism of any wrongdoing and thereby stripped demands
for self-determination of any moral authority. Said's argument here is a
fairly traditional, materialist explanation for how and why Orientalist
ideology came to occupy such a prominent place in European culture in
the modern period. Just as any system of domination creates an ideological
discourse to justify and naturalize its superordinate position, so too colonialism created a legitimizing discourse of its own. The key here is that the
causal arrow runs *from* imperial domination *to* the discourse it created –
simply put, colonialism created Orientalism.

This is undoubtedly the argument for which *Orientalism* is best known.
But it is also the component of Said's argument that is the most conventional and familiar. Said was not by any means the first anti-imperialist to
describe modern Orientalism as being tied to the colonial project. Or, to

put it more broadly, he was not the first to show that much of the social scientific and cultural scholarship produced by colonial powers was in fact geared to justifying their rule over Eastern nations. As Said noted, albeit somewhat belatedly, his book was preceded by scores of works that made the same argument from scholars belonging to the postcolonial world.[3] Many, if not most, belonged to the Marxist tradition in some degree of proximity. What set Said's great book apart, then, was not the argument he made but the erudition and literary quality that he brought to it. For even while others had made claims that were identical to his, no one had made them with the same panache and, hence, to the same effect.

But Said also makes another argument, running through the entirety of his book, that reverses this causal arrow, and takes the argument in an entirely novel direction. On this version, Orientalism was not a conse-quence of colonialism, but one of its *causes*: "To say simply that Oriental-ism was a rationalization of colonial rule," Said avers, "is to ignore the extent to which colonial rule was justified *in advance* by Orientalism, rather than *after* the fact."[4] In other words, Orientalism was around far before the modern era and, by virtue of its depiction of the East, it created the cultural conditions for the West to embark on its colonial project. That depiction had at its core the urge to categorize, schematize, and exoticize the East, viewing it as mysterious and unchanging, in contrast to the familiar and dynamic West. Hence, the West was ordained the center of moral and scientific progress, and the exotic and unchanging East, which was an object to be studied and apprehended, but always alien, was always distant.

Said traces this tendency back to the Classical world, continuing through the medieval period, and culminating in the great works of the Renaissance and after.[5] This implies that Orientalism is not so much a product of circumstances specific to a historical conjuncture, but some-thing embedded deeply in Western culture. To push this argument, Said makes a distinction between *latent* and *manifest* Orientalism.[6] The latent components are its essential core, its basic moral and conceptual architec-ture, which have been in place since Homer and define it as a discourse. Its manifest elements are what give Orientalism its form in any particular era and, hence, the components that undergo change in the course of history. Manifest Orientalism organizes the basic, underlying bits compris-ing latent Orientalism into a coherent doctrine, and its most coherent incarnation is, of course, the one synthesized in the modern era.

This distinction enables Said to accommodate the obvious fact that, as a discourse, Orientalism has not remained unchanged across space and time.

He readily admits that Western conceptions of the East have undergone innumerable transformations in form and content over the centuries. Still, "[W]hatever change occurs in knowledge of the Orient is found almost exclusively in *manifest* Orientalism." In other words, the changes have only been in the way Orientalism's essential principles are expressed, their essence remaining more or less the same across the centuries. Said continues, "[T]he unanimity, stability, and durability of *latent* Orientalism are more or less constant [over time]."[7]

It is not just that latent Orientalism imbricates itself into the pores of Western culture. It is also that, once embedded so securely, it goes beyond simple bias to becoming a *practical orientation* – an urge to bring reality in line with its conception of how the world ought to be. To Said, this practical stance has been a defining characteristic of the Orientalist mindset, from Antiquity to the modern era, despite all the changes that it experienced across time. This has enormous consequences for the fate of East-West relations. Said poses the following question: Once the world is carved up analytically the way Orientalism enjoins us to, "can one survive the consequences humanly? [Is there] any way of avoiding the hostility by the division, say, of men into 'us' (Westerners) and 'they' (Orientals)."[8] The question is rhetorical, of course, because for Said the answer is obviously in the negative. The hostility bred by latent Orientalism is passed on from one generation to another as a pillar of Western culture, always viewing the East as inferior. And as it becomes internalized and fixed as a cultural orientation, the urge to *improve* the natives, to help them clamber up the civilizational hierarchy, becomes irresistible. It slowly generates a momentum toward a transition from gaining *knowledge* about the Orient to the more ambitious project of acquiring *power* over it. Said's own description of this process is worth quoting:

> Transmitted from one generation to another, it [latent Orientalism] *was a part of the culture,* as much a language about a part of reality *as geometry or physics.* Orientalism staked its existence, not upon its openness, its receptivity to the Orient, but rather on its internal, repetitious consistency about its constitutive *will-to-power* over the Orient.[9]

Latent Orientalism came packaged as a *will-to-power.* This was the practical orientation that it embodied. Hence, the obsessive accumulation of *facts,* Said suggests, "made Orientalism fatally tend toward the systematic *accumulation of human beings* and *territories.*"[10]

Notice that this version of his argument just about completely inverts the first, materialist, one: instead of a system of domination creating its justifying ideology, it is the latter that generates the former: An ideology now creates the power relations that it justifies. One is not sure how far Said wishes to press this point – whether he takes Orientalism to merely be an enabling condition for colonialism's rise, as against a stronger, more propulsive role. I will consider the merits of both interpretations later in this essay. But it seems clear that, on this second argument, he views Orientalism as in some way responsible for the rise of European colonialism, not just its consequence.

Now *this* argument, unlike the first, does add considerable novelty to the critique of Orientalism. As Fred Halliday observed in a discussion of the book, critiques of Orientalist constructions had typically been materialist in their approach and grounded in political economy. Said's originality derived in his formulation of an argument that gave a nod to this older approach, but then veered decisively away from it, offering what was an unmistakably culturalist alternative. Hence, "[W]hile much of the other work was framed in broadly Marxist terms and was a universalist critique, Said, eschewing materialist analysis, sought to apply literary critical methodology and to offer an analysis specific to something called 'the Orient.'"[11] It is to this innovation that we now turn.

Two Early Critics

Said's second argument attracted some attention in the early years after *Orientalism* appeared, most pointedly in Sadik al-Azm's biting critique in *Khamsin*, and then in Aijaz Ahmad's broadside in his book *In Theory*. As al-Azm correctly observed, Said's second argument was not only in tension with but also fatally undermined his objective of criticizing Orientalist views of modern history. For to say, as Said did, that Orientalism had been the defining element in the Western constructions of the East, without attributing it to any social or institutional matrix, strongly suggested that Orientalism was in some way part of the enduring cognitive apparatus of the West. It led inexorably to the conclusion, al-Azm suggested, that "Orientalism is not really a thoroughly modern phenomenon . . . but is the natural product of an ancient and almost irresistible European bent of mind to misrepresent the realities of other cultures, peoples, and their languages, in favour of Occidental self-affirmation."[12] But if this is what Said was saying, then did it not resurrect the very Orientalism that he disavowed? A defining characteristic of this worldview, after all, was the idea of an ontological chasm separating East and West, which the fields, categories, and theories emanating from the West could not traverse. The

Western mind, in other words, was not capable of apprehending the true nature of Eastern culture. Said's implantation of Orientalist discourse as an unchanging component of Western culture seemed to reinforce this very idea – of the inscrutability of the Orient to Western eyes – from the Greeks to Henry Kissinger.

The same questions about Said's second argument were raised by Aijaz Ahmad in a landmark assessment of his broader oeuvre, published almost a decade after al-Azm's review.[13] Ahmad speculated that Said's second rendering of the connection between Orientalism and colonialism was perhaps attributable to the influence of Foucault; though, for Ahmad, it was questionable whether Foucault would have supported the idea of a putative continuity in Western discourse from Homer to Nixon.[14] The critical problem for Ahmad, however, was not Said's fidelity to Foucault, but the theoretical and political consequences of locating Orientalism in the deep recesses of Western culture, rather than among the consequences of colonialism. Ahmad raised two issues in particular.

First, Said seemed to take the Orientalist mind-set to be so pervasive in scope and so powerful in influence that the possibility of escaping its grip appeared exceedingly remote. Hence, even thinkers known to be fierce critics of British colonialism are blandly assimilated into the rogues' gallery of European Orientalists. The most prominent figure in this regard is Marx, who Said relegates to this ignominious status with only the flimsiest of explanations. Ahmad's foregrounding of this issue was surely justified, given the role that Marx and his followers had played in not only criticizing the racism of colonial apologists but also in their leading role in anticolonial movements – from Ireland, to India, from Tanzania to Said's own homeland of Palestine. Ahmad pointed out, again correctly, that the very passages that Said singled out as instances of cultural parochialism could easily be read in a very different vein as describing, not the superiority of Western culture, but the brutality of colonial rule.[15] In any case, regardless of one's judgment about Marx, what was at issue here was whether Said could justifiably claim that Orientalism not only stretched back to Classical Greece but also exercised such power as to absorb even its critics.

Further, Ahmad pointed to a second, equally important implication of the analysis. Said's argument, and also his vocabulary, pushed strongly toward displacing the traditional interest-based explanations for colonialism in the direction of one relying on civilizational clashes. Conventional accounts of colonial expansion had typically adverted to the role of interest groups, classes, and state managers as its animating force. For Marxists it had been capitalists, for nationalists it had been "British interests," and for liberals it was overly ambitious political leaders. What all these explanations had in common was the central role that they accorded to material interests as the motivating factor in colonial rule. But if in fact Orientalism as a body of thought propels its believers toward the accumulation of territories, then it is not interests that drive the project, but a deeply rooted cultural disposition – a discourse, to put it in contemporary jargon. As Ahmad concludes:

> This idea of constituting identity through difference points, again, not to the realm of political economy in which colonisation may be seen as a process of capitalist accumulation but to a necessity which arises within discourse and has always been there at the origin of discourse, so that not only is the modern orientalist presumably already there in Dante and Euripedes but modern imperialism itself appears to be an *effect* that arises, as if naturally, from the necessary practices of discourse. (182; emphasis added)

Ahmad is registering his agreement with al-Azm's judgment that Said has reversed the causal arrow that normally went *from* colonialism *to* Orientalism. Naturally this means that the study of this phenomenon moves from the ambit of political economy to cultural history. But it is not just that colonial expansion appears to be an artifact of discourse. The dispositions that it comprises are placed by him, not in a particular region or historical era, but in an undifferentiated entity called "the West," stretching back two millennia. This is, of course, a classically Orientalist assertion on Said's part. But its implications for the study of colonialism are profound. For colonialism now appears, not as the consequence of developments particular to a certain era, but as an expression of a deeper ontological divide between East and West, a symptom of the cultural orientation of Europe's inhabitants. We have gone from the culprit being British capitalists, to its being "the West" – from classes to cultures.

Said never addressed either al-Azm or Ahmad's criticisms – a shame because they remain among the most important and devastating engagements with his work to date.[16] In a private exchange with al-Azm, he promised to reply at some length, and indeed to dismantle al-Azm's entire critique point by point.[17] But he never delivered on that promise, nor did he respond in print to Ahmad's critique. In the rest of this essay I purpose to build upon those early interventions to push further in the same direction. Ahmad and al-Azm were justified in their observation that Said's argument had turned the corner from materialist critique of ideology to an idealist argument. But while their accusation was correct, their justification of it was not fully developed – perhaps because they took the weakness of idealist Said's argument for granted. In today's context, however, it is important to further develop the line of argument they opened up, and demonstrate why Said's view is wrong *by virtue* of its idealism.

The crux of what I wish to argue is that Said's second argument – that colonialism was a consequence of Orientalism, not its cause – was not only disturbing in its implications but also that it could not possibly be right, on Said's own admission. In other words, what al-Azm and Ahmad failed to observe was that *the second argument was contradicted by Said's own evidence*. Orientalism *could not* have generated modern colonialism or even contributed to it in any significant way. Its roots therefore have to be sought in political economy, not in European culture – much as materialists had argued for decades.

Culture and Colonialism

Said is correct in his observation that ethnocentric and essentializing depictions of the East were widespread among European observers from the earliest times. The question is what explanatory role such depictions are accorded in the rise of European colonialism. We have seen in the preceding section that Said clearly assigns considerable importance to them in this regard. Just what the causal chain is that connects them to it, and how important they are compared to other factors, is murky. But we can be confident that the role is important because he never qualifies it, nor feels compelled to embed it in a wider discussion of how it combined with other forces that pushed Britain and France outward in the modern era. The problem with Said's view is that, in his own description of the content of Orientalism, and his empirical discussion of its relation to other cultures' own discourses about the West, the argument for its importance as a factor in the advent of modern colonialism breaks down. And by extension, the promotion of culture as a central explanatory factor in the latter process must also be demoted.

The central problem with which Said must contend is that there was nothing unique in the West's highly parochial understanding of the Orient. The same essentialized and ethnocentric conceptions were typical of Eastern understandings of the West. Hence, the texts we have from Arab, Persian, and Indian descriptions of European culture from pre-colonial times are no less parochial in their descriptions of Europe and its people, and no less prone to generalize across time and space. Indeed, it is hard to imagine any description of a culture that can escape the tendency to categorize, generalize across cases, and schematize in some way or form. The fact is that aspects of Western scholarship of the East that Said takes to be Orientalist are in fact found in many instances of cross-cultural observation or scholarship.

Said of course knows this and readily admits to it. Hence, he observes,

> One ought again to remember that all cultures impose corrections upon raw reality, changing it from free-floating objects into units of knowledge. The problem is not that conversion takes place. It is perfectly natural for the human mind to resist the assault on it of untreated strangeness; therefore cultures have always been inclined to impose complete transformations on other cultures, receiving these other cultures not as they are but as, for the benefit of the receiver, they ought to be.[18]

But this admission raises a fundamental problem for Said's insistence that Orientalism was in some way responsible for modern imperialism. For if the urge to categorize, essentialize, and generalize about other cultures – which Said insists is what Orientalism does – is common to *all* cultures, then how can it explain the rise of modern colonialism, which is a project specific to *particular* nations? In other words, if this mind-set was common to many cultures, then it cannot have been what generated colonialism because the latter was particular to a few nations in (mostly) Western Europe.

One way to save Said's second argument would be to weaken the claim for Orientalism's causal role. As I suggested in the preceding section, because of Said's ambiguity regarding its status, there are a variety of ways that we could construe his claim. At the very least, we can distinguish between a strong version of it and a weak one:

> *Strong version*: Latent Orientalism was *sufficient* to launch colonialism. On this account, the motivational push coming from cultural essentialism was all that was needed to launch a colonial project. No other preconditions were necessary.

> *Weak version*: Latent Orientalism was necessary *but not sufficient* to launch colonialism. On this account, the racism associated with latent Orientalism was an indispensable precondition for colonialism, but it needed other factors to also be present – perhaps political and economic ones. But the latter cold not have been effective had the Orientalist mind-set not been gestating.

The strong version proposes that once the Orientalist mind-set was in place, it could, on its own, generate modern colonialism. On this view, no other contributing factor was needed to bring about the result. Hence, it would predict that any country that viewed other cultures through this prism would embark on colonial expansion. Clearly this view is contradicted by the observation that the number of countries with an "Orientalist" mind-set (as described in the preceding text) far exceeded the number that in fact embarked on colonial expansion. So the strong version cannot be sustained.

Another strategy to save Said's second argument would be to resort to its weak version. The burden here would be to propose that even if latent Orientalism could not, by itself, generate colonialism, it was nonetheless an essential part of the combination of factors that did bring it about. Hence, it was still necessary, even though it wasn't sufficient and even though it had to act in tandem with other factors.[19] Thus, it might be that economic interest or political ambitions were also critical in generating the British or French thrust into the Middle East. The search for oil, the desire to find new markets, the need to secure geopolitical advantage by capturing key ports – all these might have been critical motivating factors for the European powers. The weaker argument would be able to accommodate all these into an explanation for the rise of modern imperialism. It would not have to claim that racial prejudice alone was what drove the Europeans outward. But it could still insist that these other factors on their own would not have been sufficient for the outcome. Without the mind-set created by the already existing latent Orientalism, the other factors might have remained inert, unable to muster the force needed to launch the project.

This would probably be the commonsensical defense of Said's argument, and it is certainly the most effective. But while it has a surface appeal, this version also fails for two reasons. The first has to do with the internal structure of the argument. Nobody doubts that factors like economic or political motivation had to play a role in colonialism's rise. In that sense, the place of the broader causal complex is secure. The question is, once the economic motivation is in place, will its proponents also require the psychological orientation generated by Orientalism to undertake the colonial project? It might seem that the answer is an obvious yes because it could be claimed a process as brutal and costly as colonialism could not be undertaken without some moral or ethical justification – not just for the wider public but also for its practitioners. Moral agents could not engage in oppressive practices, they could not terrorize other human beings, unless they believed that the endeavor served a higher purpose. And this is what Orientalism provided them, with its claims to civilize and educate the natives. The ethnic and racial domination implied by modern colonialism would thus be perceived by its progenitors as a moral undertaking, not just the naked pursuit of power and profit. This is the sense in which Orientalism might be suggested to be necessary, albeit insufficient, as a causal factor in the expansion of European rule.

But what this argument would overlook is that it is not the rationalizing function of Orientalism that is in question but the need for it to be *already present* in European culture at the *inception* of the imperial project. Thus, materialist arguments could easily allow that an economically motivated project is greatly facilitated by a discourse that rationalizes the project on moral grounds. But they would deny the stronger proposition that, had the discourse not been in place, the project would have stalled or failed to be launched. This is so because, once the economic interest is in place, there is an endogenously generated pressure to *create* a justifying discourse for the project, even where such a discourse does not already exist. Dominant agents are not impeded by the fact they do not have, ready at hand, a rationalizing ideology. Where it does not exist, they cobble one together. This is, after all, the main function of intellectuals – to serve ruling groups by crafting an ideology that justifies their dominance on moral grounds. So the absence of such a discourse at the project's inception cannot be deemed an obstacle to its launching.

But this is exactly what is implied in Said's claim that *latent* imperialism was in some way responsible for the modern colonial project. For even the weak version of his second argument to succeed, it has to establish that, had British and French elites not had the intellectual resources of Orientalism already available to them, this absence would have been an obstacle to their colonial project. Without this claim, the second argument collapses into a materialist one. If Said were to agree that, even if Orientalism had not been available as an academic discipline, even if latent Orientalism had been absent from the scene, its basic elements could have nonetheless been crafted *ex nihilo* to justify colonial rule – then he would be suggesting that *latent* Orientalism was not in fact a necessary part of the causal complex that brought about colonialism. If it is conceded that colonial elites were capable of generating their own rationalizing discourse, then latent Orientalism fails even as a necessary component of the forces behind colonialism. We are now back to the materialist argument that ruling classes *create* the ideology needed for their reproduction, and not the other way around.

Hence, Said's second argument cannot be sustained, even in its weak form. Once it is admitted that essentializing descriptions of other cultures were common across East and West, and once we recognize that other motivations were enough to propel states outward, then it cannot be maintained that the mind-set created by these descriptions was *in any way* responsible for the colonial project. What was in fact responsible was what Marxists and progressive nationalists had been suggesting for a century prior to the publication of *Orientalism* – the material interests and capacities of particular social formations in the West. It is to Said's credit that he acknowledges the fact of cross-cultural parochialism – but quite astonishing that he is unaware of how devastating the admission is to his argument. The admission injects a deep and unresolvable contradiction in one of his fundamental claims. Once this part of his book is rejected, as it should be, what remains standing is his first argument – that the basic function of Orientalism was to serve as the justification of colonial rule, as its consequence, not cause.

Legacy

Said never addressed the ambiguity in his book regarding the relationship between Orientalist discourse and the colonial project – in chief, the copresence of two diametrically opposed enunciations of that relationship. But, in many ways, that very ambiguity played a role in the easy assimilation of *Orientalism* into the broader shifts underway around the time of its publication. The early 1980s was when critical intellectuals ceased to be enamored of Marx and Marxist theory, turning to the warm embrace of poststructuralism and, soon thereafter, postcolonial theory. In this context, Said's incipient culturalism, his nod to the potentially primary role of ideas and discourse in the initiation of colonialism, folded seamlessly into the shifts that were occurring in the scholarly world. His explicit overtures to Foucault, his adoption of some of the latter's conceptual vocabulary, packaged the book in a fashion that made it easily digestible, even familiar. Substantively, the culturalism of his second argument – which elicited censure from Marxists like al-Azm and Ahmad – barely raised an eyebrow in the wider firmament because this was the very direction in which critical theory was evolving. Indeed, the reaction from broader circles was directed, not at Said, but at Ahmad, whose important critique of Said was met with a campaign so vicious and personalized that it is jarring to revisit it even a quarter-century later.[20]

But the second aspect of Said's book that ensured its warm reception had to do with his treatment of Marx. Said did not just present his book as a scholarly work on colonial ideology but also as a representative of the *anticolonial* tradition. It was packaged as a work of critical theory – deeply erudite, intensely scholarly, but never neutral. In this respect, it was intended to be part of the anticolonial tradition associated with the global

Left in the twentieth century. But as he well knew, that tradition had been led by, and associated with, Marxist and socialist theory since the late nineteenth century. Even mainstream nationalists drew on the theories and the political ambitions of the Marxist Left, from India and China to South Africa and Peru. The only political currents that were explicitly hostile to that tradition were those associated with conservative nationalists and religious groups. For a century prior to the publication of *Orientalism*, the progressive critique of colonialism had always orbited around, and drawn upon, Marxism.

Said's innovation was to be the most significant intellectual who claimed the mantle of radical anticolonialism, *while also* denouncing Marx as a purveyor of an alien and highly parochial values and analysis. This was significant in several respects. First and foremost, for the rapidly professionalizing New Left – now tenured and looking for acceptance in the American academy – it provided an ideal instrument to distance themselves from Marxist theory *while still* identifying as radicals. It was now possible to reinvent colonial critique so that it defended the idea of self-determination, while eschewing any association with socialist or Marxist ideas. Indeed, the preferred motif now became to criticize the Marxist legacy as *not radical enough* – hence to outflank it rhetorically from the Left.

These strategies were neatly exemplified in an influential series of essays on Marxism and colonial critique, by the Indian historian Gyan Prakash. Writing in the early 1990s, when Said's influence was well established, Prakash upheld the banner of anticolonialism, calling for a root-and-branch excision of Orientalism from colonial historiography – in which one of the main targets turned out to be Marx and his followers.[21] What was significant here was not just the novelty of turning Marx into a proponent of the "colonial gaze" – to use a bit of postcolonial jargon; but equally, for Prakash to draw explicitly on Said, on *Orientalism*, and to drape his argument in that book's conceptual vocabulary. This strategy was soon just about ubiquitous in all the fields in which area studies played any significant role, so that by the second decade of this century, it was taken for granted that the only way in which Marxist theory could have anything to offer in colonial critique was if somehow it could be rid of its Western bias and its putative endorsement of colonialism – for which Said's work was, and still is, taken to be the remedy.

Second, a central implication of Said's description of Marx as an Orientalist was that the analytical categories associated with him were similarly demoted. It had been common, even typical, in the critical

anticolonial tradition to approach the subject through the prism of political economy – even if the analyst did not mobilize its categories, the deep
and enduring relation between colonial expansion and capitalist motives
was at least assumed, if not highlighted. But in a book devoted to the
explication of colonial ideology, to the connection between that ideology
and the colonial project, Said studiously distances himself from any
reference to capitalism. Neither the word nor its cognates even make an
appearance in *Orientalism*, except in reference to others' works or in irony.
The entire issue is presented and analyzed through the framework of
cultural analysis, in which the thinker who receives a positive endorsement
is not Marx, nor Lenin and Luxemburg, who wrote the two most influential analysis of imperialism in the twentieth century – but Foucault.

What made the marginalization of political economy all the more
significant was the framework he seemed to offer in its place. At the core
of the traditional materialist understanding of colonialism was the analysis
of capitalism and the wider theory bound up with it – the manner in
which class interests shaped imperialism; the relation of laboring classes to
it; the question of whether, and how much, they might have benefited to
it; the mechanisms by which local elite interests were harnessed to the
project; and of course, the role of the state. But few of these concerns make
their way into Said's framework. The categories that drive his analysis are
civilizational and geographical – East and West, Orient and Occident.
Capitalists and workers, peasants and landlords – the normal concepts of
political analysis are displaced by the very categories that Said ought to
have been anxious to set aside. Rather than interests, what motivates
colonialists is the West's "will to power," a concept that is connected to
interests only semantically, if at all.

The evacuation of materialist categories, the turn to culturalism, the
positing of what appears to be a cognitive divide between West and East,
the pillorying of Marx as another in a long line of European Orientalists –
all these elements in Said's argument were entirely in line with the
evolution of critical scholarship in the era of Reagan and Thatcher. As
social theory went from materialist to culturalist, and from culturalist to
postcolonial, overtures to *Orientalism* remained a fixture throughout. And
Said, a humanist and lifelong critic of cultural essentialisms, became
associated with an intellectual turn that has resurrected the very Orientalist
tropes that he spent much of his career trying to undermine. Said was
apparently never entirely at ease with this circumstance, as Timothy
Brennan has observed.[22] But he did little to overturn it, far less to resist
it. For better or worse, he not only tolerated but also presided over his
enshrinement as one of the foundational thinkers of the postcolonial turn.

For those who seek a return to the materialist roots of the anti-colonial tradition in scholarship, the dimensions of Said's *Orientalism* I have highlighted – his second argument, the essentialism that it entailed, the demotion of political economy, and the positing of an East-West dichotomy – will have to be set aside. This means that one of the tasks is to revive the critical approach endorsed by scholars such as al-Azm and Ahmad, against the mountainous and deplorable calumny to which they have been subjected. Most of all, it will mean placing the question of class and capitalism back at the center of political and historical analysis of colonialism – and also of the postcolonial states that followed in its wake. But this does not by any means entail a rejection of *Orientalism*. The materialist core of Said's work remains valid, untouched by the infirmities of his "Orientalism-in-reverse," as al-Azm correctly described his second argument. It still offers an imposing edifice upon which the anticolonial tradition can build. It is just that this dimension of Said's great work will have to be embedded in an analytical framework that draws upon, and returns to, those categories that are missing from *Orientalism*, and that postcolonial theory has worked for more than a generation to either bury or forget – back to political economy, for which, even today, Marx remains the indispensable starting point.

Notes

1 Edward Said, *Orientalism* (New York: Vintage, 2003), pp. 3, 4, 41, 42, 95, 201.
2 *Orientalism*, p. 107.
3 Said, "Orientalism Reconsidered," *Cultural Critique* 1 (Autumn 1985), 93.
4 Ibid., p. 39. Emphasis added.
5 *Orientalism*, pp. 56–60.
6 The distinction is introduced in *Orientalism*, pp. 206. The discussion of the relation between the two and their functions comprises chapter 3, part 1, pp. 201–225.
7 Ibid., p. 206.
8 Ibid., p. 45.
9 Ibid., p. 222. Emphasis added.
10 Ibid., 123. Emphasis added.
11 Fred Halliday, "Orientalism and Its Critics," *British Journal of Middle Eastern Studies* 20.2 (1993), 145–163 (148).
12 Sadik al-Azm, "*Orientalism* and Orientalism in Reverse," *Khamsin: Journal of Revolutionary Socialists of the Middle East* 8 (1981), pp. 5–26.
13 Aijaz Ahmad, "*Orientalism* and After: Ambivalence and Metropolitan Location in the Work of Edward Said," *In Theory* (London: Verso, 1992), pp. 159–220.
14 Ibid., pp. 165–167.

15 For the most thorough and quite decisive engagement with Said's arguments about Marx, see Gilbert Achcar, "The Specters of Marx in Edward Said's *Orientalism*", *Welt des Islams*, 53–2 (2013), 149–191.

16 In correspondence, he promised al-Azm that he would respond. But to my knowledge he never did. Ahmad's critique was met with silence by Said and with aggressively *ad hominem* arguments by his followers.

17 He warned al-Azm, "I don't think you've ever tangled with a polemicist of my sort … I propose to teach you a lesson in how to argue and how to make points." Said to al-Azm, November 10, 1980. http://pastandfuture presents.blogspot.co.uk/2016/12/edward-saidsadik-al-azm-1980.html (accessed September 24, 2017).

18 *Orientalism*, p. 67.

19 It would be what John Mackie referred to as an INUS condition – a necessary but insufficient component of an unnecessary but sufficient causal complex. See Mackie, "Causes and Conditions," *American Philosophical Quarterly* 2.4 (October 1965), 245–264.

20 A flavor of the tone taken by critics may be had in the symposium organized by *Public Culture*, Fall 1993. The most personalized attacks, noteworthy for their combination of a patronizing tone with a near-complete absence of engagement with Ahmad's arguments, are probably by Neil Lazarus and Benita Perry. See Parry, "A Critique Mishandled," *Social Text* 35 (1993), 121–133 and Neil Lazarus, "Postcolonialism and the Dilemma of National-ism – Aijaz Ahmad's Critique of Third-Worldism," *Diaspora: A Journal of Transnational Studies* 2.3 (Winter 1993), 373–400. For a rare instance of actual engagement, see Neil Larson, "Determination: Postcolonialism, Post-structuralism and the Problem of Ideology," *Dispositio* 20.47 (1995), 1–16.

21 Gyan Prakash, "Postcolonial Criticism and Indian Historiography," *Social Text* 31/32 (1992), 8–19, esp. 13–14.

22 Timothy Brennan, "The Illusion of a Future: 'Orientalism' as Traveling Theory," *Critical Inquiry* 26.3 (Spring 2000), 558–583.

CHAPTER 4

Culture and Imperialism
Errors of a Syllabus

Seamus Deane

Edward Said's *Culture and Imperialism* (1993) is widely regarded as perhaps the last echo of the great work of European humanism, Erich
Auerbach's *Mimesis: The Representation of Reality in Western Litera*ture
(1946), a book that Said revered. The fiftieth anniversary of the first
English translation of *Mimesis* was published in 2003, with an introduction by Said, in the year Said died. Both books give memorable accounts of
an extensive range of works of art that belong to a common tradition.
Auerbach's presiding idea is that European realism evolves out of an
opposition between the formal and hierarchical modes of representation
and the biblical mode; over the centuries they gradually yield one to the
other to produce realism, a fusion or an evolution through which we
achieve the representation of access to the inner consciousness, the modern
domain of "reality." Said's *Culture and Imperialism* deploys what he calls a
"contrapuntal" method of reading or listening to the nuances of texts in
which the tacit reliance of European claims to universality on imperialism
and the note of resistance to them become simultaneously audible. Such
stethoscopic readings release a "nomadic" energy that passes beyond the
limits of those congealed ideas of racial essence and servile mimicry by
which colonial texts are bound. Humanism would thereby be extended in
its geographic range and in its moral compass. Further, it would have to
survive Fanon's accusation that "Europe is literally the creation of the
Third World" and Sartre's amplification of it, as quoted by Said: "There is
nothing more consistent than a racist humanism, since the European has
only been able to become a man through creating slaves and monsters."[1]
Said had already demonstrated in the marvelous essays of *The World, the
Text, and the Critic* (1983) the existence of that truly global and secular
humanism Fanon and Sartre had dismissed as a possibility.

Culture and Imperialism and *Mimesis* are synoptic and miscellaneous;
they imply a totality that neither can realize. The examples they choose to
embody or illustrate their general themes simply cannot be exemplary

enough – always open to the complaint that they are arbitrary, forced, instances of special pleading. Yet both have also been accorded the status of serene overviews of a whole field. Auerbach's position in this regard is more secure, not least because Said has helped to elevate it but also because Auerbach's work has been around longer. There is also the *timing* of the appearance of each. Auerbach's book appeared after World War II. He wrote it while teaching in Istanbul, expelled from the center of Europe by the Nazis, isolated from the great libraries he felt he needed for a work of such scope. These are among the often-rehearsed circumstances that gave the book its wide appeal. Its title and its timing, the common word *reality*, the political–cultural word *representation*, the prestigious Greek word-concept of the short title – all had special resonance in the moment of European recovery after what seemed like total collapse. Culture had not only survived but also had expanded its role, perhaps had even reached an apogee with Woolf and Proust; that was one implication. Another was that here we had a defining narrative of the collapse, an overview that mapped, historically and geographically, a process in which fragmentation was the latest, perhaps even the last, phase. The book thus combined a sense of reassuring mastery with a sense of foreboding. It was a modernist work, punctually recording how modernism had discovered the means of representing (and thus to some degree understanding and even overcoming) the experience of breakdown. *Mimesis* was perhaps the first cultural history to marry a sense of totality and serenity to the miscellaneous and fragmented.

Said's work chiefly belongs to the era when the notorious "clash of civilizations" had begun.[2] *Orientalism* (1978) now appears in the short retrospect of just under 40 years to have had all its omens and warnings about willed cultural distortion realized in the West's wars on the East, British-led from the 1920s, American-led since the 1990s. *Culture and Imperialism* (1993), however, had a less prophetic dimension; there was little need for it. US imperialism had already begun what it imagined or hoped would be the final phase of its global domination. Said's sections on various artists – Forster, Malraux, Camus, Conrad, Yeats, and others – illustrate culture's historic complicity with imperial systems. There is no such dimension in Auerbach's *Mimesis*. As in his *Scenes from the Drama of European Literature* (1959), his aim is to show how European humanism was altered by the arrival of modernism. A new sensibility was formed in the aftermath of the French Revolution, reaching its first paroxysm in Baudelaire's *Fleurs du Mal* (1857) in which we witness the demolition of Europe, for which that of Haussmann's Paris was the analog.[3] In Said's *Culture and Imperialism*, imperialism plays the role modernism had in

Auerbach, a destructive energy for the representation of which a new consciousness had to be formed. It was a consciousness, born of the "culture" of nineteenth-century Europe; it was new and yet it too had universal scope. This is the humanism that they share. But Said's version of modernism needs to include imperialism, although it remains uncertain here if the two are wholly identical. It is a claim that *must* be made for the sake of the general argument but that nevertheless includes a certain reservation, often audible in the syntax of his sentences: "I would like to suggest that many of the most prominent characteristics of modernist culture, which we have tended to derive from purely internal dynamics in western society and culture, include a response to the external pressures on culture from the *imperium*" (227). Yet such pressures *do* produce inquiries, not only about our common culture but also about our common human nature. Is that a fiction, perhaps *the* fiction, that had underpinned European humanism? Said's work had already shown that an adjoining, subordinate fiction, Orientalism, was central to the ideology of imperialism. Could the amalgam that had been known as humanism survive the shocks of modernism and of imperialism? Thus, Said and Auerbach raise the prospect of humanism's disappearance, if for different reasons. Both rescue it in the long run, claiming that its newly expanded consciousness has (or may have) redeemed it. Such a consciousness would require a more inclusive and democratic reach than humanism had so far displayed.

Imperialism's alliance with colonialism, although open to dispute is not open to doubt; some of its effects are so brutal and obvious that it is sometimes surprising to find that they are also subtle and often concealed. Said stresses that they both create a strange dialectic of distance and intimacy with their subject territories; white settlers, especially, anxiously both maintain and abolish that distance, initiating many debates, both specious and authentic, about their identity, near-identity, or difference from or intimacy with those they rule. This is the seedbed for *culture*; with it, we face so many varieties of meaning and so many questions of definition that, as with a word like *money*, it is easily understood and also an abstruse term of art. In *Mimesis* and *Culture and Imperialism*, the term refers to literary works that deploy various techniques of "representation" for an historical reality that changes with time; through representation, and the interpretation of it, we believe we can gain an unrivaled apprehension of what *culture* means. Said's most memorable interpretations of this sort are centered on novels of the classic Western tradition, chosen to illuminate their unwitting complicity with the imperialist world in which they were embedded. It is in the pursuit of the historically explicable changes in methods and techniques of representation that *Mimesis* and *Culture and Imperialism* reveal their affinities. Yet whatever general resemblances the books share, they end abruptly with chapter 4 of *Culture and Imperialism*, "Freedom from Domination in the Future."

Culture and Imperialism is a gathering of various lectures and addresses and so risks being repetitious and, to certain degree, disheveled. Yet in his effort to achieve a concluding momentum, Said only manages in chapter 4 to emphasize the book's repetitions that have, by this stage, become clamorous; a note of desperation is now and then audible. The proffered cure for the contemporary form of desolation – one of the products of a disciple's contrapuntal method of reading – is Homi Bhabha's "hybridity," a recognition of global interdependence, a refusal and dismissal of the fake consensus of uniformity, especially in its nationalist versions, of a privileged special destiny for some, of the so-called inferiority of "others."[4] Yet such a cadenced awareness and inclusiveness, great as its merits are, is not a comprehensive form of resistance. Marxism, which is such a form, is sharply rebuked by Said for its failure to recognize the role and power of imperialism in the world system. Given the record of Marxist analysis of imperialism and its relations to capitalism, this is a remarkably unjustified conclusion on Said's part.[5] Theory, as then understood, was dismissed for its alarming weightlessness, especially for its antihumanist abolition of the subject, and for a shallow new humanism that selects its cultural texts from a menu free of canonicity, now determined by caprice. There is also an attack on those whose version of the disintegration of traditional values is itself an imperial ruse. This long catalog of fake or failed critiques of the global condition is not so much a defense of humanism as a strident advocacy for *some* alternative to the atonal political uniformity that the United States required at home for its marauding foreign policy in the Middle East.

The complaints are loud but do not carry weight. Cultural diversity, as the price of political consensus, is readily paid by the "liberal" state. The cultural wars waxed and waned, Christian/American fundamentalists fumed, women made notable advances in their status, although against formidable opposition, and ideas of stable sexual identity were up-ended – yet none of this made any difference to the military coercion and civilizational propaganda, domination, and hegemony together that the West enjoyed at the turn of the millennium. Said's historical self-awareness, so often exquisitely attuned, seemed slowly to desert him in those years. It was replaced by a dry anger at what he considered the obvious insufficiency of the forms of and recommendations for resistance. What he called "the partial tragedy of resistance" was that it often had "to recover forms already established ... by the culture of empire" (253). *Culture and Imperialism* illustrated this. War had been established by the United States as the condition of the world. Yet, in these dramatic conditions, *Culture and Imperialism*'s historical importance was slight. In stark contrast to what he had achieved in *Orientalism* and in *Covering Islam* (1981), Said seemed to have flashed his credentials here and little more. A decade before, he was "speaking to power"; now, in this anticlimactic chapter and conclusion of *Culture and Imperialism*, he hopes for "a community or culture made up of numerous anti-systemic hints and practices for collective human experience ... that is not based on coercion or domination" (406). We see fleeting possibilities but no sustained comparison, for example, of the structures of imperialism and of globalization, perhaps the first as prelude to the other, an "infantile disorder" as the French historian Marcel Gauchet called it, that we have finally outgrown.[6] Instead we are told that "a new critical consciousness" is needed. Auerbach pops up again, quoting from a twelfth-century monk on how "to transcend the restraints of imperial or national or provincial limits" (407). But nothing more substantial. Perhaps this chapter belongs elsewhere. It reads now as an add-on and retrospectively damages the preceding chapters. The book, at this point, escapes the gravities that had just about held its troubled spirit to the realms of politics and culture and peters out into a shopping list of what we need to get now, in the most forbidding circumstances.

Said's crusade for justice for Palestine never wilted in the face of the organized hatred and unremitting hostility that it aroused in the United States. There was, however, another critique of his work that had nothing to do with this poisonous propaganda. Aijaz Ahmad's attack of 1994 on *Orientalism* in his *In Theory: Classes, Nations, Literatures* aroused a furor that still has reverberations because, I would suggest, it asked questions (in the form of accusations) that still need to be pondered, particularly in relation to the shape of Said's career.[7] (It should be remembered that Ahmad was a Marxist and that his book arose out of a dispute with the Marxist Fredric Jameson's claim that allegory was now a form specific to the Third World.) These questions turn on the issues of distance and intimacy that are fundamental to Said's thinking, but not only in relation to Orientalism, theme or book. In that relation and at that time the question challenged Said's authority. Was he guilty, as a metropolitan intellectual, of a profound inauthenticity in presenting Orientalism as a Third World problem to a metropolitan audience for which it promptly became a fashion? The Ahmad question gathered weight (and debris) as it rolled on. Said, the accusation went, pretended to an intimacy with this fictive world that was enabled by his distance from it. His version of distance provided him with objectivity, impartiality, and, in the fatally ambiguous word, "oversight." Representing distance as a requirement for overview is a standard technique of the novel (writer's point of view), television, and film. War propaganda displays the technological as moral superiority; the aerial view of bombing (silent, exact, surgical) versus the street view of the car bomb, atrociously close, fearsomely noisy, the characteristic implement of a low technology and of an engulfing fanaticism. Distance is embedded in humanistic ideology; it makes many claims, none so effective as having the capacity for "objective" representation. Intimacy, equally desirable, empirically rich, affectively warm, with no need for technology, is its polar opposite. According to Ahmad and others, Said was disabled by his distance from what he aspired to represent; his struggle to do so, the condescension that unavoidably went with it, his infelicitous mixture of sophistication and naivety, all identified him as an unwitting representative of the humanism that supported and reproduced the imperialism he affected to expose and weaken. Said in response insisted on his committed role as a Third World intellectual, working in the First World but never assimilated by it. It was impossible to be who he was and where he was without the questions of distance and intimacy besieging as well as inspiring him. Further, these were questions of representation that had immediate political applications, most obviously in relation to Palestine, or in the advanced technology of Desert Storm, the war that "happened only on screen." "Faced with war . . . we must become objectors to the objectivity of its representation."[8] Said was a fierce opponent of that war, but he seemed to be unaware that it was in the realm of the "theory" that he had dismissed that he could have found the theoretical resource to analyze the problems of representation that this war brought to a climax. This was not an abstract issue, it was political. The question of distance and objectivity was central to his own position. Yet he did not really take it into account on this convulsive occasion. As he paid a price in his analysis of imperialism with his dismissal of Marxism, so too he paid a price on the issue of representation with his dismissal of "theory."

I suggest that Said never found an answer to Ahmad's question; it dragged on him for years because it made the issue of Orientalism central to all that he did or said thereafter and bound it up with his good faith as a writer. His political enemies pounced on the opportunity to make this question unavoidable. Everything became, as a result, an element in a war between, for instance, scholarship and propaganda. Was Orientalism the truth in a general sense or was *Orientalism* an attack on the West? What should be left in, taken out, added on; what about the scale of the German contribution, a pointed question because Auerbach and his generation had been so important in the formulation of what humanism was? The questions were inexhaustible.

Ahmad had touched on a neuralgic point. Much that was rich in Said's reflections on, for example, ideas such as filiation and affiliation could be perverted to questions of political loyalty or betrayal. They could be transferred from being aesthetic ideas about the enrichment of conscious-ness – especially in both Auerbach's and Said's analyses of novels – to political acts of disloyalty to one's origins or of accommodation with the presiding powers that be, the "system." The relation of the aesthetic to the political, which was important in Said's earlier repudiation of the claims to aesthetic autonomy by the American New Critics, lost much of its philo-sophical weight in this atmosphere. Because it was also a contentious issue in the journalistic accounts of the effect of French theory in the American academy, and because Said had already played a major part in that by his initial acceptance of Foucault in *Beginnings*, he too was classified as one of those foreign influences that had joined in the death of the author, the destruction of "meaning" and all the other crimes committed daily against traditional humanism in the university classrooms that should have been defending it. This misreading of Said was politically motivated to such a degree that it ignored his own disaffection with theory and with Foucault, a writer determined to become a celebrity. It is also worth noting that in his staged clash between power and culture, Foucault conceded victory to power.[9]

Prior to its strategic importance in the reception of *Orientalism*, the "distance" question in Said, as we may call it, was part of his inquiry into the techniques by which objectivity and authority were established in fiction. The inquiry *Joseph Conrad and the Fiction of Autobiography* (1966) and *Beginnings* had opened and developed, *Orientalism* in a sense brought to a premature end. Only flashes from it survive in the great essays of *The World, the Text, and the Critic* and in *Culture and Imperialism*. Many of the formative presences in his earlier work – Lukács, Raymond Williams, Kierkegaard, Foucault – are dismissed; others, like Gramsci, are granted only a highly contrived role in *Culture and Imperialism*. With these names go the worlds of thought, Marxism and theory, they represented. Marxism was transmogrified into an inflexible positivism without revolu-tionary potential, despite the global emancipatory effects it had already had. "Theory," as it was grossly called, had ingeniously found ways to discover and then demolish the idea of authority, in the process creating a radical reputation in the most esoteric language for a phantasmal politics. Said, alert to the depoliticizing dimension of theory, failed to see –in Derrida, for one – how his own interrogations of authority as a fictive strategy had been enriched, even transformed.[10] Dogged by Ahmad's electric insight into the politics of "distance," ensnared in the polemics of Orientalism, he abandoned what had promised to be an unprecedentedly wide-ranging reconsideration of the conventional relationship between the categories of the aesthetic and the political. His appreciation of some Marxist thinkers had been deep and fruitful – Lukács and Williams – but it was now concealed by the fuss he makes about the *marxisant* posturing of others. From Sartre to Bobbio and Habermas, he had witnessed a series of defections that lowered Marxism's prestige; later, the servility of the latter two in particular before American power made an already sorry spectacle vile.[11] Foucault's increasing pessimism about the possibility of systemic change became Said's rationale for turning from theory's refusal of metanarratives, the suspect overview and voiceover, teleology in any guise. Said was able, through his own great rhetorical skills, and the harsh experience of the Palestinian cause, to dismiss the feigned or failed assaults of Marxism and contemporary theory as so much shadowboxing. As a consequence, his two careers, so to speak, one as a literary critic and promoter of humanism, one as a celebrated intellectual who had exposed the cultural tactics of imperialism, never fused. There was, intellectually speaking, no necessary dichotomy between them. He created one, choosing the intellectual over the professorial career. The one remnant of the linkage between them was his advocacy of an Auerbachian humanism, expanded and enriched, that had endured the calamities of contemporary imperialism as it had earlier endured its Nazi cousin and predecessor.

"The colonized man liberates himself in and through violence," declared Frantz Fanon in *The Wretched of the Earth* (1961).[12] In that book, he addressed the violence and hatred that rose perpendicularly from a situation in which, as with Algeria, the insurgent colony was integrated into the metropolitan nation that ruled it. This had happened in 1916–1922 in Ireland. There was a similar structure to the hatreds of the Irish-British war; they had the fury of a warped intimacy, the rage of an empire in decline, the ingredients of distance and closeness that played so pronounced a role in Said's reflections. (This perhaps explains Said's almost instinctive sympathy with and insight into Jonathan Swift's rage in his Irish-English-British quandary.)[13] Said speaks of Yeats's efforts "to lay hold of a distant yet orderly reality as a refuge from the turbulence of his immediate experience."[14] As with Said's teacher, R. P. Blackmur, whom he both criticizes and imitates, there is a willed mystification about the question of violence. Yeats "situates himself at that juncture where the violence of change is unarguable but where the results of the violence beseech necessary, if not always sufficient, reason" (284). This is pure Blackmur, where the effort to avoid saying something produces the impression that a profundity has been perpetrated.[15] There is no ambiguity about Fanon's attitude toward the colonisers. They must be killed as they had killed and would kill. This was a war of survival for the Algerians, for all colonized peoples. "But isn't the colonial status the organized enslavement of a[n] entire people?"[16] At stake was the possibility of a real humanism, not the botched version Europe had produced and imposed on Africa and Asia. The debates made famous by Simone de Beauvoir, Sartre, and Camus prefigured those of the 1980s in the aftermath of Orientalism. Fanon became the icon of colonial revolt. Said, however, used Fanon's bluntness on the question of violence to deflect his own evasion of it, even as, on the same page almost, he criticizes American journalists for quoting Yeats in their reports from the Middle East to sanction their condemnation of violence without asking where it originated (283–284). This was a standard example of the West's abuse of the word *culture* to mask its own violence.

While Said was a warm supporter and admirer of the first Intifada (1987–1991), he was severely compromised by his position in New York, the man of the First World, on the question of violence. By the late 1990s, he was facing the question of internal violence, of civil war, within the Arab world. Therefore, in *Culture and Imperialism*, when we are met with the apparently anodyne warning that in the ex-colonies violence must not become a mimic practice of the imperialists for that would be a concession to their barbarity, the contrast with Fanon's purity and clarity seems painful. Fanon's call for a new humanism morphs now into an appeal for a *refreshed* humanism, one without the constitutive violence of its European predecessor. When *Culture and Imperialism* was written, nationalism had become a source of internal violence in the postcolonial world, and Said is hard put to deal with that record. The violence was "explained" as constitutive of nationalism, the effects of colonialism, or religious feeling, or some mix of all three, not to mention the spectacular inequalities and miseries of the globalizing world. Whatever answers were given, Said seemed to be prevaricating, because he was removed from precisely that panurgic feeling of group identity that characterized the insider. Even though Said insisted that traditional European humanism was essentially Christian, it must now become secular, and this requirement was coded into his attacks on nationalism (which was becoming more and more Islamic), his view of national liberation as a step toward a global emancipation was taken by many merely to confirm his outsider status.

When Fanon's name first appears in *Culture and Imperialism*, it is in the company of T. S. Eliot (there to remind us of the copresence of past and present in the consciousness of a people); the conjuncture appears strange, almost comic. Fanon is cited to remind us that the capitalists have behaved in the underdeveloped world like nothing more than criminals (11–12) and that the removal of their flags and police does not mean their removal from Algeria or from our memories. Said's conflation of the two seems to ask that, while remembering imperial violence, "we must take stock of the nostalgia for empire . . . as well as the anger and resentment it provokes and look carefully and integrally at the culture that nurtured the sentiment, rationale and, above all the imagination of empire" (12). This is a moment in which the relation between imperialism and culture is newly conjugated; now we hear increasingly of the importance of "culture" in the "empire" and the dangers of misreading European novels that treat of imperialism. The fact that imperialism was or is violent, that it was the criminal basis of much Western wealth, is conceded over and over again. But the "cultural" product of the interaction between imperial rule and the places it dominated and the common culture that might be formed as a result, supervenes over all else: "[M]ost of us should now regard the experience of empire as a common one" (xxiv). The juxtaposition of Eliot and Fanon makes more sense if we read *Culture and Imperialism* as being an account of the moment that succeeded the defeat of imperialism. The West has not yet absorbed that defeat imaginatively, nor has victory in any real sense been realized by the former victims. Fanon, the revolutionary, and Eliot, the humanist, do share an alliance in the composite culture that has emerged. Violence has had its day, emancipation is almost achieved; how can this be represented, for example, in the literary canon? Said, by this rather risky maneuver of putting Eliot and Fanon in a companionate relation, has turned the question of violence as such into the question of culture.

Because imperialism was integral to the experience of the West (as of the colonized), Said argued that it needed to be incorporated and represented, particularly in works of art where the depth of its saturation could be registered. There was no communal identity that was autonomous, "[F]or it is the case that no identity can ever exist by itself" (60). The effect, he claimed, would be mutually beneficial. Still, in metropolitan areas, there was resistance to this disturbance of the canon that had once had, like empire, virtually unanimous support, even from those now prominently opposed to it. "It is perhaps embarrassing that sectors of the metropolitan culture that have since become vanguards in the social contests of our time were uncomplaining members of this imperial consensus. With few exceptions, the women's as well as the working-class movement was pro-empire" (62). Now, after the success of resistance movements, "[W]riters and scholars from the formerly colonized world have imposed their diverse histories on, have mapped their local geographies in, the great canonical texts of the European centre." There follows an account of "the uneasy relationship between nationalism and liberation" in which intellectuals, apart from some of bad faith, have established the primacy of national communities and produced "a critical literature." These are, for the most part, "exiles, expatriates, or refugees and immigrants in the West," but their work has not been accepted by those "that betrayed the liberationist ideal in favour of the nationalist independence reality." And even among those and their metropolitan supporters, there is a need for vigilance "since there is an inherent danger to oppositional effort of becoming institutionalised . . . resistance hardening into dogma." So, "there is always a need to keep community before coercion, criticism before mere solidarity, and vigilance ahead of assent" (63).

I have cited so much from this sequence to highlight the effects of Said's vision of himself and of the structural role such a self "must" maintain against "mere" solidarity with the various groupings directly or indirectly mentioned (or traduced) here. Within the attack on the dangers of groupthink and the assertion of the claims of "criticism" against it, a prime example of the precious individualism of the "liberal" subject, we can see how rare is the "humanism" that Said is reconfiguring as the enchanted perspective that grants objectivity: overview. (Fanon has an excoriating passage on the "eternal" values taught to the "colonized intellectual" the first and most specious of which is "individualism.")[17] The *profanum vulgus*, in its Third World or First World habitat, is a *class* that scarcely deserves the rescue it has been given. It will always yield to the dangers of conformity, to which it is peculiarly susceptible; it typically exists as a mob. This is an expression of disillusion with one group and of disdain for the other. Ahmad's accusations still have force. For it is at this point that Said says "my themes here are a sort of sequel to *Orientalism*" (64). It is a surprising sequel because Said has here risked losing two audiences – that of the colonized, who have betrayed liberation for nationalism, and that of the metropolitan world that, formerly unthinkingly pro-empire, has now adopted anti-imperialism as a fashion. This is, in each case, a "mere" solidarity from which Said must keep his distance.

Yet it is the fate of Palestine, abandoned and ill-led, that grossly determines the positions of Said the American and Said the Palestinian adoptee. His lifetime had seen the creation by the Western powers of a colonial state, Israel, endowed by the Christian West with immunity for all its crimes, the weaponry to commit them, and the ideology (once used in Germany against the Jews) to justify them. *Culture and Imperialism*, as I have been describing it, has to be read in that context. Palestine is proxy for the world dominated and ruined by imperialism. All his recommendations, especially in chapter 4, are directed to the United States, deliberately denuded of any connection with conventional bogies of the American imagination – socialism, avant-garde theory – that might make them less appealing, more likely to find a response. Any advance in that regard would be to Palestine's advantage. There was none, of course, rather the reverse; and the "professor of terror" had to watch as the war on "terror," the term Israel reinvented in 1970 to describe any Palestinian resistance to it, unrolled from Bush *père* to Bush *fils*. In 2002, on the lip of the invasion of Iraq, he wrote:

> As someone who has lived my life within the two cultures, I am appalled that the "clash of civilizations," that reductive and vulgar notion so much in vogue, has taken over thought and action. What we need to put in place is a universalist framework for dealing with Saddam Hussein as well as Sharon ... and a whole host of countries where depredations are endured without sufficient resistance. The only way to re-create or restore this framework is through education, open discussion and intellectual honesty that will have no truck with concealed special pleading or the jargons of war, religious extremism and pre-emptive "defence."[18]

Said's real affection for the academy and his touching respect for that Auerbachian humanist tradition that it housed, combined with his grief for Palestine, give his writing a tone, collegial and personal, that is highly distinctive. In the passage from the first-person singular to plural, from "I" to "we," he is always conscious of how important and precarious it is to master the tonal change that is involved. In the American climate, to sustain that tone was a triumph for a fastidious politics, for the claim of the imperial West to the pronoun "we" was the basis for legitimizing any action, any atrocity. Said recognizes that the "we" of literary humanism embraced the idea of "our common culture," although he was compelled to try to keep the word *culture* clear of the ideological appeal of capitalism, that which most monotonously appeals to human nature as its basis and the individual as its hero, alchemizing egoism into a form of community.

The history and geography of the humanist community was embodied for him in the figure of Auerbach, who appears in several incarnations in *Beginnings,* in *The World, the Text, and the Critic*, and in *Culture and Imperialism*. Situated between West and East, defining the West in the East, he appears to Said to have performed "an act of civilizational survival" (54), for that "a marvellous, symphonic whole [that] . . . could be studied exclusively as a concerted and secular historical experience, not as an exemplification of the divine" (54). Said's contradictory versions of humanism's history only emphasize his idealization of it. Compromised by "the striking rise of nationalism" (55) in the two centuries between 1745 and 1945, the achievements of specific national cultures took precedence over the European. Yet it was the spontaneous Eurocentric dimension of these national literatures that animated Said's interest in the study of Orientalism. Further, it was the work of Auerbach, Leo Spitzer, Ernst Curtius, and the like who, as practitioners of world of comparative literature, replaced that compromised version of Europe with the older conception of "Romania." This serene "anthropological Eden" (52) had Dante's *Divine Comedy* as its founding text, and "within recurrently renewed structures," according to Auerbach, its literature continued to attest "to the abiding dialectical order represented by Europe" (55). However, behind Auerbach was an "even longer tradition of humanistic learning" that we associate with the Enlightenment; yet previously mentioned Romania was under threat from the emerging languages and cultures that suddenly seemed to appear after World War II, although it had already begun to be rescued in 1926 by having its geographical limitations exposed by Gramsci showing that the gulf dividing the wealthy North and impoverished South of Italy revealed their interdependence. This "fissure" was *in parvo*, like the fissure between the West and imperialism, its abiding reality. Once exposed, Europe ceased to have a legitimate claim to universality, and the "Orient," one of imperialism's greatest fictions, stood forth as the inescapable "Other" by which Europe had successfully learned to define itself by the laborious expedient of dividing culture from the social and political. Here again, the North-South division of Italy provided the telling analog. *Culture and Imperialism* was, in turn, by implication, the classic work in which the liberated and greatly expanded Europe would become a true world literature, finally becoming global in the political as well as the cultural sense. It is only on closer reading that this global literature – Auerbach, Spitzer, Goethe, and so forth – reveals itself to be the version of world literature that began in the West in, of all places, the department of comparative literature at Columbia University in 1891, and that the names of the great German *Philologen* operate here as a rebuke to the contrasting shallow (and monolingual) scholarship – if that it could be called – of the English department(s) members (unnamed) who were manifestly incapable of bearing the immense and grave weight of this Germanic tradition (53–54). The climactic event in this sequence was the launch of Sputnik in the late 1950s and the subsequent changes in American educational policy. And so on. In the midst of such confusion, all that we learn is that Auerbach, *Mimesis*, and humanism have a range beyond anything contemporary teachers can match. Further, now that former imperial cultures need to be included as well, the demands of humanist education have become so taxing that few can meet them. Humanism is in danger.

The audience for the straight message in this rather garbled history is the American Academy, and its chief provocation was the loud quarrel over what constituted the literary canon, as that was understood and taught, chiefly in the departments of English and of comparative literature in the United States. Said was arguing for the broadening of the traditional (imperial) canon to include works from the hitherto peripheral countries (see 67–68). For a comparatist like Said, it was inevitable that the reading list should include French and German as well as English, although the major colonizing nations, Great Britain (or England; he never refers to the United Kingdom) and France outbid Germany by quite a distance (50–60). The relationship between the novel as a form, its "patterns of narrative authority," and "a complex ideological configuration underlying the tendency to imperialism" (82) is a tantalizing prospect that is never realized; but then we realize that it never could be because a phrase such as "a tendency to imperialism" belongs to no knowable condition or place. Another apparent oddity is that, of all the many "cultural critics" mentioned – here Eliot belongs, along with Arnold, John Stuart Mill, Carlyle, Ruskin, Renan, and a half-dozen others – two of Said's most admired and leaned-upon authorities in his earlier work, Foucault and Raymond Williams, are excluded because they have no (or not enough) interest in imperialism. His authorities are impeccably conservative; all shades of radical opinion are expelled. Even if authors are cited to show their provincial bigotry (say Macaulay and Mill on India), they still have names that resonate in the Anglosphere, not just in relation to empire but also more generally in relation to culture. Lists of names proliferate throughout; they are endorsements of the main arguments or they are like lists for further reading in this rich and varied, conventional, and yet eccentric syllabus. The aim of that syllabus is to further enrich, not disturb, the canonical list. Here is a moment in the American culture wars in which a list of entirely palatable texts for the new humanism is recommended. These are all Names of the Fathers. Indeed, where a female author, George Eliot, is quoted in the midst of a discussion of Kipling, it is to show that a moment of moral reawakening in *Middlemarch* is paralleled by one in Kim in which the Irish boy recognizes himself as a Sahib and that India is his (173–174). That may be a characteristic awakening in Kipling, but it is disturbing to find Said, of all people, adapting Eliot's moment of emancipation to such a gross example of imperial annexation.

Ultimately, *Culture and Imperialism* is not about either culture or imperialism in the sense that Said gave to those words. It now reads, after the Oslo accords and Said's powerful and yet wounded repudiation of Palestinian concession, as a last attempt on his part to woo the American academy by means of culture into something approaching an ethical response to imperialism. It was like cajoling a cat into altruism. This is the reason, I believe, that in a startling and sudden shrinkage, the book concludes as a syllabus that suggests how works from the colonized cultures of the West might be included into the Western canon. It is part of the American debate of the early 1990s about liberal education. It looks at first, because it has many brilliant moments, to belong to a larger and wider world than the humanism that it intermittently evokes and confusedly describes. We stumble here with Said into a very small clearing in an immense forest. "Deep in the forest there's an unexpected clearing which can be reached only by someone who has lost his way."[19]

Notes

1 See Frantz Fanon, *The Wretched of the Earth*, trans. by Richard Pilcox, with commentary by Jean-Paul Sartre and Homi K. Bhabha (New York: Grove Press, 2004), p. 237.
2 Samuel P. Huntington, *The Clash of Civilizations and the Remaking of World Order* (New York: Simon and Schuster, 1996); see Edward W. Said, "The Clash of Ignorance," *The Nation*, November 22, 2001, 11–14.
3 *Scenes from the Drama of European Literature* (Manchester: Manchester University Press, 1984).
4 Homi K. Bhabha, *The Location of Culture* (London: Routledge, 1994).
5 See V. G. Kiernan, *Marxism and Imperialism* (London: Edward Arnold, 1974).
6 *L'Avènement de la démocratie. Vol. 2, La Crise du libéralisme* (Paris: Kampen, 2003), p. 232.

7 Aijaz Ahmad, *In Theory: Classes, Nations, Literatures* (London: Verso, 1992), pp. 159–220.

8 Paul Virilio, *Desert Screen: War at the Speed of Light* (London: Continuum, 2002), p. 28.

9 I make no attempt here to engage with Said's subtle accounts of Foucault's work in *The World, the Text, and the Critic*, especially in the essay "Criticism between Culture and System." See also his remarks in "*Orientalism* and After," in Edward Said, *Power, Politics and Culture*, ed. by Gauri Viswanathan (London: Bloomsbury, 2004), p. 214.

10 In the same essay in *The World, the Text, and the Critic*, Said engages with both Derrida and Foucault and with their disagreements.

11 See Perry Anderson's essay, "The Affinities of Norberto Bobbio," *A Zone of Engagement* (London and New York: Verso, 1992), pp. 87–129.

12 Fanon, *Wretched of the Earth*, p. 44.

13 See "Swift's Tory Anarchy" and "Swift as Intellectual" in *The World, the Text, and the Critic*.

14 Edward W. Said, *Culture and Imperialism* (London: Vintage, 1994 [1993]), p. 287.

15 See R. P. Blackmur, *Selected Essays of R. P. Blackmur*, ed. by D. Donoghue (New York: Ecco Press, 1986). The echoes of Blackmur, Lionel Trilling, Fred Dupee, and many others of that era in the American Academy are audible in Said's *Humanism and Democratic Criticism* (New York: Palgrave McMillan, 2004).

16 Fanon, *Wretched*, p. 48, n.7.

17 Ibid., p. 10–11.

18 "We Know Who 'We' Are," *London Review of Books*, October 17, 2002, 25.

19 Tomas Tranströmer, "The Clearing," *New Collected Poems*, trans. by Robin Fulton (New York: New Directions, 2007).

CHAPTER 5

Exile as a Political Aesthetic

Keya Ganguly

Is there an aesthetic appropriate to the predicament of exile? Or, to put it another way, is there a style particular to the representation of exile? If these questions merit an answer at all, it would have to be in the negative, because there is no singular experience of exile just as there cannot be a single aesthetic form that expresses the myriad ways in which exile is inhabited, let alone understood or narrated. Terms that have cropped up in conventional discussions of this issue such as *nostalgia*, *in-betweenness*, *estrangement*, or *bifocality* are inevitably partial, even inadequate, given that they rely on a form of inductive reasoning that is, at its core, positivistic – insofar as they build their case from particular instances in which one can point to exilic nostalgia, marginality, alienation, and so on, to propose a general argument about the condition of exile at large. In these approaches, the critic's preference for a specific idea serves as the basis of a totalizing description, more often than not resulting in the assimilation of exile into an exclusively existential or ontological problem.

If, however, exilic existence is seen less as an ontological condition than an intellectual outlook that must, of necessity, function without the securities of home and tribe, then the preceding questions are better reframed as follows: What form of *critical consciousness* can the experience of exile generate and, relatedly, does the provisional nature of exile call for representational strategies that refuse a state of rest? Another way to pursue these questions is to mark the distinction between the rooted cosmopolitan's desire to be everywhere at home and the exilic subject's impulse to resist that seduction in the first place. In this way of looking at the issue, the importance of the contrast between the cosmopolite and the exile turns on the former's voluntary mobility as against the impossibility of the latter's return to a native land (to echo the title of a famous poem by Aimé Césaire).[1]

These are some of the directions on exile as an intellectual and political *standpoint* – rather than existential dilemma – that emerge in Edward

Said's meditations on the topic. We see the conviction about standpoint reflected in Said's references to the exiled subject's "median state, neither completely at one with the new setting nor fully disencumbered of the old, beset with half-involvements, half-detachments, nostalgic and sentimental on one level, an adept mimic or a secret outcast on another."[2] If such a description reveals the exile's state of mind to be fraught with anxiety, it is also, and indeed by that very token, appropriate for the skeptical intellectual attitude Said consistently favored; it is an attitude secured less on the grounds of certainty than in the practical difficulties, blind alleys, trials and errors, as well as settlements that a genuinely critical consciousness must embrace.[3]

The metaphor that best characterizes such openness to the unknown and, especially, to the unknown fraught with danger, is that of a "bend in the river," a phrase Said at one point borrowed from V. S. Naipaul's novel of the same name.[4] With this adaptation, he captures both the confusion and possibilities that the turn brings into view, past the bend, as it were. But whereas Naipaul condemns his exiled main character Salim as confused and weak, Said is as concerned about the immense difficulties that attach to the condition of exile as he is to what he calls "the marvels of adjustment."[5]

Accordingly, heroism, innovation, and a capacity for survival are always aspects of the rigors, along with the rigorousness, even discipline, that exile imposes. Said's model for this principled form of thinking is, above all others, the Frankfurt School social philosopher Theodor W. Adorno (who was for more than a decade himself an exile from Nazi Germany). Adorno's philosophical pronouncements on how to *think* exile – to grasp it as a modality of thought and to embrace the openings it makes possible – provided Said with the means to advance the most deeply felt arguments about exile as an intellectual disposition whose principal impulse is to challenge the comforts of home.[6] I will return later to his reliance on Adorno's conception of a politicized aesthetics, but first let us take a look at some of the powerful imagery that inspired Said's writings on exile.

Resistance contra Nostalgia

A line fragment from Mahmoud Darwish's poem "The Earth Is Closing on Us" serves as the title of *After the Last Sky*, Said's 1986 portrait of Palestinian lives (with photographs by the Swiss photographer Jean Mohr).[7] The poet asks where his people should go "after the last frontiers," linking their flight with that of birds: "[W]here should the birds fly after the last sky?" This image, yoking the plight of a frontierless people with that of other scattered creatures, becomes in Said's hands a *mise-en-abŷme* of Palestinian existence. Scattering is also a metaphor for his varied explorations in the book, which range from meditations on loss to reports of historical and political events in the years leading up to the ill-fated Oslo accords. History and memory are thus fused in this chronicle of the past, evoking what was possible as well as the impossible stuff of longing, one active and real, the other idealized.

The phrase "after the last sky" embeds the duality of reality and desire, summoning an opening, on the one hand, and a closing, on the other, in the translated rendition of Darwish's words. For its English readers, this phrase stitches together what comes *later* with the finality attached to what came *last*, at the end. In this doubling of contingency and finality, the phrase prompts us to consider what Said, writing on Darwish in the journal *Grand Street*, called the "esoteric and certainly an exotic situation" of the poet's "survival after the aftermath."[8] With the idea of surviving *after* the aftermath, a third sense seems to interpose itself articulating the staggered and scattered nature of exilic time with revival. That is to say, the third sense splices together fracture and reconsolidation (to be distinguished from resignation), and it is this sense that urges both poet and critic onward. Their individual and combined insights into survival have themselves survived into the present, if we consider that the decades intervening between Darwish's or Said's death and the present still retain the impact of their shared struggle to live with catastrophe and beyond it.

Much of the commentary on Darwish's poetry as well as Said's book has focused on the melancholic aspects of their stances, which is not surprising given that melancholia accords with the general feeling tone of our times – affecting not only those who have experienced exile or suffered the deracination that comes with it, but also those who identify with the sense of loss it conjures. As an existential disposition, melancholia has its effect on all who are drawn to the modernist aura of what Georg Lukács derided as "transcendental homelessness" (and we should recall that Lukács was an exile from Hungary, even if Said did not enlarge on this historical fact in his writings).[9] But this is simultaneously the lure and the limitation of the melancholic mode: it enables mourning but not resistance.

Lukács's view that melancholy is seductive though emphatically not transformative makes it all the more important to note that "The Earth Is Closing on Us" bespeaks a different and resistant emotion as well, one whose charge is less consoling than openly agitational. For the poem shifts from its muted and melancholic opening to a tone that is militant and angry, voicing feelings that are not only in stark contrast with the with-drawal characteristic of melancholia but also actively channel the determin-ation of Palestinians as a people to fight and even to die for the larger cause of freedom.

This sense of active rather than passive resistance characterizes some of the most uncompromising positions on history and political consciousness that Said avowed, especially in the final decade of his life. But the influence of Darwish's aesthetic of confrontation can be glimpsed earlier – as is evident in his writing of *After the Last Sky* – exemplifying, among other things, a shift in his focus from questions of representation (treated most elaborately in *Orientalism*) to the epistemological predicament of the repre-senting subject.[10] We might think of this as a transition from a conven-tional literary critic's interest in the politics of texts to a meta-political concern with the encoding of a consciousness of resistance within aesthetic forms. In fact, I would submit that Said is at his best when giving voice to the lessons of endurance under duress, seeing in this mode a crucial aspect of the politics of art that only comes to light when its conditions of possi-bility are restricted from above (and sometimes from below).

Exemplifying as it does the combination of Said's investments in life history, journalistic writing, memoir, photographic commentary, and essay, *After the Last Sky* certainly constitutes a mixed genre calling upon its author's many skills and subject positions as a reader of images, a storyteller, a political critic, as well as an ethical representative of his people. In addition, Said's borrowing of a line from Darwish's poem for his title is indicative of a larger debt because, as I have suggested previously, the poem provided him with an encompassing model for conceptualizing political defiance in an aesthetic register. The lines following the invocation of the last sky are the final ones of the poem, stridently expressing the need for confrontation and sacrifice:

> Where should the plants sleep a`fter the last breath of air?
> We will write our names with scarlet steam.
> We will cut off the hand of the song to be finished by our flesh.
> We will die here, here in the last passage.
> Here and here our blood will plant its olive tree.[11]

These lines speak of the plants that suffocate from lack of air as well as the suffering of humans whose fight against injustice is rendered a fight unto death: their blood rendered "scarlet steam," their severed limbs marking "the last passage." The note Darwish strikes here unambiguously repre-sents the Palestinian struggle as active, willed, and deliberate; this, we should recognize, is quite in opposition to the doleful and nostalgic emotion found in many narratives of loss. Indeed, the resoluteness of the utterance "We will die here" rings with the determination of the just warrior who welcomes death not in an act of nihilism but as its obverse: by negating the *lie* of the life to which he has been condemned.

To put it differently, if the here and now has produced a living death, the poet intimates a time when this betrayal of life can be overcome; as he declares when "our blood will plant its olive tree." Through this fold in figurative language, Darwish recasts the olive branch from being an empty symbol of a nonexistent peace into a more radical marker of the quiddity of existence. It is as if to say, the olive tree will grow again, if only in the wake of the bloodshed that precedes it. Metaphorically conveying the intransigence of a people whom neither occupation nor displacement has defeated, the poem's militant tone is ill-suited to the elegiac mode that has become the preferred one to describe exilic writing. As an aside, we should also remark on the distance of such militancy from the older Arabic tradition of the *marthiya* or mourning poem in which ritualized grief is the primary expression.

Ultimately, then, in choosing his title from a text that is only *apparently* a lament, Said indicates that at least one appropriate strategy for representing exile is an aesthetic of anger. Discerned across many of his writings on the resistance to power, Said leaves us with the forceful insight that the melancholia suffusing "the last sky" has to be seen as accompanied by the defiance that is a counterpoint to elegy and lamentation.[12]

Counterpoint: Culture and Administration

Returning to the question as to whether there is a style (or styles) peculiar to the representation of exile, one must remember that this is not simply a matter of devising an autonomous aesthetic strategy as we would find, for instance, in Bertolt Brecht's deployment of the *Verfremdungseffekt* (alienation effect) to subvert narrative illusion.[13] Rather, what is at stake in Said's perspective on exile is his emphasis on expressive forms that are adequate to the remit of a particular experience. So, while we may think of Brechtian method as centered on theatrically politicized responses stemming from aesthetic interventions (e.g., epic theater), Said draws attention to the links between narrative and experience that bind strategies of representation to particular communities of response.

We can, for example, find parallels between exilic style and styles prevalent in working-class fiction, the cinema of hunger, or peripheral aesthetics. In all these cases, the narrative form in question elucidates a particular modality of thought and experience – what the Welsh literary critic, Raymond Williams (one of Said's most respected sources), called a "structure of feeling."[14] But whereas Williams placed his greatest emphasis on the feelings embedded in literary structures, both generic and situational (such as a Chekov play or a Hardy landscape), Said modulates the dual emphasis on structure and feeling by proposing that it is the disjunction between them that deserves notice. In fact, his attention is not so much on literature's ability to shape or reflect a given structure of feeling as it is on the relationship *between* abstract structures (of power, authority, and institution) and feelings concretely expressed in representational forms.

Much has been written about Said's adaptation of Williams's coinage, including the way it inflects his own formulation of "contrapuntal" criticism.[15] For now, let us simply say that what remains implicit in Williams's somewhat vague articulation of structure (an objective constraint) and feeling (a subjective proposition) is brought to the surface in Said's advocacy of the contrapuntal mode. Of course, his oft-cited familiarity with Western musical vocabulary is also at work in Said's deployment of counterpoint – which we can gloss as the existence of a mediating relationship between two or more elements (melodic lines) and, at the same time, their independence or individuality.

Thus, what Williams had emphasized as the "precipitate" of objective and subjective constituents in literary and cultural texts, Said elevates as the dynamic of representation itself.[16] Instead of relying on Williams's conceptually imprecise admixture of structure and feeling to explain the ideological make up of texts or social formations, Said's nuance lies in teasing out the systemic or structural dimensions of an experiential problem within the totality of its lived expression and limned in narrative forms.

We see glimpses of his profitable modulation of the idea of a structure of feeling in as early a text as *Orientalism*, even if Said's reliance on Williams's term is not explicitly attributed there as such. For example, in the important second chapter of *Orientalism* "Orientalist Structures and Restructures," Said pays a good deal of notice to Richard Burton – the English Orientalist who, among his other contributions as a scholar and chronicler, is famous for translating the *Arabian Nights*. Describing Burton's attitude to the Orient Said says:

> Burton's most extraordinary characteristic is, I believe, that he was preternaturally knowledgeable about the degree to which human life in society

was governed by rules and codes. All of his vast information about the Orient, which dots every page he wrote, reveals that he knew that the Orient in general and Islam in particular were systems of information, behavior, and belief, that to be an Oriental or a Muslim was to know certain things in a certain way, and these were of course subject to history, geography, and the development of society in circumstances specific to it. (195)

Of note is the dialogic or, to use Said's preferred term, "contrapuntal" relationship between the governing of life by "rules and codes" and the knowing of "certain things in a certain way." The intuitive dimensions of culture are thereby shown to be dependent upon extensive and structural determinants, but the whole is only discernible in the overall point-counterpoint of codification and instinct. As Said explains, Burton's accomplishment was to have intuitively grasped the patterns of Oriental life – suspended between rule-governed and unstudied elements that constitute being an Oriental or a Muslim. Bringing Williams's phrase into this context, we might then say that Burton had successfully inhabited an Oriental structure of feeling in ways that, as Said also suggests, went deeper than the more flamboyant figure of T. E. Lawrence, another British Orientalist and military officer (familiar to many readers from David Lean's 1962 film *Lawrence of Arabia*).[17]

There are other instances of the affinities between Said's mode of reading in *Orientalism* and Williams's development of structure of feeling, although constraints of space do not permit their enlargement here. However, my point is less to emphasize this unstated affinity (openly acknowledged in Said's later writings, e.g., *Culture and Imperialism*) than to suggest the growing salience of the idea of "administration" as a particularly forceful node in the exercise, representation, and analysis of power. In this particular emphasis, Said diverges from Williams's focus on social and, especially, sociological aspects of culture into a more direct confrontation with the logic by means of which imperial and neo-imperial styles reinforce themselves. The long reach of this logic of what might be termed "the administrative mode" into the conduct of empire but also, covertly, into cultural understanding, is evident in the example Said gives of Burton as well as in his elaboration of the ways that much of what went into imperialist policy making in the Orient depended on the expertise of professional Orientalists and, crucially, vice versa.[18]

I would contend that it is because of his increasing attention to the administrative mode in modern affairs that Said ultimately found Michel Foucault's "micro-political" and "capillary" theories of power to be unsatisfactory.[19] The more generative if philosophically complex ideas of Adorno provided him with the means to avoid the hypostasis of culture in Williams and discourse in Foucault. So even though Adorno's specific form of materialism made a relatively late entry into Said's thought, it is reasonable to suggest that it was intuitively anticipated.[20]

In retrospect, one can see that Adorno's emphasis on the hand-in-glove nature of culture and administration, his monumental exposition of the "culture industry," as well as his conceptualizations of the Hegelian idea of "historical consciousness" (in writing about subjects as varied as surrealism, natural history, and Beethoven) are all decisive in Said's own efforts to harness an understanding of the mutuality of culture and politics. Relating this general Adornian impulse to the specific topic of exile, we should recall that Said consistently rejected the thought that exile was exclusively or primarily a cultural phenomenon; on the contrary, its political determination and history were for him overwhelmingly administrative matters – above all in the case of Palestine. Consequently, many of his discussions, whether openly dealing with the problem of exile or on other topics, center on the layered and contradictory effects of administrative and institutional imperatives on social forms.

One needs to acknowledge that Said's framework was by no means uniformly successful in detailing the penetration of the administrative mode into all the facets of aesthetics, culture, and politics that he sought to amplify. Nonetheless, it should be of interest to us, as latter-day readers of his critical oeuvre, that his first reckonings with this mode are already present in *Orientalism*, even if Adorno's specific theorizations of the entwinement of culture and administration were yet to make their mark on him.[21] What is particularly remarkable about the conceptual approach of this influential book is that, in a time of hypersensitivity toward and celebration of "the text," Said risked advancing a critical method that fully displaced the stifling preoccupations of traditional New Critics with textual meaning and, more daringly perhaps, the self-styled literary radicals of the 1970s swept up in Louis Althusser's pronouncements about the "relative autonomy" of culture.[22]

That is to say, Said's scrutiny was unfailingly on the objective pressures on cultural statements, seeing this neither as a matter of overt determination (what one is accustomed to hearing as the charge against "vulgar Marxism") nor quite so concealed as to be immaterial. If Williams had overemphasized the "solution" and, hence, dissipation of structure into feeling – in propositions like "structures of feeling can be defined as social experiences in solution" – Said foregrounded the *fact* of structuration and constraint without subordinating it to other influences.[23] In this way, he carefully skirted the criticism that his was just another base-superstructure argument.

It is a testament to Said's rhetorical skill that he was able to underscore administration as a major lever of Orientalist discourse without falling prey to the charge of being insufficiently attentive to the "open-ended" nature of discourse. For we should also remember that his rise to fame in the academic setting of the 1980s was not unrelated to his deft negotiation of the conceptual differences between an ascendant poststructuralist criticism (predicated on the idea that one cannot appeal to a reality outside language) and the alleged determinism of a Marxist outlook that seeks explanations of culture and history on materialist terms. To the extent that Said stressed the direct effects of administration on culture without appearing to sound deterministic or Marxist, he outmaneuvered the most visible, if repressive, doxa of the times, at least in the context of the US academy: the dismissal of the Marxist tradition that, as others have documented, produced some of the most important anticolonial intellectuals of the twentieth century (from Aimé Césaire, Ho Chi Minh, C. L. R. James, James Connolly, or M. N. Roy, to the towering figures of Lenin or Trotsky). Moreover, this very tradition had influenced Said's own critical style, as the final imprint of Adorno on his thought also attests.[24]

Parataxis and Late Style

Said's efforts to distance himself from Marxism, especially from what he saw as its doctrinaire tendencies, have been remarked upon by many commentators so there is no need here to rehearse his positions or the limitations thereof.[25] What seems more productive, again given the passage of time and our obligation to be attentive to the movement of ideas, is to look for nuances in his arguments that are either consistent with a Marxist approach or amenable to dialectical Marxism in ways that Said did not himself clarify.

Before we can proceed to mine these openings, it is important to distinguish between a methodological allegiance to Marxist protocols of understanding, on the one hand, and Marxism's political goals, on the other. To say this is not to deny the value of the former or fixate on the latter; rather, it is to note that while Said's hopes for Palestinian sovereignty were always aligned with the ideals of socialist self-determination, his references to Marxism or dialectics in his cultural criticism were not always fully worked out. For this reason, a certain amount of conceptual work has to be undertaken to extract the ways in which Said annexed dialectical ideas for situating his contrapuntal analysis of problems straddling the domains of culture and politics.

One such idea centers on the figure of *parataxis* – which appears early on in *Orientalism*'s collocation of Orientalist knowledge and imperial administration. This figure is subsequently taken up in *Culture and Imperialism* when Said coordinates Jane Austen's world with plantation economy and still later, paratactic effects are noted, albeit glancingly, in Said's lengthy introduction to Erich Auerbach's *Mimesis*. As we know, parataxis characterizes a relationship of adjacency between two clauses (in a sentence) or two propositions (in a syntactic unit) without the use of a subordinating or coordinating word or phrase. Over the course of his writing, Said often used this trope to analyze the relationship between representation and history in which the two are coordinated but do not admit to the subordination of either. In any discussion of Said's style, I think it is justifiable to consider parataxis an important weapon in his arsenal because of the ways it enabled him to posit – by means other than Hegelian and Marxist – a thesis-antithesis relationship between source and effect, ideas and representations, or culture and administration.

Thus, whether explicitly or implicitly, paratactic formulations allowed Said to overcome the stalemate of needing to decide whether representations reflect or deform reality (a standard problem in theories of representation), furnishing instead a figurative basis for elaborating the co-dependency often featured in what he preferred to label the contrapuntal dynamic of the real and the representational. Whether considering Orientalist ideology, the far-flung entailments of the imperialist imagination, or the more abstract case of realism in literature and expressionism in music, the paratactic mode provided Said with an interpretive key to demonstrate the juxtapositions of historical experience and the narration of that experience, without prioritizing either. By design or serendipity, he found it a way to circumvent both the materialist emphasis on economic determinants of social life and the reigning dictate of the "linguistic turn" of the 1980s and 1990s regarding the dominance of discourse. This was prominently championed, for example, by Ernesto Laclau and Chantal Mouffe in their advocacy of "post-Marxism" as against the alleged economic determinism of Marxism,[26] but the "exorbitation of discourse" (as Benita Parry put it in her critique of mainstream postcolonial thinking) was also everywhere in discussions of the politics of representation.[27]

Strategically, then, in his introduction to *Mimesis*, Auerbach's classic exploration of the links between literature and social context, Said takes a different turn from the theoretical elevation of discourse, consistently lauding Auerbach's focus on how the "*world* affects the transformation of reality and consequently of style."[28] Auerbach permitted Said to make the case that if reality is transformed, so are the styles that accompany its representation; there is, in other words, the same weight placed on the transformation of both reality and style. Sharing this conviction with Auerbach about the consonance of the two, Said's commentary focuses on aspects of the latter's argument that illustrate how the best writers conjure this nexus of reality and style in key part by transmitting changes in the world through changes in styles of narration.

What strikes one is Said's unapologetic endorsement of Auerbach's disregard for the impediment to understanding that is supposed to result from the mediation of reality by language. Consider the following statement:

> Most of all, however, in Auerbach's searingly powerful and strangely intimate characterization of the Christian Thomist poet Dante – who emerges from the pages of *Mimesis* as *the* seminal figure in Western literature – the reader is inevitably led to the paradox of a Prussian Jewish scholar in Turkish, Muslim, non-European exile handling (perhaps even juggling) charged, and in many ways irreconcilable sets of antinomies that, though ordered more benignly than their mutual antagonism suggests, never lose their opposition to each other.[29]

Antinomies, antagonism, irreconcilable, and opposition are the words that leap out in this passage. They of course point to the existential paradox of Auerbach's situation in Istanbul, but they also constitute the elements of an orientation that admits to the absence of reconciliation in life no less than in writing or representation. At the heart of Auerbach's approach to realism in literature, this orientation inflects his consideration of manifold objects – Homer, the Bible, Dante, Goethe, Stendhal, Flaubert, even Joyce – illuminating, as Said quotes him, "the abiding order and ... interpretation of life which arise from life itself."[30]

Parataxis is part of the overall machinery of Auerbach's narrative outlook, especially in the chapters in *Mimesis* on biblical and classical literature, although Said makes reference to this device only once in his introduction. Nonetheless, as the preceding quotation demonstrates, he represents the paratactic and contradictory aspects of Auerbach's predicament as a scholar in exile – remarking on his Prussian nationality, Jewish ancestry, European formation, and Islamic location, all of which are irreconcilable aspects that catch Said's eye. By the same token, he needs no more than a single mention of this trope in his commentary on the text because Auerbach calls attention to the function of parataxis on his own, staking many of his claims about literature and experience on propositions that coexist without being put in any relationship other than their adjacency.[31]

Paul Bové, one of Said's early admirers, has discussed the distinction Auerbach made between the contrapuntal and the paratactic, particularly with respect to Dante's poetry. According to Bové, Auerbach's daring approach rests on emphasizing counterpoint as the hallmark of a modern and secularizing sensibility, thereby breaking with all traditional criticism (which had regarded Dante's poetry as a treatise on the divine). He argues that Auerbach's achievement was to show the departure of Dante's compositional mode from parataxis in the Bible or the classics to a contrapuntal pitting of divine and human for syntactic effect. This shift in focus toward the complex *human* drama enfolding the *Divine Comedy* is for Bové the way forward in modern criticism's attention to the "historicality of the human" – a conviction that Said was the first to share with Auerbach through his championing of humanism as well as in his promotion of contrapuntal criticism.[32] Of course, the point about humanism, seen moreover from a historicist perspective, is made by Auerbach to show how Dante's language is "dependent upon the setting, the physical and moral climate . . . [presenting] the journey of an individual and his guide through a world whose inhabitants remain in whatever place is assigned to them."[33]

The main issue for Auerbach is Dante's essentially secular investments and his corresponding innovation lies in coordinating historical and stylistic complexities, a point that Said brings to the surface at many moments in his introduction. Bové's concern, however, is with establishing that counterpoint is the formal strategy for capturing the "momentary tonalities" of the modern – to be distinguished from the "stiffness" of parataxis that sets scenes "stiffly side by side and in the same key," he says, quoting Auerbach.[34] For us, the point has less to do with the relative merits of these tropes than the fact of their prominence in the style of criticism Said both inherited and practiced. This was constitutively premised on recognizing that, with the classical and biblical world left behind, the emergent modernity of Dante's environment could only be explained by the cross-fertilizations of culture, trade, and thought in the Italian city-states of his time, and that also find expression in the existential confrontations of the scenes, especially in the tenth canto of the *Inferno*.

My purpose in referring to Bové in the present context is also to show the subtle differences between his emphasis and Said's, both of them eager in their own way to claim Auerbach's historicism for a cause other than historicism's own. Still, it should be added that Said was less driven to downplay historicism's accent on historical causality; by contrast, Bové's later contentions reveal a poststructuralist viewpoint that seeks to retain for itself a purchase on understanding history while abjuring Auerbach's idea that history is determined by material conditions identifiable on their own terms.[35] A simpler way to say this is to suggest that rhetorical figures such as parataxis or counterpoint can *equally* serve as the means to avoid contending with historical determination by emphasizing, instead, the purely discursive juxtaposition of events, movements, or actions. And such a celebration of semiotic free play certainly accounts for the valorization of parataxis in forms of modernism that have sought to detach aesthetics from politics (the idea of "art for art's sake"); it may also, however balefully, account for the privileging of paratactic strategies of representation (such as collage and montage) in our own "postcritical" era.

That said, it is important to keep in mind that in most if not all of Said's work, the objective of criticism was always less theoretical or hermeneutic than political; as he once put it in response to a question, "some historical questions cannot be resolved theoretically."[36] To this we can also add that his abiding goal was to keep the philosophical flame of humanism lit (an ideal most broadly expressed in *Humanism and Democratic Criticism* published in 2004, the year after his death).[37] As a result, his engagement with the figure of parataxis or its more prominent musical analog, counterpoint, was staged with the possibilities of human understanding in mind – conveying far greater interest in what such figures might enable scholars and critics to know about the world than what they foreclose.

This brings me to my final consideration: to the question of "late style" and, especially, to the ways that it sutures the problem of exile – as a matter of banishment, estrangement, and, ultimately, death. Let us recall that the idea of late style had preoccupied Said for a number of years prior to his death, leading to the posthumous publication of a lambent collection of essays entitled, *On Late Style: Music and Literature Against the Grain.*[38] The inspiration for his meditations on late style derived, as we also know, from Adorno's own posthumously published book on Beethoven; but whereas Adorno was mostly preoccupied with the problem of historical subjectivity as it is expressed in Beethoven's late works, Said translates this concern into his explorations of "the last or late period of life, the decay of the body, the onset of ill health."[39]

Since the publication of this book in 2006, reviewers and commentators have amply observed the connections between Said's thinking about lateness and his illness, along with its highly personal investment in the form and content of aesthetic works – a discernible "style," in other words, proper to a philosophical confrontation with death.[40] While the gravity of Said's discussion of late style may appear distant from the less consequential issue of the differences between parataxis or counterpoint as hallmarks of the modern that I took up in the preceding section, there is sufficient reason to connect the figure of parataxis with the problem of late style. This is not least because at the heart of both conceptions lies the twinned issue of the lack of resolution in life and the disavowal of harmony in art.

Crucially, too, Adorno provided Said with the ultimate example of a philosopher-critic whose treatment of parataxis in the poetry of the German Romantic poet Friedrich Hölderlin stands as perhaps the last word on the rejection of metaphysical or ontological notions and their replacement by a form of writing that presses our recognition of the fragmentary nature of existence to its limit.[41] Adorno's philosophical ideas about parataxis and late style are much too difficult to be glossed quickly or with ease, so let me stay close to some of what Said took from him in thinking about music and literature "against the grain" (as he put it in the subtitle to *On Late Style*).[42] In that context, it is perhaps sufficient to hint at the outline of Adorno's argument about parataxis – which settle on Hölderlin's use of this figure in his late works as the reflection of a "constitutive dissociation" that undermines both an idealized notion of the self as well as the reverence toward poetic language.[43]

Another point to keep in mind here is that Adorno's reading against the grain of Hölderlin's Romanticism was also a reading against Martin Heidegger's rightwing existential idealization of being. Correspondingly, in the book on Beethoven's music, late style betokens, for Adorno, all the means by which aesthetic works express their severed relationship to history. This problem – of overcoming the historical disjunction between subject and object – is at the core of Adorno's attention to parataxis; consequently, in reading Hölderlin's poetry or Beethoven's late works against the grain, his interest lay in offering an immanent critique of German Idealism's notion of a self-reflective consciousness. Paratactical structures are, by this token, the linguistic (or sonic) equivalents of historical irresolution whose overcoming constitutes the program of dialectics. In his own approach to read against the grain, Said picks up Adorno's dialectical impulses, albeit at a distance and without the same critical or materialist edge. Instead, he found great sustenance in the musicological nuances of Adorno's ideas about Beethoven, mobilizing the idea of disjunction to endow nonreconciliation with a productive and even positive inflection.

The essays in *On Late Style* derive from Adorno's emphasis on the "disorderly" and even "catastrophic" nature of Beethoven's late works, prompting Said to state that, "For Adorno, lateness is the idea of surviving beyond what is acceptable and normal."[44] The late works are the emblem of this survival *beyond* – a way of thinking that, we might recall, takes us back to the theme first elaborated in *After the Last Sky* on exile as a form of survival "after the aftermath." Unsurprisingly as well, Said took this seemingly unfinished, disharmonious music to be "a form of exile," and in so doing, he once more followed Adorno into the idea that, however contradictorily, music, literature, and by extension, other forms of art, have something profound to say, if only in their negation of present reality.[45]

In Said's hands, the problematic of late style is thus turned into a reckoning with the many ways of not being on time: the expression of "apartness and exile and anachronism."[46] Along the same lines, the problem of untimeliness is conveyed through the catchword of "irreconcilability." As Michael Wood states in his introduction to the collection, the note about irreconcilables is one that is struck throughout, whether the discussion has to do with so-called road maps in the Middle East or the propensity of artworks, particularly late works, to resist reconciling with the derangements of history and experience. We might then close by noting the remarkable if paradoxically harmonious ways that Said was able to join lateness and exile in his deliberations on style – as a very particular mode of the confrontation with death. By these means, he was also able to link his lifelong interest in music with his equally long-standing focus on the affiliations between the world, the text, and the critic, seeing them as especially resonant under circumstances in which expression and existence are both threatened.

Notes

1 Aimé Césaire, *Notebook of a Return to the Native Land*, trans. by C. Eshleman (Middletown, CT: Wesleyan University Press, 2001).
2 Edward W. Said, "Intellectual Exile: Expatriates and Marginals," *Grand Street* 47 (1993), 112–124 (114).
3 Seamus Dean gives an inspired account of Said's critical humanism in S. Deane, "Edward Said (1935–2003): A Late Style of Humanism," *Field Day Review* 1 (2005), 189–202.
4 V. S. Naipaul, *A Bend in the River* (New York: Vintage, 1989).
5 Said, "Intellectual Exile," p. 115.
6 See, for instance, T. W. Adorno, "The Meaning of Working through the Past," in *Critical Models: Interventions and Catchwords*, trans. by H. W. Pickford (New York: Columbia University Press, 1988), pp. 89–103.

7 Edward W. Said (with Jean Mohr), *After the Last Sky: Palestinian Lives* (New York: Columbia University Press, 1999).
8 Edward W. Said, "On Mahmoud Darwish," *Grand Street* 48 (1994), 112–115 (115).
9 Georg Lukács, *The Theory of the Novel*, trans. by Anna Bostock (London: Merlin, 1971 [1916]), p. 40.
10 Edward W. Said, *Orientalism* (New York: Pantheon, 1978).
11 Mahmoud Darwish, "The Earth Is Closing on Us" in *Victims of a Map*, trans. by Abdullah al-Udhari (London: al-Saqi Books, 1984), p. 13.
12 Drawing on the musical idea of "counterpoint," the idea of "contrapuntal criticism" is developed in Edward W. Said, *Culture and Imperialism* (New York: Alfred A. Knopf, 1993).
13 Brecht formulated his *Verfremdungseffekt*, or alienation effect, as a strategy of distantiation intended to discourage audiences from identifying with illusory characters and actions in narrative situations. See *Brecht on Theatre: The Development of an Aesthetic*, ed. and trans. by John Willett (London: Methuen, 1964).
14 Raymond Williams, "Structures of Feeling," *Marxism and Literature* (Oxford University Press, 1977), pp. 128–135.
15 See Bill Ashcroft and Pal Ahluwalia, *Edward Said*, 3rd ed. (New York: Routledge, 2008); Abdirahman A. Hussein, *Edward Said: Criticism and Society* (London: Verso, 2004); Valerie Kennedy, *Edward Said: A Critical Introduction* (Cambridge: Polity, 2000).
16 Williams, *Marxism and Literature*, p. 13.
17 There are those who deny that Said gave any credit to Orientalists for their understanding of the Orient. See, e.g., Robert Irwin, *For Lust of Knowing: The Orientalists and Their Enemies* (London: Allen Lane, 2006); see also the critical review of this book by Timothy Brennan, "Settling Scores: The Orientalists Strike Back," *Race and Class* 48.3, (2007), 94–113.
18 *Orientalism* is filled with passages describing the interplay between culture and administration, with figures such as Curzon and Cromer serving as examples of the ideological transformation of space into administered territory in the context of British imperialism. Said also provides examples of their French counterparts, especially in the final chapter, Said, *Orientalism*, "Orientalism Now," pp. 201–328.
19 Michel Foucault, *Discipline and Punish: The Birth of the Prison*, trans. by Alan Sheridan (New York: Vintage, 1977). Foucault's discussions are notable for their emphasis on the indirect and "capillary" rather than "juridical" nature of power; he also asserts, however counterfactually, the "productivity" of power – seen as a diffusive rather than hierarchical exercise in modern society.
20 See Keya Ganguly, "Roads Not Taken: Notes on the Legacy of *Orientalism*," *History of the Present* 5.1 (2015), 65–82; see also Lecia Rosenthal, "Between Humanism and Late Style," *Cultural Critique* 67 (2007), 107–140.
21 See Adorno's influential essay on the ineluctable joining of administration and culture under capitalism in T. W. Adorno, "Culture and Administration,"

The Culture Industry: Selected Essays on Mass Culture (New York: Routledge, 1991), pp. 93–113.

22 Said also pursues these themes elsewhere; see Edward W. Said, *The World, the Text, and the Critic* (Cambridge, MA: Harvard University Press, 1983).

23 Williams, *Marxism and Literature*, p. 133.

24 For an elaboration of this influence, see Timothy Brennan, "Edward Said as a Lukácsian Critic: Modernism and Empire," *College Literature* 40.4 (2013), 14–32.

25 See, for their varying critiques, Benita Parry, "Edward Said and Third-World Marxism," *College Literature* 40.4 (2013), 105–126; Bryan Turner, *Orientalism, Postmodernism, and Globalism* (New York: Routledge, 1994); and Gilbert Achcar, *Marxism, Orientalism, Cosmopolitanism* (New York: Haymarket Books, 2013).

26 Ernesto Laclau and Chantal Mouffe, *Hegemony and Socialist Strategy: Towards a Radical Democratic Politics* (London: Verso, 1985). The weaknesses of this work are exposed in two key essays by Norman Geras, "Post-Marxism?," *New Left Review* I.163 (May–June 1987), 40–82, and "Ex-Marxism without Substance: Being a Real Reply to Laclau and Mouffe," *New Left Review* I/169 (May–June 1988), 34–61.

27 Benita Parry, "Problems in Current Theories of Colonial Discourse," *Oxford Literary Review* 9 (1987), 27–58.

28 Edward W. Said, "Introduction to the Fiftieth-Anniversary Edition," in Erich Auerbach, *Mimesis: The Representation of Reality in Western Literature*, trans. by W. R. Trask (Princeton, NJ: Princeton University Press, 2003), p. xvii, emphasis added.

29 Said, "Introduction," p. xviii.

30 Ibid., p. xxxi.

31 The following are the only statements in *Mimesis* where Said explicitly mentions the function of parataxis: "If we go back to Homer, as Auerbach does in the celebrated and much-anthologized first chapter of *Mimesis*, the style is paratactic, that is, it deals with reality as a line of externalized, uniformly illuminated phenomena, at a definite time and in a definite place, connected together without lacunae in a perpetual foreground [which technically speaking is parataxis, words and phrases added on rather than subordinated to each other]; thoughts and feelings completely expressed; events taking place in leisurely fashion and with very little of suspense." Ibid., p. xviii.

32 Paul A. Bové, *Poetry Against Torture: Criticism, History, and the Human* (Hong Kong: Hong Kong University Press, 2008), p. 42.

33 Auerbach, *Mimesis*, p. 178.

34 Bové, *Poetry Against Torture*, p. 42.

35 For an early and clear charting of the concept of "historicism," see D. E. Lee and R. N. Beck, "The Meaning of 'Historicism,'" *The American Historical Review* 59.3 (1954), 568–577.

36 Edward W. Said, "Late Style: Adorno, Cafavy, Lampedusa," lecture delivered at the University of Minnesota, Minneapolis, February 24, 1999.

37 Edward W. Said, *Humanism and Democratic Criticism* (New York: Columbia University Press, 2004).

38 Edward W. Said, *On Late Style: Music and Literature Against the Grain* (New York: Pantheon Books, 2006).

39 Ibid., p. 6.

40 See, for instance, Edward Rothstein, "Twilight of His Idols," *Sunday Book Review, New York Times*, July 16, 2006, www.nytimes.com/2006/07/16/books/review/16rothstein.html (accessed July 27, 2017); also Frank Kermode, "Going Against," *London Review of Books* 28.19 (2006), 7–8.

41 T. W. Adorno, "Parataxis: On Hölderlin's Late Poetry," in *Notes to Literature*, trans. by S. W. Nicholsen, vol. 2 (New York: Columbia University Press, 1992 [1963]), pp. 109–149.

42 For a longer treatment of Adorno's ideas about parataxis, see J. M. Bernstein, *Adorno: Disenchantment and Ethics* (Cambridge: Cambridge University Press, 2001), esp. pp. 356–358.

43 Cited by Beatrice Hanssen, "'Dichtermut' and 'Blödigkeit': Two Poems by Friedrich Hölderlin, Interpreted by Walter Benjamin," in *Walter Benjamin and Romanticism*, ed. by Beatrice Hanssen and Andrew Benjamin (New York: Continuum, 2002), p. 140.

44 Said, *On Late Style*, p. 13.

45 Ibid., p. 8.

46 Ibid., p. 17.

CHAPTER 6

Said and the "Worlding" of Nineteenth-Century Fiction

Lauren M. E. Goodlad

At an important juncture in Jane Austen's *Mansfield Park* (1814), Fanny Price, who has been visiting Sotherton, the estate of her cousin Maria's fiancé, sits down on a "well shaded" bench "looking over a ha-ha into the park."[1] There Fanny stays during a sequence of events stretching over two chapters and more than an hour of diegetic time. At first, she listens while her cousin Edmund Bertram converses with Mary Crawford, the vivacious young sister-in-law of Mansfield's new parson; then, after Mary grows "weary" of rest and the couple departs, Fanny sits alone and becomes "surprised at being left so long" (77). Several brief encounters with other characters take place before Fanny, "quite impatient," at last leaves her perch without ever seeing the avenue of trees she had hoped to enjoy (82).

Anyone who writes on *Mansfield Park* must take note of the exceptional status of this most debated of Austen's novels. For Lionel Trilling, the work's "greatness" is "commensurate with its power to offend."[2] Barbara Bail Collins, possibly the first to call *Mansfield Park* a "Victorian" novel, points to the heroine's childhood, long denouement, scenes of déclassé Portsmouth, clerical focus, and moralizing narrator.[3] William Galperin, noting that *Mansfield Park* was never reviewed, counters that the novel is less "Victorian" than futural – albeit to "perplexing" and "dystopic" effect.[4] Louise Flavin marks the increased complexity of Austen's free indirect style; Ann Banfield, the heightened social connections to place; and many others, the apparent lack of irony.[5] For my purposes, all of these claims resonate in demonstrating how the exceptionally "worlded" and "world-ing" aesthetic features I describe in this essay generate formal disruption of many kinds, making *Mansfield Park* a set piece for the nineteenth-century novel and its relation to empire. But before I make that case, I will take a page from Austen's book, leaving Fanny seated at the ha-ha while we take another view of the subject.

Contrapuntal Rereading

In "The Novel and Empire," Elaine Freedgood writes that the nineteenth-century novel, like the map and the newspaper, contributed "to the imagining of empire." Indeed, she adds, "The enterprise of empire depends upon the *idea of having an empire*" a quotation she draws from the opening chapter of Edward Said's *Culture and Imperialism* (1993).[6] In the passage in question, Said explains that imperialism, more than a simple desire to extract profit, springs from a "structure of attitude and reference" that culminates in an "almost metaphysical obligation to rule" (xxiii, 10). Said's loosely Gramscian theory of culture's work – elaborated across realist, modernist, and postcolonial examples – prompts him to conclude: "Without empire, there is no European novel as we know it" (69). This consummately epigrammatic formulation – no empire/no novel – has, on the one hand, made the anthologizing of essays like "The Novel and Empire" part of literary criticism as we know it and, on the other hand, provoked decades of contestation and debate. Thus, if scholars of the novel are, by now, "after Said" in a number of ways, the critical project of theorizing culture and imperialism, I suggest, is an unfinished project that may be as important now as it was in the 1990s.

In defining his method as *contrapuntal rereading*, Said sought to engender "a simultaneous awareness both of the metropolitan history and of those other histories against which (and together with which) the dominating discourse acts" (51). In this way he responded to critics who had seen his *Orientalism* (1979) as a study too focused on imperial power and too little on resistance.[7] By adopting a notion of counterpoint from classical music, Said set out to reread works that, despite being "shaped and perhaps even determined" by the histories of colonization and resistance (51), suppressed this imperial provenance. Moreover, critical theory conduced toward Eurocentric myopia. The result was a European culture "exonerated of any entanglements with power" – an "act of complicity" on the part of theorists whose "model of critique" ignored "continuing struggle over" imperialism (56–57).

But in making this case, Said's goal was not to break with critical theory. The point of contrapuntal rereading was to "draw out, extend, [and] give emphasis and voice" to the "silent or marginally present or ideologically represented" (66). The twinned ambition of *Culture and Imperialism* is to reclaim the encounters with otherness that an imperial culture has repressed as well as to describe the emergence of a new kind of metropolitan subject – an exilic consciousness whose mature form is the postcolonial intellectual. This "new presence within Europe" surfaces first in striking modernist tropes such as Thomas Mann's plague, James Joyce's "wandering Jew," and Marcel Proust's "inverts." Modernism thus captures a new proximity: "[I]nstead of being *out* there," now "they are *here*,'" Said writes (188). But to recognize the "non-European cultures" that imbue this art, Said forecast, will require a "huge and remarkable adjustment in perspective and understanding" (242–243).

Has any such adjustment been made? That Austen, Kipling, and Conrad are frequently taught alongside Olaudah Equiano, Mary Seacole, and Chinua Achebe; that British literature courses now include such authors as Monica Ali and Caryl Phillips, suggests that in some significant part, the answer is yes. Nonetheless, looking back to *Culture and Imperialism* in 2018, in the midst of a world-historical reaction against both the legacy of the Enlightenment *and* the legacy of postcolonial critiques of the Enlightenment, one can hardly judge the work of giving voice to the silenced as a fait accompli. When Said asks what kind of contrapuntal rereading might help to address the crises of the present, he poses a question that scholars today must continue to explore from new millennial vantage points.

We might begin by recalling that critics friendly to Said's project have long charged *Culture and Imperialism* with a too-narrow account of the postcolonial condition. When Mary Louise Pratt's early review pointed out that the same breathless drive for accumulation which fueled the scramble for Africa drove comparable events in Spanish America, it anticipated Benita Parry's criticism of Said's "disconnection" of empire from the globalization of capital.[8] We have seen how Said's effort to distinguish imperialism's "structure of attitude and reference" from a mere economic by-product entailed positing an "almost metaphysical" culture of domination that takes on a life of its own. At the same time, Said overlooked distinctions within the diverse modes of imperialism that, for centuries, had developed unevenly across cultural and geographic borders. As the historian John Darwin emphasizes, it was by drawing together the disparate logics of plantation slavery, white settlement colonies, "free" trade imperialism, and territorial dominion – while "exploiting" the "benefits that each had to offer" – that Britain sustained the geopolitical edge it had won in Austen's time.[9] Understood as such, the British empire – a sprawling web of uneven structures developed in response to particular economic, geopolitical, and cultural rationales – was both a world-system in Darwin's sense as well as a formation subject to global networks of trade and finance, colonial resistance in multiple contact zones, as well as competition from other geopolitical and commercial actors. For all these reasons, Said's tendency to portray imperialism as a unified structure of domination is, by contemporary lights, too doctrinaire to foster capacious contrapuntal rereading.

Nonetheless, it is worth comparing Said's account of imperialism to the Eurocentrism and nation-centrism that dominated most scholarship well into the 1990s. Weighing in a few years after *Culture and Imperialism*, Franco Moretti's *Atlas of the European Novel: 1800–1900* (1999) proffered a map of Austen's fiction that reinforced the dyad of novel and nation-state. Countering Said's contrapuntal thrust – but confirming the insularity of Austen's fiction – Moretti insisted that *Mansfield Park* "defines the nation as *the sum of all . . . possible stories.*"[10] On this view, Sir Thomas Bertram departs for an estate in Antigua "because Austen needs him out of the way."[11] Said points to Raymond Williams, whose influential *Culture and Society: 1780–1950* (1958)[12] – to which his own title nods – "does not deal with the imperial experience at all" (65). Williams's passing notice of immigrants in a later work, according to Said, does little justice to those "voyages in" which brought the politics of decolonization to the metropole (244). For Said, the "hybrid cultural work" this migrant presence enabled countered the old conceit of a unidirectional history that traveled from center to periphery (244–245). Such deprovincializing of Europe has engendered a compelling responsibility to otherness that makes it possible to think beyond the stalemate between Marxist and postcolonial theory.

Yet another important influence on *Culture and Imperialism* is the prevailing understandings of nineteenth-century realism that Said shared with Moretti, Fredric Jameson, and many others. In direct contrast to the deprovincializing account of modernism's debts to colonial migration, Said depicts realist fiction as largely trapped in a binary of "here"/"out there." Discussing Joseph Conrad, he describes the "unsettling anxiety" and "ironic awareness" of the "post-realist modernist sensibility" (188). By contrast, realism, he assumes, invariably "consolidates" the institutional "status quo" (77) – its "main purpose" to "keep the empire more or less in place" (74). In particular, realism generates "patterns of narrative authority" that affirm the abstract and positivistic versions of geographic space that authorize "power and privilege abroad" (70, 76). Said thus affirms a realism/modernism antithesis that homogenizes the aesthetic and material complexity of novels during a period of remarkable geopolitical and literary ferment. In Britain especially, the decades from the 1830s to the 1870s – a period that saw the burgeoning of a serialized print culture that included landmark novels by authors like Wilkie Collins, Charles Dickens, George

Eliot, and Anthony Trollope – were also "the critical phase of Britain's emergence as a global power in command of a world-system."[13]

In the years since *Culture and Imperialism* was published, scholars of the novel have begun to challenge the perception of realist fiction as an ideological bulwark programmed to consolidate vision and support the status quo. A cluster of noteworthy scholarship has demonstrated realist fiction's potentially dynamic engagement with the long and ongoing history of capitalist globalization, inside and beyond the structures of colonization and imperial domination.[14] In fact, the long-standing critical tendency to uphold modernist innovation at the expense of realism dates back to the turn of the nineteenth century when proto-modernists like Henry James, as well as modernists such as Virginia Woolf, launched strong critiques of realist aesthetics. These antirealist attitudes were adapted and amplified by scholars working under the auspices of New Criticism, Marxism, structuralism, poststructuralism, and the New Historicism.

Critiques of realism in this vein – though often unnervingly lax in defining their object – tended to foreclose or ignore the "worlded" and "worlding" qualities of the novels in question. By *worlded,* I have in mind the existing processes and materialities that a realist literature so-called takes for its subject; by *worlding,* I allude to the new ways of seeing, knowing, and thinking that such a literature may palpably express in response to those worlds. Rather than a prop for imperial power, nineteenth-century realism, on this view, might be understood as an archive, the formal contours of which may at times evoke that "simultaneous awareness" of metropolitan and colonial histories that contrapuntal rereading sets out to gauge and explore.

The Nineteenth-Century Geopolitical Aesthetic

How might scholars of the nineteenth-century novel begin to research the worlding and worlded dimensions of a "realist" archive so conceived? In a 1995 book on cinema and the world-system, Jameson coined the term *geopolitical aesthetic* to describe how artistic forms articulate "an unconscious, collective effort" to "figure out" "the landscapes and forces" specific to global situations that are at once lived and beyond individual experience and cognition.[15] The term *geopolitical aesthetic* can help to identify nineteenth-century modes of disavowal, irony, anxiety, and spatial disruption inviting scholars to reconsider the formal variations realist literature undertook as it strove to "figure out" the expanding world-systems established between Austen's time and the modernist era proper.[16]

To see how this works let us consider E. M. Forster's *Howards End* (1910) – a novel that, according to Jameson, strikes out a new modernist aesthetic through a moment of "spatial perception."[17] Jameson has in mind the passage in which Mrs. Munt speeds northward on a train: "At times the Great North Road accompanied her, more suggestive of infinity than any railway awakening, after a nap of a hundred years."[18] This evocation of the "empty endlessness" of a nation-spanning motorway, according to Jameson, answers a distinctly imperial condition of spatial disjunction in which metropolitan and colonial conditions are materially fused but phenomenologically divided. Imperialism, that is, "means that a significant structural segment of the economic system . . . is now located elsewhere . . . outside of the daily life and existential experience of the home country, in colonies over the water whose own life experience" remains "unimaginable for the subjects of the imperial power."[19]

Yet, according to Jameson, realist fiction is doubly incapable of any comparable perception: first because realism is formally driven "to avoid recognition of deep social change" or "contradictory tendencies"[20] and, second, because it is a materially preimperial form – a "national literature" that, unlike Forster's novel, depicts a fully bounded lifeworld, with no "missing piece" to provoke any glimpse of a ghostly imperial "outside."[21] Imperialism, on this view, begins with the scramble for Africa; nineteenth-century fiction, as in Moretti's account of *Mansfield Park,* is portrayed as an intrinsically nation-centered form.

Said's treatment of realism, by contrast, is potentially more favorable to nuanced geopolitical understanding given his greater attention to the long history of empire, commitment to contrapuntal perspectives, and sensitivities to the "particular genius" of individual literary works (67).[22] When he claims that Sir Thomas Bertram's Caribbean "possessions" fix his "social status" and "make possible his values," Said harks back to the premise that novels such as *Mansfield Park* are "shaped and perhaps even determined" by imperial histories (62, 51). Nonetheless, Said shares Jameson's assumption that realism papers over such ideological contradictions. In contrast to Conrad's anxiety or Forster's stirring geospatial perception, realist fiction simply "excludes" the other (as in *Mansfield Park*) or "ideologically represents" the other (as in *Kim*) (66). Indeed, the realist construction of space as Said construes it, all but determines this lamentable outcome. Harnessed to the imperatives of "cartographic," "military," "economic," and "historical" discourses, realist space assures that Austen will depict Sir Thomas's property in Antigua as the "natural extension of the calm . . . beauties of Mansfield Park" (78–79).

In the last decade or so, as critics have increasingly questioned the worn-out premise of a realism-modernism antithesis, the understanding of realist space has diverged from this tendency to assume a passive adherence to imperial mapping, or nation-centric "grid."[23] The "great breakthrough of nineteenth-century novels," writes Rosa Mucignat, is their enhanced visualization of spatial depth and movement.[24] In *The Victorian Geopolitical Aesthetic: Realism, Sovereignty, and Transnational Experience* (2015), I explored a wide range of powerful spatial figures derived from nineteenth-century fiction. The rendering of space in these novels, as with Forster's road, helps to visibilize the existing twining of metropole and colony – throwing light on those disavowed affects and shared materialities that contrapuntal rereading explores. Readers of Collins's *The Moonstone* (1868), for example, will recall the striking space of the Shivering Sands. This occult Yorkshire landscape, likened to a "broad brown face" and invoking "hundreds of suffering people,"[25] concentrates the layers of imperial violence that Collins's multipart narration encompasses: the storming of Seringapatam in 1799, the conquest of the Punjab and surrender of the Koh-i-Noor in 1848, as well as the Indian rebellion in 1857.[26]

Armadale (1864–1866), the work that Collins took for his best, is saturated with the archeological traces of Atlantic slavery: a topic that Britons memorialized – in effect, suppressed – through the triumphalist narrative of abolition. In narrating an improbable story that reaches back to the largest plantation in Barbados, *Armadale*'s most distinctive feature is a weird topography that crisscrosses Britain, the Continent, and the Caribbean and includes such exceptional locales as the semisovereign Isle of Man and the labyrinthine Norfolk Broads. The novel's most memorable event is the resurfacing of a sunken ship from the preabolition era, ironically named *La Grace de Dieu*.[27] As *Armadale* resurrects a "guilty ship" that epitomizes the secret connection between its white protagonist and his mixed-race namesake, the novel evokes W. J. M. Turner's *The Slave Ship* (1840), itself inspired by the 1781 massacre on the *Zong*, an atrocity publicized by Equiano and discussed by the abolitionist Thomas Clarkson among others.[28]

Perhaps the most memorable spatial figure in mid-Victorian realist fiction is the Tenway Junction in Trollope's *The Prime Minister* (1875–1876) – scene of the self-obliteration of Ferdinand Lopez, one of British literature's most disturbing antiheroes. Signaling Trollope's turn from the comic irony that had elevated him to fame in his Barsetshire novels, *The Prime Minister* splits between the story of Plantagenet Palliser's disappointing political achievements and Lopez's darker narrative of alien identity, fraudulent speculation, and marital despair. Though he is a suspected Jew with unknown origins as well as a callous husband, Lopez never entirely loses his pathos. His estranged condition anticipates the exilic experience of Said's modernist works.

In providing the stage for Lopez's suicide, the Tenway Junction becomes the spatial bearer of ambivalence and uncertainty. The narrator's teasing introduction first declares that "[i]t is quite unnecessary to describe" the Tenway, "as everybody knows it," only to describe at length "a marvelous" place that is "quite unintelligible" though it is "daily used by thousands." "From this spot . . . lines diverge east, west, and north, north-east, and north-west, round the metropolis in every direction."[29] So far from a reassuring cartography, Trollope's "spot" is a metonymically super-charged epicenter of global traffic, psychic damage, and multidirectional space. Connecting mid-Victorian London to histories and experiences beyond its metropolitan sightlines, the Tenway Junction heightens the perception of an existing worldedness that individuals can sense but never fully cognize.

The work of the nineteenth-century geopolitical aesthetic is, thus, to visibilize the formation of world-systems in motion. But these perceptions of worldedness and their worlding effects are not exclusively spatial. A geopolitical aesthetic may sharpen vision through new types of charac-terization such as the racially hybrid and futuristic Ezra Jennings in *The Moonstone*, or the voiceless Indian prince whose ambiguous narrative of dispossession weaves in and out of the wry marital plots of *The Eustace Diamonds* (1871–1873), another Palliser novel.[30] It can be figured through chronotopic objects like *Armadale*'s guilty ship, *The Moonstone*'s titular diamond, or the spectacularly flawed wedding present at the center of James's *The Golden Bowl* (1904).[31] It may determine narrative form as in the forks between "Jewish" and "English" plots that organize *The Prime Minister* as well as George Eliot's contemporaneous *Daniel Deronda* (1876).[32] Or it may refigure realist conventions more radically as when the fused histories of violation in *The Moonstone* – a Hindu shrine "there" and an English country estate "here" – call forth multiple voices to take the place of a single and all-knowing narrator. Alternatively, it can be expressed thematically as in the "adulterous geopolitical aesthetic" that connects a range of mid-century novels in which global finance infects the structures of bourgeois marriage, from Dickens's *Dombey and Son* (1848) and Flau-bert's *Madame Bovary* (1856), to the later works of Eliot, Trollope, James, and George Meredith.[33] Raymond Williams has described such works as species of "country-house" fiction in which "the country-house" is "not of land but of capital." In such works, "[H]ouses, parks and furniture are explicitly objects of consumption and exchange. People bargain, exploit and use each other . . . Money from elsewhere is an explicit and dominant theme."[34] The particularly geopolitical perception of such works is, thus, the long-evolving spatial and social phenomenon through which money from "there" became money "here" – a rich (and as yet unplumbed) opportunity for contrapuntal rereading.

"They are here": The Country, the City, and the World System in *Mansfield Park*

Let us return to *Mansfield Park* to see what the notion of a nineteenth-century geopolitical aesthetic can contribute to rereading this much-discussed novel contrapuntally. Can Williams's story of "money from elsewhere" be backdated to explore the spatial twining of "here" and "out there" during the critical decades of an emerging imperial world-system? The proposition makes sense given the rising class of speculators enriched by constant wars as well as the lucrative services in trade, shipping, and finance that colonialism ushered in. But it is also important because *The Country and the City* is a frequent launching point for scholarship on Austen.

Moretti, for example, enlists Williams to help establish nation building as the genius of Austenian space. "What [Austen] sees," according to Moretti's quotation, "is a network of propertied houses and families" in a "tightly drawn mesh" through which "most actual people are simply not seen."[35] This emphasis on seen/unseen buttresses Moretti's case for a pattern of "exclusion."[36] By joining land and money into "a large, exquisite home," Austen invents a form for making "sense of the nation-state" during "the harshest class struggle" in "modern British history."[37]

Like Moretti, Said begins his analysis with Williams's contrast between Austen's fiction and William Cobbett's *Rural Rides* (1822–1826).[38] Thus, while Said criticizes Williams's Anglocentric focus on a crisis of enclosure that, in actuality, coincided with imperialism (83), he affirms the Austen-Cobbett contrast. Cobbett, "riding past on the road," names "classes," says Williams, while "Austen from inside the houses, can never see that." Her "intricate" social description is, "understandably, internal and exclusive." Said thus reprises an analysis that predicates the discernment of *class* on a kind of mobility that female authors, immured in the country house, "understandably" lack. Such an Austen "can never see" what lies beyond the morals of her elite repertoire – "people who, in the complications of improvement are, repeatedly trying to make themselves into a class."[39] That these "complications" do not themselves indicate a noteworthy class analysis is, for Williams, quite clear: "Where only one class is seen, no classes are seen,"[40] he writes, in a judgment Said deems to be "dead right" (84). The Austen of this interpretation is so conditioned to regard land as the sole "index of revenue and position" – and so insensible to the physical labor producing wealth – that her novels abstract the moral conduct they authorize from the modes of exploitation beyond her purview.[41]

In thus opposing a (female) novelist, to a (male) journalist and polemicist, Williams turns differences of genre, style, and content into a set of gendered binaries between inside/outside, house/road, unseen/seen, and (in Said's variation) "here"/"out there." Here is the ground both for Said's assertion that Austen turns a slave plantation into the "natural extension" of Mansfield Park's "beauties" and for Moretti's that she translates "the harshest class struggle" in "modern British history" into the unifying vision of an "exquisite" house.

To be sure, Williams rightly upholds *Rural Rides* as the prelude to new forms of novelistic art. As Cobbett calls out the large landholders whose children marry "paper-money people," "big brewers," and "Jews" – as well as the arrival of "nabobs," "negro drivers," and "admirals,"[42] he anticipates the "money from elsewhere" that, as Williams shows, pervades the naturalistic country-house novels of the 1870s and after. What is surprising, however, is the disregard of comparable forces in *Mansfield Park*. Whereas the country houses of later fiction stand in for "events prepared" and "continued elsewhere," Austen's cultivated gentry, according to Williams, projects a reassuring "morality of improvement."[43] But even granting that Sotherton and Mansfield are not the decadent estates of a James novel, in *Mansfield Park*, the characters who most eagerly seize on improvement – Rushworth, Henry Crawford, and Mrs. Norris – clearly talk this talk to forward self-promoting designs. If these self-anointed improvers stand at some remove from Cobbett's "nabobs," "paper-money people," and "Jews," the Crawfords' uncle is an "admiral" known for "vicious conduct" (32) while the relevance of "negro drivers" speaks for itself.[44] The readiness to commodify country-house life, moreover, is already at work in Mary's sizing up of Tom Bertram's patrimony as a "gentlem[a]n's seat" that "might do" (38). As Fraser Easton writes, "[N]o human interaction" – "from the marriages of the Ward sisters, to Fanny's questions about the slave-trade" – eludes the novel's networks of "economy and exchange."[45]

Of course, the geopolitical and literary conjunctures interweaving "here" and "out there" are complicated by the uneven world-systems in question. Terms such as *colonialism* and *imperialism* denote various practices only some of which directly advance modern capitalism. While *capitalism* strives to assert its demands for growth through economic compulsion in the context of "free" market conditions, *imperialism* can never wholly deny its reliance on conquest and domination.[46] As a committed contrapuntalist, Said sets out to explore "what is involved when an author shows" that "a colonial sugar plantation" is "seen as important" to "maintaining a particular lifestyle in England." But he goes on to suggest that when Austen "referred to Antigua," and "to realms visited by the British navy," she did so "without any thought of possible responses" by Caribbean or Indian people (93). Said tenders this claim without appearing to recognize that Austen's intended brother-in-law died in a campaign in the Caribbean in 1796, when the French republic's forces included Toussaint L'Ouverture's army of emancipated slaves. As Ruth Perry notes, this costly battle was so "scandalously unpopular" that it helped to fuel "growing disapproval" of West Indian slavery.[47] Significantly, then, the critical years between 1806 and 1808 – encompassing passage of the 1807 Abolition of the Slave Trade Act (as well as publication of the book on this topic that prompted Austen to declare herself "in love with" Clarkson) – provide the setting for *Mansfield Park* as well as *Persuasion*.[48] When Fredrick Wentworth, the hero of the latter, joins the 1806 battle of Santo Domingo, Austen's character – unlike Cassandra's betrothed a decade earlier – is part of a force helping to defend Toussaint's Haiti against "Napoleon's attempt to re-enslave it."[49] The appearance of a mixed-race West Indian heiress in the unfinished *Sanditon* further suggests that Austen's "thinking" about Afro-Caribbean people was ongoing.

For contrapuntal rereading, the point is less to insist on the author's abolitionist fervor than to recognize that, contra Said, no such claim would be "silly" (115).[50] As Katie Trumpener suggests, the most salient difference between *Mansfield Park* and explicitly proabolition works such as Amelia Opie's *Adeline Mowbray* (1804) is Austen's groundbreaking realist form which eschews stark divisions of good and evil.[51] Nonetheless, that Sir Thomas Bertram is a species of "negro driver," that Mrs. Norris bears the name of a notorious overseer described in Clarkson's book, and that Fanny occupies the symbolic position of a slave are just some of the arguments that scholars have raised against Said's readiness, in Susan Fraiman's words, to make *Mansfield Park* "exhibit A in the case" for European "culture's endorsement of empire."[52]

Contrapuntal rereaders should also remember that slavery is not the novel's only sign of exceptional worldedness. The novel opens with Fanny's mother seeking help from Lady Bertram for the ten-year-old William, "a fine spirited fellow, who longed to be out in the world." Though such a lad, as Mrs. Price proposes, might help Sir Thomas with "his West Indian property," he might instead be situated at "Woolwich" or "sent out to the East" (4). Austen's very first page thus traces an imperial network beyond and within the country-house ambit: from West Indian sugar colonies and a territorial empire in "the East," to the diverse military and maritime employments signified by Woolwich. Nor, despite her sedentary habits, does Fanny lack ways to go "out in the world." Once mocked by her cousins for geographic ignorance, she matures into a reader of *Crabbe's Tales* (which elegize the enclosure of common land), Cowper's *The Task* (which cries out against slavery as well as enclosure), and the memoirs of George Macartney.[53] By teasing Fanny that she "will be taking a trip into China" (123), Edmund spotlights Macartney's role as Britain's ambassador to an important new center of "informal" imperialism,[54] but Macartney is also remembered as the first Briton to remark on the "vast empire on which the sun never sets."[55] The reflections of an Irishman descended from Scots, who, as Governor of Grenada, surrendered to the French, and as Governor of Madras, negotiated the treaty after the fall of Seringapatam (where Francis Austen served and which Collins later took for *The Moonstone*'s primal scene), Macartney's memoirs offer a consummate survey of Britain's transition into "a global power in command of a world-system."[56]

If Fanny's reading thus seems designed to counter the nation as the sum of all possible stories, the crucial point is that *Mansfield Park*'s geospatial map of "out there" heightens its insights into the country house. The resulting perception of a world-system in motion is more like an adjustable lens zooming in and out of diverse focal points at multiple scales, than Said's static exclusions or Jameson's "fixed-camera view."[57] As such, *Mansfield Park* is one of the first major novels to evoke "money from elsewhere" – elucidating the complex interplay of country, city, and colony in a world-systems matrix that has yet to be fully theorized.

Consider the ride to Sotherton, a road's-eye view of the Rushworth demesne dominated by the perspective of the haughty Maria Bertram, future mistress of an "ancient manorial residence with all its rights of court-leet and court-baron." Maria's evident relish in her fiancé's "consequence" inflects her declaration that the cottages at Sotherton "are really a disgrace" (65). Lamenting the appearance of rural impoverishment, she does not register it as a concerning social phenomenon. Her pluming herself on the ancient "rights" that distinguish Sotherton from the "new money" Mansfield is, thus, grimly ironic.[58] For Maria, such "rights" confirm the family's status without prompting any obligation to study the altered relations between land and labor that – thanks to the narrator's cues – the "disgraceful" cottages nonetheless pronounce. By contrast, Fanny is an attentive observer who, like a species of Cobbett, notes "the appearance of the country, the bearings of the roads, the difference of soil, the state of the harvest, the cottages, the cattle, [and] the children" (64).

The proletarianization of labor that rural enclosure helped to enact marked the onset of a capitalist imperative to maximize productivity which continues into the present day. Enclosure thus involved more than the mandatory fencing, gating, and hedging that all but one of Austen's major novels depicts.[59] It also entailed the extinction of common use rights that compelled the rural populations of England, Ireland, and Wales to accept the new way of life that Thomas Carlyle identified as the "cash nexus."[60] As Karl Marx explained in his analysis of this primitive accumulation, the expropriation of land for the benefit of the largest producers transformed England's peasant proprietors into "hirelings."[61] Citing Dr. Richard Price, a radical eighteenth-century divine whose work of which Austen knew,[62] *Capital* describes how a once independent population was compelled to labor longer for less, migrate to towns, and rely on poor relief to supplement wages.[63] The new social configuration that this primitive accumulation made possible combined a population of "free" workers forced to sell their labor; a class of producers (typically large tenant farmers) compelled to increase productivity under pressure of rising rents; and, finally, the "unprecedented division of labor" that, over time, results from the market's demand for such ever-greater efficiencies.[64] Hence, capitalism – an encompassing economic system bent on extending its imperatives to increase productivity and replicate the cash nexus at ever-greater scale – originated in the 300-year-long rural transformation that was reaching its apex during the decades of Austen's writing.

Mansfield Park highlights this advent by locating the Bertram estate in Northamptonshire. A hotspot for eighteenth-century enclosure, the county was one of two singled out by Price – thus making the "new lordships" he described in 1772 roughly contemporaneous with the origins of the "modern-built" Mansfield Park (48).[65] Scholars quoting the 1813 letter in which Austen queried whether Northamptonshire was "a Country of Hedgerows" have pointed out that the county and its hedges are telltale signs of a rural enclosure reaching its peak in the period of the novel's setting.[66]

But, of course, agrarian capitalism's story transcends the borders of any one county. Already in Price's book, one perceives that the same labor-for-hire that fueled Britain's revolutions in agriculture and manufacturing, had begun to enlarge the network of settler colonies that evolved into, and beyond, the Anglophone heartland.[67] In this way, John Locke's influential notion of undercultivated land as "waste" helped to legitimate enclosure inside Britain's borders as well as settler colonialism beyond them. In *Chartism* (1839), Carlyle called "emigration" one of the two "great things" (the other being education) that "all thinking heads in England" had been dwelling on for more than a decade.[68] White settler colonies, notable for their devastating impact on the indigenous peoples inhabiting the supposed waste, were the first "form of imperialism driven by the logic of capitalism."[69] Their underlying motive force was a drive to expand the imperative to produce that emigrant Britons took up as a God-given mission.

The ideology of "free" labor that underwrote this material condition was at odds with a "slave-powered globalization" that was still highly profitable in the early nineteenth century.[70] Many of the antislavery activists who pressed for abolition were thus enthusiasts of political economy who anticipated a rapid transition in the West Indies from the cruel oppression of slave-grown sugar to the supposed liberty of English-style agrarian capitalism.[71] Ironically, then, critics of enclosure often likened Britain's agricultural laborers to slaves. Poems like "The Village Minstrel" (1819), by the Northamptonshire poet John Clare, called on a "boasted land of liberty" to acknowledge the "parish-slaves" that enclosure had created in "every village."[72] In *Mary Barton* (1848), Elizabeth Gaskell's condition-of-England novel, John Barton invokes "slavery" to reject both old economy and new. Describing the Manchester masters who "pile up their fortunes with the sweat" of their "slaves," Barton regards domestic service as another "species of slavery."[73] Such metaphorical usages, though powerful in depicting the exploitation of labor, decouple "slavery" from the specific materiality of the Atlantic world-system, including the discourses of race that structured its aftermath. Moreover, when nineteenth-century feminists used similar metaphors to describe gender inequality as a retrograde feature of British life – akin to the "backward" Orient – their discourse "helped consolidate" the "sense of Western superiority" Said describes.[74] As scholars have noted, the title character of Charlotte Brontë's *Jane Eyre* (1847), who repeatedly describes herself as a "rebel slave," achieves her "feminist" independence through a legacy that may be as tainted by the triangle trade as is Bertha Mason's Jamaican fortune.[75]

By contrast, Cowper's *The Task* (1785), which Fanny quotes on behalf of Sotherton's trees, explicitly criticizes enclosure as well as Atlantic slavery, but, in doing so, distinguishes British from Caribbean labor: "We have no slaves at home – then why abroad?," the speaker asks.[76] Similarly, *Mansfield Park* ties metaphoric slavery to the self-aggrandizing Aunt Norris who boasts of "slaving" over costumes for *Lovers' Vows* (130) just as she earlier declares herself the enemy of "waste" (112). Austen's novel thus represents enclosure and Atlantic slavery as contiguous features of an emerging world-system while marking the difference between them. Indeed, post-Saidian scholars who liken Fanny's subordination to slavery arguably project a metaphorical equivalence onto the relation of country house and colony in place of the novel's subtler metonymic linkage. Though Fanny's situation enables keen social insights, as the poor relation of a wealthy family she is neither an Antiguan slave nor a rural laborer. To assume otherwise is to adopt Aunt Norris's logic; it is also to isolate Fanny from the matrix of characters and objects that "world" her story.

Consider the exchange between Edmund and Fanny that describes the "dead silence" after the novel's single conversation about the slave trade (155). As George Boulukos notes, many critics mistakenly assume that slavery was a shocking topic for Fanny to raise: Instead, he contends, Fanny likely "congratulates" Sir Thomas for ameliorating a brutal practice.[77] Yet, what we read in *Mansfield Park* is quite different. Although Sir Thomas travels to oversee the "better arrangement" of "affairs" in the wake of "recent" West Indian "losses" (25), nothing suggests that he undertakes ameliorative reforms in preparation for abolition of the slave trade – or, for that matter, some other course of action (such as the sale of land to offset the costs of Tom's "extravagance" [18]).

Instead, the slave trade comes up obliquely. After Fanny declines to affirm her cousin's pining for the Crawfords, he relates Sir Thomas's notice of her "countenance" and "figure." When Edmund urges her to talk more, so as to demonstrate her "beauty of mind" as well, Fanny protests that when she asked her uncle about the slave trade she "longed" to inquire further, but for the "dead silence" that followed. By her own account, she discontinues the conversation so as to avoid "set[ting] [her]self off" at her cousins' "expense, by shewing a curiosity and pleasure" in Sir Thomas's "information which he must wish his own daughters to feel" (155). Distinctive in the passage is the indirection through which Sir Thomas's return from Antigua brings Fanny's sexual maturation to light. When Edmund speaks of his father's "admiration" for the niece he regarded as girlish upon his departure, he links his father's untold Caribbean experience to the female narrative of development that readers have followed in his absence. Hitherto set apart, uncle and niece are increasingly entwined as his recognition of patriarchal failure develops alongside her courtship plot. Of his views on the slave trade, we learn nothing beyond his niece's "curiosity and pleasure" in his "information." The Bertrams' "silence" on this increasingly deplored economy must speak for itself.

Instead of a faulty patriarch holding forth on amelioration, the novel spotlights careful (female) attention to material worlds in transition. Fanny's powers of observation and love of information offer exemplary rejoinders to the dizzying effects of an expanding world-system. The novel contrasts a niece who reads about Britain's ambassador and asks about the slave trade to a vacuous aunt who desires shawls from "the East" (239).[78] As one whose study of local conditions connects people and landscapes, Fanny also differs from Mary, who regards "nature, with little observation" – perhaps because the restless Henry refuses to settle them in any permanent "abode" (64, 33). Though Mary exudes the sophistication Fanny lacks, her acculturation to "the true London maxim, that everything is to be got with money" leaves her slow to fathom why laborers harvesting hay cannot hire out their cart (47). And when Edmund calls on her to reckon the distance between two points at Sotherton, "She would not calculate, she would not compare." The episode presages a character whose "cold-hearted ambition" derives from such refusal to affirm the material underpinnings of shared reality (76, 342).

These deficiencies, moreover, extend beyond those "great cities" where, as Edmund concedes, the "best morality" won't be found (73). When Fanny refuses Henry's proposal, her frustrated uncle deems her powers of "comparing and judging" to be "diseased." A "little abstinence" from Mansfield's "elegancies," he reasons, will "teach her the value of a good income" (289). In actuality, removal to Portsmouth enlarges Fanny's social awareness and strengthens her judgment.[79] Sir Thomas learns that his own faculties of "comparing" are diseased – through overreliance on the same instrumental calculus that has nurtured the deracinated individualism of the Crawfords as well as the decadence of his heir, the egotism of his daughters, and the "dead silence" of his family on matters of consequence to the world at large.

Looking Over the Ha-Ha

In her compelling case for *Mansfield Park* as a groundbreaking novel of "social consciousness," Ann Banfield suggests that the work's "triadic contrast between aristocratic Sotherton," lower-class Portsmouth, and "the country seat of a man with West Indian holdings" is the "formal expression" of a rapidly transforming "society at large."[80] As a groundbreaking novel of *geopolitical* consciousness, we might add, *Mansfield Park* makes space the substrate for, and supplement to, its developing character arcs. Space so conceived is not an abstract imperial cartography, a positivistic reification of the given, or a mere device for inflecting character. Rather, as the medium of a realist variation on the geopolitical aesthetic, space is the textured and dynamic fabric of metonymic connections, the bearer of vividly rendered material histories in motion, and the occasion for momentary glimpses (like Forster's road) of the encompassing linkages between "here" and "out there." From this view, *Mansfield Park* is at its most aesthetically cogent, certainly at its most contrapuntal, when it breaks the spell of developing subjects, slows the rhythms of its country-house social worlds, and turns the reader's attention to the stories that space has to tell. Nowhere is this turn more powerful than during the scenes at Sotherton in which Fanny looks "over a ha-ha into the park."

To be sure, the visit to Sotherton enlarges Fanny's experience and advances the marriage plot, framing amorous triangles that foment rivalry and portend adultery. At the same time, each space radiates particular meaning, including the unused chapel, the formal terrace, the simulated wilderness, and the ha-ha with its history of military, architectural, and agricultural usage. Yet, from a formal standpoint, what stands out most is the elongation of time: "[W]hen people are waiting," says Fanny, "they are bad judges of time, and every half minute seems like five" (81). As with slow motion in film, this temporal deceleration magnifies spatial perception, producing surreal effects that imbue everyday happenstance with the intensity of dreamwork. Ordinary objects – an open door to a flight of stairs, a man who has forgotten his key, a locked gate – take on multiple levels of meaning.

As the least mobile of Sotherton's visitors, Fanny is largely solitary; yet, despite her vaunted "spectatorship," the bench at the ha-ha restricts what she sees and hears.[81] As her companions appear and disappear while they follow their impulses "at the expense of someone else's feelings,"[82] Fanny experiences "surprise," "anxious desire" (77), anger, astonishment (79), "dread," "ill-use" (80), impatience, and, finally, "disappointment and depression." In fact, no one finds the day either "useful" or "productive" (82, 83) – an affective listlessness that directs attention to space.

The art historian S. A. Mansbach describes the ha-ha as a "curious feature of garden enclosure" that marks an English repurposing of

"European military engineering and French landscape planning."[83] As a species of dry ditch or sunk fence, the ha-ha's agricultural utility is to prevent farm animals from crossing into gardens. In his *Theory and Practice of Gardening*, translated in 1712, Antoine D'Argenville explained the name's French derivation. Because the visual trick of a sunken barrier "surprises the eye coming near it," he writes, it "makes one cry, "Ah! Ah!"[84] "[W]hat adds to the beauty" of the garden at Stowe House, wrote a visitor in 1724, "is that it is not bounded by walls, but by a ha-hah, which leaves you sight of the . . . woody country, and makes you ignorant how far the walks extend."[85] That is to say, the low perimeter of a ha-ha may recede into the distance, combining an "empty endlessness" akin to Forster's road with a ditch that "surprises the eye coming near it."

If this expectation of surprised delight gives the ha-ha its name, the impact at Sotherton is quite different. Only Fanny's readiness for a brief "look upon verdure" takes the ha-ha on its own terms, embracing the unobstructed view while ignoring the evidence of a barrier (76). But, for Mary, no obstacle is tolerable: "I have looked across the ha-ha till I am weary," she declares, "I must go and look through that iron gate" (76). In this way she obliges Edmund to join her for a stroll, leaving Fanny behind. Maria soon follows suit: "That iron gate, that ha-ha, give me a feeling of restraint and hardship" (78). At Henry's prompting, she slides past the gate, leaving Fanny to deliver the news to the "mortified" fiancé who went off to fetch the key (80).

Though the vogue for sunken fences lasted only a few decades,[86] the ha-ha – more than a feature *of* Sotherton's space – is an optic for understanding it. The ha-ha's presence suggests that the elaborate gardens singled out for improvement date back to the early eighteenth century. Yet, while much attention is given to the avenue of oaks and the "low" placement of the Tudor-era house (which impede a wide-open prospect), the ha-ha escapes the improvers' notice. That is so even though ha-has had been out of favor ever since "Capability" Brown started the trend for more (ostensibly) natural and open styles of gardening. By the time of Austen's setting, the designer of note was Humphry Repton. Scholars have stressed that *Mansfield Park* satirizes the improvers' pompous invocations of Repton, rather than Repton's ideas – not least because the designer himself had begun to criticize the craze for open prospects that Rushworth attributes to Reptonian genius.[87] Like Mary and Maria, moreover, he was hard on the ha-ha: Its "imaginary freedom," he wrote in 1806, is "dearly purchased by actual confinement."[88]

Rachel Crawford describes the ha-ha as an "ephemeral yet vastly power-ful ideal of landownership" which harnessed the illusion of openness in "the service of proprietary status." By means of the ha-ha, "[T]he world could be appropriated as an extension of the landowner's property and a purchase on a view become a gentleman's mark."[89] In seizing on the ha-ha's unique spatial effects, Crawford endows it with a relevance that far exceeds its "ephemeral" place in the history of gardening. Hence, while her book says little about Austen, it helps explain why the ha-ha is Sotherton's symbolic center as well as the anchor for its slow-motion events.

At one level the ha-ha is an emblem of enclosure that calls us back to the "disgraceful" cottages; at another, it is a functional threshold between the distinct worlds of wilderness and park. If one version of this bound-ary returns us to the tensions between "country" and "city," another reminds of the deceptive duality of "here" and "out there." As contra-puntalists committed to "simultaneous awareness," we know that the absolute proprietorship that the ha-ha makes visible and that, for Rachel Crawford, authorizes imperial expansion, is, at the same time, the legal and social condition for capitalism. Without the primitive accumulation enclosure enabled, the ha-has, hedgerows, and fences distinct to Britain's countryside would lack the "vast power" with which Crawford (rightly) invests them.

As Williams makes clear, the aestheticizing of the country house was an aestheticizing of enclosure and, thus, of agrarian capitalism. Citing Alexander Pope, who admired the "natural" style of the gardens he saw at Stowe, Williams calls it the ability of a "new class, with new capital" and skills to organize "nature" according to "their own point of view."[90] Even in our own day, the tendency to position the "country" as a space of stasis in contrast to the "city's" bustle and change, obscures what *Mansfield Park* makes so remarkably clear. Whether the fashion of the day touted tall avenues or imposing vistas, what the country house figures is "the wealth of English agriculture in the period of agrarian capitalism."[91] The "new money" in question might be that of "nabobs" and "negro drivers" or that of an "ancient hereditary gentleman" infected by the "pursuit of gain."[92] In reply, *Mansfield Park* proffers a modest choice between getting "as much beauty" as we can for our "money" (as Mary advises) or (as Edmund prefers) staying out of the "hands of" improvers altogether (45). But whatever we choose, the novel makes clear, "they are *here*." The ha-ha at Sotherton is the world-system in motion: at once visible and invisible, real and surreal, open and restraining, here and out there. Ah! Ah!

Notes

1 Jane Austen, *Mansfield Park* (Oxford: Oxford University Press, 2003 [1814]), p. 75. All future references will be cited parenthetically in the text.

2 Lionel Trilling, "Mansfield Park," in *The Opposing Self* (New York: Harcourt Brace, 1955), pp. 181–202, p. 185.

3 Barbara Bail Collins, "Jane Austen's Victorian Novel," *Nineteenth-Century Fiction* 4.3 (1949), 175–185.

4 William H. Galperin, *The Historical Austen* (Philadelphia: University of Pennsylvania Press, 2003).

5 Louise Flavin, "*Mansfield Park*: Free Indirect Discourse and the Psychological Novel," *Studies in the Novel* 19.2 (1987), 137–159; Ann Banfield, "The Influence of Place: Jane Austen and the Novel of Social Consciousness," in *Jane Austen in a Social Context*, ed. by David Monaghan (London: Palgrave, 1981), pp. 28–48; e.g., Marvin Mudrick, *Jane Austen: Irony as Defense and Discovery* (Berkeley: University of California Press, 1952).

6 Edward Said, *Culture and Imperialism* (New York: Vintage Books, 1993) p. 11; qtd. in Elaine Freedgood, "The Novel and Empire," in *The Oxford History of the Novel in English*, vol. 3, *The Nineteenth-Century Novel 1820–1880*, ed. by John Kucich and Jenny Bourne Taylor (Oxford: Oxford University Press, 2011), pp. 377–391, p. 377. All future references to Said's book will be cited parenthetically in the text.

7 Edward Said, *Orientalism* (New York: Vintage Books, 1979).

8 Mary Louis Pratt, in "Edward Said's *Culture and Imperialism*: A Symposium," *Social Text* 40 (1994), 1–24 (5); Benita Parry, "Countercurrents and Tensions in Said's Critical Practice," in *Edward Said: a Legacy of Emancipation and Representation*, ed. by Adel Iskanadar and Hakem Rustom (Berkeley: University of California Press, 2010), pp. 499–512, p. 512n. See also Neil Lazarus who argues that postcolonial theory's understanding of imperialism is "routinely severed from the conception of 'capitalism,'" *The Postcolonial Unconscious* (Cambridge: Cambridge University Press, 2011), p. 39.

9 John Darwin, *The Empire Project: The Rise and Fall of the British World-System, 1830–1970* (Cambridge and New York: Cambridge University Press, 2009), p. 58.

10 Franco Moretti, *Atlas of the European Novel, 1800–1900* (London: Verso, 1999), p. 20.

11 Ibid., p. 26.

12 Raymond Williams, *Culture and Society: 1780–1950*, 2nd ed. (New York: Columbia University Press, 1983).

13 Darwin, *Empire Project*, p. 30.

14 I discuss this work in Lauren M. E. Goodlad, "Introduction: Worlding Realisms Now," *Novel* 49.2 (2016), 183–201.

15 Fredric Jameson, *The Geopolitical Aesthetic: Cinema and Space in the World System* (Bloomington: Indiana University Press, 1992), p. 3.

16 See my *The Victorian Geopolitical Aesthetic: Realism, Sovereignty and Transnational Experience* (Oxford: Oxford University Press, 2015).

17 Fredric Jameson, "Modernism and Imperialism," in *Nationalism, Colonialism, and Literature*, ed. by Terry Eagleton et al. (Minneapolis: University of Minnesota Press, 1990), pp. 41–66, p. 53.

18 E. M. Forster qtd. in Jameson, "Modernism," p. 52.

19 Jameson, "Modernism," pp. 50–51.

20 Fredric Jameson, "A Note on Literary Realism in Conclusion," in *Adventures in Realism*, ed. by Matthew Beaumont (Oxford: Blackwell, 2007), pp. 261–271, p. 261.

21 Jameson, "Modernism," p. 55, p. 51.

22 Occasionally, however, Said uses "imperialism" to denote a largely twentieth-century and, thus, modernist-era phenomenon; e.g., his description of *Mansfield Park* as a "pre-imperialist novel" (84).

23 Fredric Jameson, "The Realist Floor-Plan" in *On Signs*, ed. by Marshal Blonsky (Baltimore, MD: Johns Hopkins University Press, 1985), pp. 373–383, p. 377.

24 Rosa Mucignat, *Realism and Space in the Novel, 1795–1869: Imagined Geographies* (New York: Routledge, 2013), p. 71.

25 Wilkie Collins, *The Moonstone* (London: Penguin, 1998 [1868]), p. 39.

26 See Goodlad, *Victorian*, ch. 5.

27 Wilkie Collins, *Armadale* (London: Penguin, 1995 [1864–1866]).

28 I borrow "guilty ship" from John Ruskin's praise for the painting in *Modern Painters,* vol. 1, 1843, in *The Works of John Ruskin*, vol. 3, ed. by Edward Tyas Cook and Alexander Wedderburn (London: George Allen, 1903), p. 572.

29 Anthony Trollope, *The Prime Minister* (London: Penguin, 1996 [1875–1876]), p. 517.

30 Anthony Trollope, *The Eustace Diamonds* (Oxford: Oxford University Press, 1983 [1871–1873]).

31 Henry James, *The Golden Bowl* (London: Penguin, 1985 [1904]).

32 George Eliot, *Daniel Deronda* (London: Penguin, 1995 [1876]).

33 Goodlad, *Victorian*, ch. 6.

34 Williams, *Country*, p. 249.

35 Ibid., p. 166 qtd. in. Moretti, *Atlas*, p. 13.

36 Moretti, *Atlas*, p. 15.

37 Ibid., pp. 15, 18, 20, 27.

38 William Cobbett, *Rural Rides*, (New York: Cosimo, 2011 [1822–1826]).

39 Williams, *Country*, p. 117; qtd. in Said, *Culture and Imperialism*, p. 84.

40 Williams, *Country*, p. 117.

41 Ibid., p. 115. Clara Tuite perceives the influence of the "leading male heavyweights of the British left," Williams included, in Said's allusion to Austen's "aesthetic frumpery" (p. 96): "Domestic Retrenchment and Imperial Expansion," in *The Postcolonial Jane Austen,* ed. by You-Me Park and Rajeswari Sunder Rajan (New York: Routledge, 2000), p. 112.

42 Cobbett, *Rural*, p. 305, p. 38; qtd. in Williams, *Country,* pp. 112–113, p. 115.

43 Williams, *Country*, p. 249, p. 115.

44 Though Williams notes that Sir Thomas is "presented as . . . 'a great West Indian'" the observation makes no apparent impact on his judgment of what Austen "sees," *Country,* p. 114.
45 Fraser Easton, "The Political Economy of *Mansfield Park*: Fanny Price and the Atlantic Working Class," *Textual Practice* 12.3 (1998), 459–488 (460).
46 Said distinguishes between "imperialism" – "the practice, theory, and the attitudes of a dominating metropolitan center ruling a distant territory" – and "colonialism" – the "implanting of settlements on distant territory" (9). He thus glosses over the difference between West Indian colonies – where Britons settled to produce commodities such as sugar (often, like Austen's Sir Thomas, delegating oversight to others) – and colonies of settlement such as Canada and Australia, which attracted the wholesale exportation of British people and culture. By contrast to either, the vast territorial empire on the Indian subcontinent was typically regarded as a "dependency" – in part because relatively few Britons sought to settle in this densely populated and climatologically un-English space. The expansion of British commerce, more-over, relied on naval power to impose "free" trade in regions such as China and Latin America while Britain's self-appointed efforts to police the post-abolition slave trade created yet another geopolitical agenda. Said is well aware of this imperial crazy quilt, but does not make it a factor in his contrapuntal method.
47 Ruth Perry, "Jane Austen and Empire: A Thinking Woman's Guide to British Imperialism," *Persuasions* 16 (1994), 95–105 (94).
48 Austen's oft-cited remarks on being "in love with" Thomas Clarkson (on a short list of other favored authors), appears in an 1813 letter to Cassandra, qtd. e.g., in Peter Knox-Shaw, *Jane Austen and the Enlightenment* (Cambridge: Cambridge University Press, 2004), pp. 163–164. Austen's brothers James and Francis were sympathetic to abolition and the latter (based partly on firsthand experience in Antigua), wrote to his sister that "any trace of" slavery in England's colonies, no matter how modified, "is much to be regretted" qtd. in John H. Hubback and Edith C. Hubback, *Jane Austen's Sailor Brothers* (London: John Lane, 1906), p. 192. On the Austen family's various ties to the West Indies, see also E. Jordan, "Jane Austen Goes to the Seaside: *Sanditon,* English Identity and the 'West Indian' Schoolgirl," in Park and Sunder Rajan, *The Postcolonial Jane Austen,* pp. 29–55.
49 Perry, "Austen and Empire," p. 96.
50 See also Tuite, "Domestic Retrenchment," p. 107.
51 Katie Trumpener, *Bardic Nationalism: The Romantic Novel and the British Empire* (Princeton, NJ: Princeton University Press, 1997), ch. 4.
52 Susan Fraiman, "Jane Austen and Edward Said: Gender, Culture, and Imperialism," *Critical Inquiry* 21.4 (1995), 805–821 (809). On Fanny's slavelike positionality, see, e.g., Moira Ferguson, "*Mansfield Park*, Slavery, Colonialism, and Gender," *Oxford Literary Review* 13.1 (1991), 118–139; See also, Trumpener, *Bardic Nationalism*; Perry, "Austen and Empire"; and Mucignat, *Realism and Space in the Novel,* p. 72.

53 George Crabbe, *Tales* (London: Hatchard, 1812); William Cowper, *The Task* (London: Joseph Johnson, 1785); John Barrow, *Some Account of the Public Life, and a Selection from the Unpublished Writings, of the Earl of Macartney*, 2 vols. (London: Cadell and Davies, 1807).

54 Macartney's ambassadorship marked the beginning of China's importance to the quest for "influence" in the Far East, Jansen Osterhammel, "Britain and China, 1842–1914" in *The Oxford History of the British Empire: The Nineteenth Century, Vol. 3*, ed. by Andrew Porter (Oxford: Oxford University Press, 1999), pp. 146–169, p. 147; see also Knox-Shaw on Francis Austen's diplomatic visit to China, pp. 186–187.

55 George Macartney, *An Account of Ireland in 1773* (Privately printed, 1773), p. 55.

56 See also Robert Clark on Francis Austen's service in the Mysore campaign as well as the Austen family's connections to "the East" more generally, "Mansfield Park and the Moral Empire," *Persuasions* 36 (2014), 136–150.

57 Fredric Jameson, "Cognitive Mapping," in *Marxism and the Interpretation of Culture*, Cary Nelson and Lawrence Grossberg (Champaign: University of Illinois Press, 1988), pp. 347–358, p. 349.

58 Sarah Parry, "Mansfield Park vs. Sotherton Court: Social Status and the Slave Trade," *Persuasions* 35 (2014), 1–17.

59 *Pride and Prejudice* is the exception, see Helena Kelly, "Austen and Enclosure," *Persuasions* 30.2 (2010) (online).

60 Thomas Carlyle's actual quotation, "Cash payment is the sole nexus," appears in *Chartism* (London: J. Fraser, 1840), p. 66.

61 Karl Marx, *Capital, Volume 1: Critique of Political Economy* (London: Penguin, 1992) p. 886.

62 Knox-Shaw, *Jane Austen*, p. 175.

63 Marx, *Capital*, p. 886.

64 Larry Patriquin, *Agrarian Capitalism and Poor Relief in England, 1500–1860, Rethinking the Origins of the Welfare State* (London: Palgrave, 2007), p. 16.

65 Price qtd. in K. Marx, *Capital*, p. 886. According to Steve Hindle, "Northamptonshire was *the* county of Parliamentary enclosure" in the late eighteenth century: "'Not by Bread Only?' Common Right, Parish Relief, and Endowed Charity in a Forest Economy c. 1600–1800," in *The Poor in England: An Economy of Makeshifts*, ed. by Alannah Tomkins and Stephen King (Manchester: Manchester University Press, 2010), pp. 39–75, p. 42; see also Easton, "The Political Economy of *Mansfield Park*." Though the Bertrams' income partly depends on Antiguan property, enclosure also generated "new money." On John Dashwood's enclosures in *Sense and Sensibility*, see Celia Easton, "Jane Austen and the Enclosure Movement: The Sense and Sensibility of Land Reform," *Persuasions* 24 (2002), online.

66 E.g., Fraser, p. 466; see also Rachel Crawford who describes hedgerows as "the visual extension of the landowner's acquisition of land, labor, and profits" in *Poetry, Enclosure and the Vernacular Landscape, 1700–1830* (Cambridge: Cambridge University Press, 2002), p. 13.

67 On the Lockean "Anglophone heartland" encompassing Britain, North Amer-
    ica, and Australia, see K. van der Pijl, "A Lockean Europe?," *New Left Review*
    II.37 (January–February 2006), 9–37.
68 Carlyle, *Chartism*, p. 98.
69 Ellen Wood, *Empire of Capital* (London: Verso, 2005), p. 73.
70 Richard Drayton, "The Collaboration of Labour: Slaves, Empires, and Glo-
    balizations in the Atlantic World, c. 1600–1850," in *Globalisation in World
    History*, ed. by A. G. Hopkins (London: Pimlico, 2002), pp. 98–114.
71 Thomas C. Holt, *The Problem of Freedom: Race, Labor, and Politics in Jamaica
    and Britain, 1832–1938* (Baltimore, MD: Johns Hopkins University Press,
    1992).
72 John Clare, "The Village Minstrel," in *The Village Minstrel and Other Poems*,
    vol. 1 (London: Taylor & Hessey, 1821), p. 50, line number l.847.
73 Elizabeth Gaskell, *Mary Barton* (London: Penguin, 1997 [1848]), p. 11, p. 26.
74 Clare Midgley, "Feminist Historians and Challenges to Imperial History," in
    Re-presenting the Past: Women and History, ed. by Ann-Marie Gallagher et al.
    (New York: Routledge, 2001), p. 176.
75 Charlotte Brontë, *Jane Eyre* (London: Penguin, 2006 [1847]), p. 15; for a
    recent discussion see Elaine Freedgood, *The Idea in Things: Fugitive Mean-
    ing in the Victorian Novel* (Chicago: University of Chicago Press, 2006),
    pp. 30–54.
76 Cowper, *The Task*, vol. 2, l.37.
77 George Boulukos, "The Politics of Silence: *Mansfield Park* and the Amelior-
    ation of Slavery," *Novel* 30 (2006), 361–383 (363).
78 Said cites Lady Bertram's request for shawls to exemplify the novels
    "uninflected, unreflective" allusions the colonies (93); but surely it matters
    that the remark furthers a depiction of narrow-mindedness that borders
    on satire.
79 As Mucignat shows, Portsmouth introduces "concreteness" into Fanny's
    experience, p. 76.
80 Banfield, "The Influence of Place," pp. 33, 30, 35.
81 On spectatorship see Nina Auerbach, *Romantic Improvement: Women and
    Other Gloried Outcasts*, 2nd ed. (New York: Columbia University Press,
    1985), p. 51; see also Lynn Voskuil on Fanny's limited vision, "Sotherton
    and the Geography of Empire: The Landscapes of *Mansfield Park*," *Studies in
    Romanticism* 53.4 (2014), 591–615.
82 Julie Park, "What the Eye Cannot See: Interior Landscapes in Mansfield
    Park," *The Eighteenth Century* 54.2 (2013), 169–181 (172).
83 S. A. Mansbach, "An Earthwork of Surprise: The 18th-Century Ha-Ha,"
    Art Journal 42.3 (1982), 217–221 (217).
84 D'Argenville, qtd. in ibid., p. 219.
85 Qtd. in ibid., p. 218.
86 Mansbach offers 1730–1750 as the peak of popularity, p. 120.
87 See, e.g., Voskuil as well as R. Quaintance, "Humphry Repton, 'any
    Mr. Repton' and the 'Improvement' Metonym in *Mansfield Park*," *Studies*

in *Eighteenth-Century Culture* 27.1 (1997), 365–384. On Austen's real-life encounters with Reptonian improvers, see John Wiltshire, "Exploring *Mansfield Park:* In the Footsteps of Fanny Price," *Persuasions* 28 (2006), 81–100.

88 Humphry Repton, *Enquiry into the Changes of Taste in Landscape Gardening* (London: J. Taylor, 1806), p. 171.

89 Crawford, *Poetry, Enclosure and the Vernacular Landscape*, p. 15.

90 Williams, *Country*, p. 123. On Pope and Stowe see Mansbach, "An Earthwork of Surprise," p. 219.

91 Ellen Wood, *The Pristine Culture of Capitalism: A Historical Essay on Old Regimes and Modern States* (London: Verso, 1991), p. 111.

92 Humphry Repton, *Fragments on the Theory and Practice of Landscape Gardening* (London: J. Taylor, 1816) p. 192.

CHAPTER 7

Said and Political Theory

Jeanne Morefield

In his 2003 poem, "Edward Said: A Contrapuntal Reading," Mahmoud Darwish reflected on Said's intellectual and emotional struggles with identity, politics, and the fact of living in exile. The poem, written on the occasion of Said's death, is an imagined conversation of sorts between Darwish and Said in which, at one point, the fictional Darwish asks the fictional Said about a visit to his childhood home in Jerusalem, now occupied by Israeli Jews. The Said of the poem – Darwish's Said – explains that he did not enter the house and, instead, stood at the door, wondering what the current residents would think of him:

> Would they ask:
> Who is that prying foreign visitor? And how
> could I talk about war and peace
> among the victims and the victims' victims,
> without additions, without an interjection?
> And would they tell me: There is no place for two dreams
> in one bedroom?[1]

I have chosen to begin a chapter on political theory, imperialism, and the importance of Said's thought with Darwish's poem rather than with a straightforward unpacking of Said's method because I am interested in cultivating this approach as a *disposition* toward critique rather than a theoretical framework into which we can fit aspects of empire, like puzzle pieces, and make sense of the whole. Beginning with Darwish's contrapuntal reading allows us to back into this disposition through the eyes of another, waking up to its complexities and contradictions through the to and fro of dialogue. And it is deeply complex. For instance, Darwish's questions about Said's return to his childhood home and Said's answers appear initially to be about the possibility of peaceful cohabitation in Israel/Palestine. Importantly, however, the Said of the poem doesn't ask whether it is possible for Jews and Palestinians to coexist – for two dreams to find a place in one bedroom – because Darwish knew that for Said, the long, multiethnic history of Palestine obviated the feasibility of such a future. Rather, the poet's Said questions whether others – the victims and the victims' victims – can imagine this possible world. This latter question, so evident in the trepidation Said expresses about his reception, is not only more complicated than the former but also goes straight to the necessary tensions – between domination and resistance, identity and narration, history and the present – at the heart of what Said called *counterpoint* and the democratic form of humanism that accompanied this critical vision. These complexities are also precisely what makes a Saidian approach so potentially valuable for political theorists interested in questions of empire and imperialism.

I realize full well that suggesting Said might be useful for thinking about imperialism will no doubt strike anyone outside the deeply isolationist subfield that is political theory as absurdly obvious. This is a man whose 1978 book, *Orientalism,* ignited a scholarly movement dedicated to the study of imperialism, inaugurated the field of post-colonial studies, and became for many scholars of comparative literature, history, cultural studies, and anthropology, a virtual classic learnt "by osmosis."[2] Said was also an astonishingly productive scholar and his work has been the subject of sustained attention for decades by some of the most well-known scholars of our era.[3] And yet, aside from passing references, political theorists have largely ignored Said's writings, a strange lacunae given that over the last 15 years, increasing numbers of them have become interested in imperialism.[4] In opposition to this trend, I make the case here that political theorists would do well to embrace Said's approach because it speaks precisely to the kinds of analyses political theory does well by pushing theorists toward what they often avoid: interdisciplinarity and a willingness to engage what Said called "untidy" modes of inquiry that engage multiple political visions and identities – multiple dreams – simultaneously. Moreover, I argue, a Saidian disposition can help bridge what is often an unfortunate gap in political theory scholarship between historical analyses of imperialism and contemporary critiques of American power. The chapter first touches on the "turn to empire" in political theory, moves to an analysis of Said's interdisciplinarity, and concludes – with Darwish – by reflecting on some of the frustrations and promises of this critical disposition.

Political Theory, Imperialism, and Said

In her important 2010 review essay, Jennifer Pitts notes that political theory "has come slowly and late to the study of empire," only turning its full attention to an area of inquiry that, for decades, has preoccupied scholars in other disciplines, after September 11, 2001.[5] While political theorists may be showing up slowly and late to empire, however, they have not yet arrived at an appreciation of Said and continue to ignore almost entirely the work of a man whose influence on the study of imperialism in nearly every other academic field is incalculable.[6] A scholar of astonishing breadth, Said wrote about literature, culture, ideology, history, philosophy, and all these at the same time, as well as dozens of books and articles on the political question of Palestine and the mechanisms by which Palestinians were denied "permission to narrate" their own experiences.[7] Indeed, as a Palestinian exile – constantly negotiating the space between the history of imperialism, the Palestinian present, and the global impact of America's militarism – Said brought an acute sensitivity toward the relationship between culture, politics, imperialism, and resistance to nearly all his writings. As Akeel Bilgrami notes in his loving introduction to *Humanism and Democratic Criticism*, because of his commitment to Palestinian freedom and because politics was so integral to his most important writing, "Edward Said's intellectual legacy will be primarily political – not just in the popular imagination, but also perhaps in the eyes of academic research."[8] The centrality of politics to Said's work makes it all the more ironic then that the majority of political theorists have remained so steadfastly immune to his charms.

What accounts for this lack of engagement? In many ways, Said's critical disposition runs perfectly counter to the two modes of political theorizing that have dominated the North American academy for the last 70 years: a canon-oriented approach to the history of political thought, on the one hand, and a normative approach that abstracts questions about justice from analyses of actual politics and history, on the other.[9] More to the point, even for theorists interested in questions of empire, Said's "nomadic" orientation toward critique – his radical interdisciplinarity, the expansive palate of genres he investigated, and the breadth of interpretive strategies he employed – simply flies in the face of the subfield's general resistance to methodologies and orientations that pull from too many theoretical approaches at once or appear to lack systematic rigor. Some of Said's most important critical interventions regarding the study of imperialism, however, flow precisely from developing the insights of, in his words, "people who are unsystematic." As he explained, one "cannot derive a systematic theory" from Antonio Gramsci, Franz Fanon, or C. L. R. James precisely because they were "involved in culture, in political struggle" and in the adaptation of conventional disciplines and genres to the study of politics.[10] And yet, from Said's perspective, creative engagement with culture and politics was absolutely essential for interrogating a global phenomenon as culturally and politically complex as imperialism. He thus cultivated a perspective that straddled what he identified in his critical evaluation of Frederick Jameson's work as the "dichotomy between two kinds of 'Politics'": a politics "defined by political theory from Hegel to Louis Althusser and Ernst Bloch" and a politics "of struggle and power in the everyday world."[11] Such an approach is inherently interdisciplinary and engaged with history in ways that provide neither normative solutions to political/ethical problems nor the conceptual scaffolding political theorists often desire to explain political phenomena in systematic terms. Indeed, from the perspective of political theorists interested in conceptual clarity, Said's intellectual "nomadism" (as he called it) can seem hopelessly muddled or, in Iskander and Rustom's words, "untidy and spatially fluid."[12] In addition, because political theorists are often trained to *think through* a particular theorist's mode of inquiry into the world – to provide a Rawlsian perspective on global justice for instance – following the diverse theoretical influences that exit and enter through the revolving door of Said's prose (from Vico to Foucault, Adorno to Fanon, Auerbach to Cesaire) can feel like an exhausting form of intellectual whiplash.

In addition, political theory's avoidance of Said might also be related to one of the main institutional impediments to its engagement with imperialism in the first place: the relationship of the subdiscipline to political science. As a field, political science – particularly in North America – not only segregates thinking about domestic politics and political theory from international relations but it has also been notoriously reluctant to study global politics through the lens of imperialism. Indeed, even critics of American hegemony are loathe to utter the word *empire* aloud.[13] When political scientists do analyze the politics of empire, these analyses tend be couched almost entirely in a state-centric language that views imperialism, in Michael Doyle's terms, as "simply the process or policy of establishing or maintaining an empire."[14] The parsimony of this definition presents two problems for scholars interested in how imperialism circulates historically or in the contemporary world. First, there is nothing simple about "establishing or maintaining an empire" because the process entails constantly asserting, reasserting, rationalizing, and expanding differences in power and status between the colonizers and the colonized and among the colonized.[15] To sustain this scalar world, imperialism – as an ideology and political practice – must function on a number of different registers simultaneously. Cultivating an intellectual orientation committed to understanding these complexities thus requires the critic to challenge political science's fixation with the state and focus, instead, on unknotting the tangled set of connections between imperialism and the culture sustaining it.

Second, and relatedly, a definition of *empire* or *imperialism* that does not consider the dense ideological and cultural assemblage necessary to rationalize and naturalize domination cannot adequately grapple with the way imperialism functions in a putatively postimperial age. In other words, any definition of *imperialism* that stops at the level of state control will necessarily fail to fully account for the means through which the terminologies and institutional structures associated with our contemporary global order have been determined by former empires. Political theorists have largely emulated political science's blind spots in this regard, only recently and slowly turning their attention to what Pitts calls the "discursive features of empire," those ideological/cultural/rhetorical practices that reflect the historical presence of imperial sensibilities in contemporary American and international discourse but that frequently go unseen or misidentified because they aren't couched in explicitly imperialist language.[16] Terms such as *structural adjustment* and *development* and institutions like the World Bank mirror what James Tully describes as the "complex network of unequal relationships of power between the west and the non-west" that have persisted since the onset of European imperialism.[17] Moreover, Said argued, while it is largely true that direct colonization ended in the middle of the twentieth century, "the meaning of colonial rule was by no means transformed into a settled question," and spirited intellectual debates over imperialist practices and their sustaining ideologies continue unabated within the formerly colonized world.[18] Imperialism, in this contemporary context, necessarily overflows its definitional floodgates, filling up postcolonial space. Any theoretical approach wanting to grapple with both the presence of the imperial past and contemporary imperialist practices has to be able to think in more capacious ways about what the word *empire* means in the world now.

Said approached imperialism precisely in this spirit as a "constantly expanding," "inexorably integrative" ideological formation that buttressed domination in the past, rationalizes imperial politics in the present, and renders the impact of the former invisible on the latter.[19] For Said, imperialism was/is a dynamic process, ordering the world spatially and temporally through, first, the discursive and political construction of what he famously called "imagined geographies," forms of knowledge and carto-graphic common sense that naturalize fundamental differences between the Orient and the West, the colonizing and the colonized. The develop-ing and the developed.[20] In this sense, *Orientalism*'s most profound innovation was its assertion that understanding how the West came to dominate the East politically requires a deeper understanding of this geographic thinking and of the ways the West studied, imagined, quanti-fied, and described the Orient. Moreover, Said's inquiry also exposed the discursive mechanisms through which imperialism orders the world by telling developmental stories about peoples and places, narrowing the narrative aperture of history such that alternative accounts of colonization, precolonial time, and resistance simply disappear and "history" becomes the history of colonization alone.[21] By this logic, active traces of the imperial past on the present (including the grotesque inequality of resources between the Global North and South) appear *sui generis,* untethered from a history of imperialism, dispossession, and resource extraction – the natural order of things.

In essence, for Said, culture "works very effectively to make invisible and even 'impossible' the actual *affiliations* that exist between the world of ideas and scholarship, on the one hand, and the world of brute politics, corpor-ate and state power, and military force on the other."[22] Rendering such affiliations visible – writing back to the densely skeined, discursive land-scape that was and is the relationship between the politics of modern imperialism and its culture – required, for Said, a commodious intellec-tual disposition capable of moving between the social/cultural/political context of colonialism in the past and present and the broad geographic and military systems that sustain(ed) it. In this sense, Said argued, the "[W]ork of theory, of criticism, demystification, deconsecration, and decentralization [is] never finished." Rather, theory must commit to exceeding its boundaries in the same way as does imperialism, "to travel, always to move beyond its confinements, to emigrate, to remain in a sense in exile."[23] Such an orientation entailed, first and foremost, a rejection of specialized disciplinary attachments that produce increasingly narrow "constituencies and interpretive communities," reifying and privatizing the otherwise untidy landscape of history.[24] In an intellectual environment where academic fields tend to "subdivide and proliferate," scholars often fail to perceive the astonishingly complex overlap of the discourses, polit-ics, and cultural formations buttressing imperialism.[25] Said preferred instead what he called a "worldly" approach to inquiry committed to reading texts as objects that are "produced and live on in the historical realm," always leavened by the "insinuations, the imbrications of power" and the multiplicity of cultural and political expressions woven into the imperial experience.[26] Such an approach requires that the critic situate texts within the whole "economy" of discourses that give empire life and to expand the boundaries of what counts as "texts" worthy of inquiry to include, for instance, the rhetorical utterances of public intellectuals, travel narratives, and educational manuals. Theory must be capacious enough to travel across areas of expertise, between high and popular culture, while scholars must be willing to "make connections across lines and barriers."[27]

Making "connections across lines and barriers" was also fundamental to an approach Said called *counterpoint*. Drawing conceptual inspiration from Western classical music, he described counterpoint as the interplay of "various themes" with "only a provisional privilege being given to any particular one."[28] The "resulting polyphony," Said argued, cautioned against approaching the West's "cultural archive" as the univocal efflux of one, unsullied source flowing into the world, touching and reshaping the inert cultures of the non-West along the way. Rather, he maintained, it is essential to analyze these texts contrapuntally, "with a simultaneous awareness both of the metropolitan history" narrated by Western authors and "those other histories against which (and together with which) the dominating discourse acts."[29] Reading nineteenth-century British novels in this manner, for instance, means reading them with an awareness of how they were shaped by the often-hidden or suppressed presence of the West Indies or India. Moreover, extracting cultural forms from the "autonomous enclosures" in which they are usually analyzed and placing them back into the "dynamic global environment" created by imperialism required, for Said, that we read Western culture in the context of anticolonial revolt and the competing discourses of domination and resistance within which nationalist and liberationist movements circulate. Such attention to "the continuity of resistance" requires reframing imperialism as a multivocal, "contested and joint experience."[30]

This contrapuntal emphasis played a crucial *political* role in Said's critical vision. On the one hand, reading imperialism for both domination and resistance disrupts universalizing narratives that locate progress and "development" in the West alone, reducing the rest of the world to passive recipients of enlightened discourse. For Said, imperial history is fissured throughout by "overlapping" experiences of resistance and relationships forged between participants in protest movements in Africa, India, "and elsewhere in the peripheries."³¹ As such, it was simply never the case that the imperial encounter "pitted an active Western intruder against a supine or inert non-Western native" because "there was *always* some form of active resistance, and in the overwhelming majority of cases, the resistance finally won out."³² On the other hand, Said argued, imagining power purely through the lens of domination (as he sometimes accused post-structuralists of doing) allowed critique to draw "a circle around itself" and eschew the search for political change.³³ By contrast, he understood "critical practice as a form of resistance" whose goal was to further the emergence of "non-dominative and non-coercive modes of life and know-ledge."³⁴ Taking his inspiration from Gramsci, Said believed intellectuals to be uniquely positioned to challenge orthodoxy and dogma, to raise embarrassing questions for the power elite, and to fight for people and causes that are perennially forgotten or "swept under the rug."³⁵ Moreover, Said argued, given the global reach of American military, political, and economic power, intellectuals who benefit from that power have a "par-ticular responsibility" to analyze the relationship between the United States and the rest of the world from "within the actuality" of those relationships, not from the perspective of "detached outside observers."³⁶ Thus, the global fight for justice and against imperialism was, by Said's lights, "the functional idiom of the intellectual vocation," an idiom that could only be sustained if scholars coupled inquiry into domination with inquiry into resistance: past, present, and future.³⁷

Counterpoint and Humanism

While it is generally agreed that the 1978 publication of *Orientalism* provided the inspiration for postcolonial studies as an emerging mode of inquiry and critique, Said was not, as Rosi Bradioti puts it, "very keen" on the field that "nonetheless celebrated him as a foundational figure."³⁸ While he shared with postcolonial scholars an enduring interest in the critique of universal theory and an appreciation for the discursive apparatus enabling imperialism, he did have two major *political* complaints about much postcolonial scholarship. One way to begin unpacking Said's polit-ical thought, then, is to examine these moments of departure more closely.

Said's first objection to postcolonial studies lay in an affiliation he sometimes observed between postcolonial scholarship and identity politics, an approach to the "politics of knowledge" that, he argued, often substi-tuted "approved names" for the kind of contrapuntal theorizing he cher-ished as an intellectual.³⁹ Moreover, Said was uncomfortable with what he

saw as a similarity between identity politics and nationalism's tendency
to read domination and resistance through a singular interpretation of
oppression that eliminated multiplicity and hybridity. Fixed approaches
to origins and identity, he argued, imposed "constitutive limitations" on
historical experiences which were actually "polarized, radically uneven"
and "remembered differently," transforming these experiences into primal,
unhealable wounds.[40] Ultimately, he maintained, lassoing the experiences
of dispossession associated with the historical overlap of the "metropolitan
and ex-colonized worlds" to immutable identities resulted in a "politics of
blame" that vitiated possibilities for solidarity.[41] By contrast, Said took
inspiration from the experience of exile, arguing in a 1992 interview that,
as an exile, "you always bear within yourself a recollection of what you've
left behind and what you can remember, and you play it against the
current experience." From this perspective, he continued, "the notion of
a *single* identity" becomes especially fraught because it mutes the tensions
and contradictions of the exilic experience, demanding "simple reconciliation" between competing visions of home and identity that, from the
perspective of exile, can never be made to cohere.[42] Said's own exilic and
generous understanding of identity rejected simple reconciliation and
embraced the "many voices playing off against each other," insisting on
the need "just to hold them together."

At yet, at the same time Said argued against fixed identities and a "politics
of blame," he also resolutely refused to forget the historical and ongoing
forms of imperial domination that shaped the contemporary world. His call
to reject the insistent return of identity politics to fixed and univocal
narratives of imperial oppression thus differs profoundly from the pre-
sentism of many in the foreign policy commentariat who refuse to see the
current global political environment in terms of its imperial past. He took
direct aim at this dangerously bland species of amnesia in 2002's "Always on
Top," wherein he challenged the post–September 11th trend of nostalgically
praising classical imperialism. How convenient, Said argued, "after years of
degeneration following the white man's departure, the empires that ruled
Africa and Asia don't seem quite as bad" to imperial apologists like Niall
Ferguson, pundits who insist that the cessation of formal European rule in
the 1960s implies that the problems faced by residents of the formerly
colonized world today are entirely of their own invention.[43] Said was
troubled by this dismissal of the "enabling rift" between black and white,
colonized and colonizing that was the essence of formal imperialism at its
height, a dismissal that leads (at best) to a form of "just get over it" politics

and (at worst) to a Ferguson-like neo-imperialism. "Who decides," Said demanded to know, "when (and if) the influence of imperialism ended?"

Additionally, even as he critiqued nationalism and the "politics of blame," Said was profoundly sympathetic to the conditions in which anticolonial nationalism resonated precisely because he was attentive – in ways Ferguson and his ilk are not – to the relationship between the *ongoing* trauma of imperial occupation and the construction of national identity. Moreover, he was also well aware that his own experience – as an exiled Palestinian academic at an Ivy League, American university – allowed him to step back from trauma. As he put it in *After the Last Sky*: "I write at a distance. I haven't experienced the ravages. If I had, possibly there would be no problem in finding a direct and simple narrative to tell the tale of our history."[44] Here Said is both open to the experiences that make sense of nationalism while still resisting nationalism's capacity to reduce competing experiences to a single "plot of a logically unfolding conspiracy against us." "Holding" these two perspectives together without feeling compelled to reconcile them allowed Said to both tell imperial history through lenses focused on the "enabling rift" of occupation, dispossession, and settler colonialism *as well as* on those moments of polyphony and connection that trouble simplistic nationalist accounts of the present. It is particularly important, he argued, to hold together these competing visions when analyzing works of art and culture. For instance, he noted in "Always on Top," Kipling's *Kim* "is a sympathetic and profound work about India, but it is informed by the imperial vision just the same." The real problem, he continued, "is to keep in mind two ideas that are in many ways antithetical – the fact of the imperial divide, on the one hand, and the notion of shared experiences, on the other – without diminishing the force of either."[45]

For Said, a criticism that assumed such "holding and crossing over" between imperialism, postcolonialism, and resistance also assumed a "common enterprise shared with others," or, as he put it in his early defense of Rushdie's *Satanic Verses*, a deep awareness that, "although it contains many spheres, the contemporary world of men and women is one world."[46] It is precisely in this commitment to a "common enterprise" that we find Said's second major disagreement with much postcolonial scholarship. Thus, while the deconstructive impulses of his work resisted universalizing theories claiming to reconcile all difference – be they Orientalist geographies or Enlightenment notions of civilization – Said was also critical of the tendency he identified in postcolonial studies to abandon the very idea of "humanity" as a unifying principle in the first place. By contrast, he argued, it was possible "to be critical of Humanism in the name of Humanism" if, as scholars, we remain aware of the extent to which this historically Eurocentric conception was used to justify imperialism, civilizational improvement, racism, sexism, settler colonialism, and so forth. He thus argued for a form of humanist critique that was both explicitly cosmopolitan and "text-and-language-bound," attuned to history while remaining resolutely open "to the emergent voices and currents of the present, many of them exilic, extraterritorial and unhoused."[47]

For Said, the key to fostering a humanism capable of escaping Eurocentrism's yawning maw – always poised to swallow up difference through appeals to reason – was to keep its conceptual assumptions narrow. In other words, rather than nesting his attachment to the category of "human" in some ideal moral theory, or in a list of human attributes cobbled together from European high culture, Said was inspired by Vico's commitment to the "secular notion that the historical world is made by men and women and not by God."[48] For Vico, Said explained, human beings are fundamentally makers of history and "we know what we make" or, rather, "we know how to see it from the point of view of its human maker." Limiting humanism's definitional reach to "making history" frees it from the expansive set of specific requirements attached to Enlightenment conceptions of "reason" or "dignity." Moreover, understanding human beings as united by their shared "capacity to make knowledge" pushes back against the poststructuralist tendency to imagine people as inescapably bamboozled by power, capable only of "passively, reactively, and dully" absorbing its weight. Finally, the flip side of this definition – that we know how to see what we make from the point of view of another because we understand each other as makers – opens up humanistic practice to more expansively generative forms of reading and politics.

Said contrasted this approach with the bland universalism found in so much liberal imperialist thought and policy making. Rather than write "prescriptive articles for 'liberals,' à la Michael Ignatieff, that urge more destruction and death for distant civilians under the banner of a benign imperialism," for instance, Said suggested liberals concerned with foreign policy would do well "to imagine the person whom you are discussing – in this case, the person on whom the bombs will fall – reading in your presence."[49] Imagining the person on whom the bombs will fall as a reader and thinker shifts the intellectual authority away from the policy makers at Harvard, Princeton, or the Council on Foreign Relations, to the person being discussed. Said's insistence that we understand human beings first and foremost as *makers* of history acknowledges the person you imagine in your presence as having alternative histories to tell and – because they are also readers and therefore interpreters of experience – having different prescriptions to offer and analyses to relate. Understanding this reading person as *like you* and yet as someone who potentially reads/theorizes/ imagines history and the world *differently* from you, necessarily evokes a sense of counterpoint: of familiarity and remoteness. Said's democratic humanism thus urges the critic to begin thinking about specific events like the invasion of Iraq, or seemingly irreconcilable conflicts such as in Israel-Palestine, contrapuntally by looking for "what has been left out" (which histories, which voices) and then reading these absences against the dominating discourse, "recovering what has been left out of peace processes that have been determined by the powerful, and then placing that missing actuality back in the center of things."

Said modeled this kind of reading in both his scholarly and political writings. For instance, he argued, a contrapuntal reading of Israel-Palestine similarly refused to empty the current conflict of its history, specifically, its imperial history. In *The Question of Palestine*, he thus combined contemporary analysis with a historical critique of Zionist discourse during the period leading up to the creation of the state of Israel, focusing in particular on narratives that imagined the future state as emerging from the nearly empty ruins of an older, Arab Palestine. Said examined the way this discourse mirrored conceptions crucial to "high European imperialism"; Orientalist ideas of lazy Arabs who were passing into obscurity, rationalized plans requiring European ingenuity to make the barren desert bloom, descriptions of Palestine as a virtual *terra nullius*.[50] The Balfour Declaration of 1917, in which the British (soon to be the Mandatory power in Palestine) declared that they viewed "with favor the establishment in Palestine of a national home for the Jewish people" was, Said argued, similarly imperialist in its logic and execution.[51] Here and in many of his political writings, Said braided these evolving acts of dispossession, disclosure, and disappearing into an account of the way Palestinian voices are rendered invisible in the dominant iteration of whatever "peace process" currently consumes world leaders.[52]

Again, however, Said's exilic commitment to hold together the "polyphony of many voices playing off against each other" rather than resolve them into a single historical plot meant that the kinds of counternarratives he routinely told about Palestine were committed to revealing the lived world of the Palestinian people as a discrete nation without ever essentializing nationalism. In the wake of the failed Oslo Accords – of which he was tremendously critical – this contrapuntal vision evolved into support for a politics of "binational" citizenship that did not require either "a diminishing of Jewish life as Jewish life or a surrendering of Palestinian Arabs."[53] For Said, however, "real" as opposed to "simple" reconciliation could not take place in a context in which apartheid and denial structured everyday life but, rather, required both reciprocal recognition and a commitment to equality between Palestinians and Jews, as well as a discursive environment in which the ongoing history of Palestinian dispossession was acknowledged. In contrast to the "prescriptions" of liberal academics like Ignatieff, Said did not reach his "binational" solution through the imposition of an ideal theory. Rather, as a scholar who believed humans make and interpret history and who understood that history produces contrapuntal realities, Said found his binationalism, in part, in the history of Palestine:

> Palestine is and has always been a land of many histories; it is a radical simplification to think of it as principally or exclusively Jewish or Arab. While the Jewish presence is longstanding, it is by no means the main one … Palestine is multicultural, multiethnic, multireligious. There is as little historical justification for homogeneity as there is for notions of national or ethnic and religious purity today.[54]

A critical engagement with Palestine's polyphonous history, Said concluded, allows us to imagine a future in which "real reconciliation" between Palestinians and Jews is possible, a reconciliation rendered invisible to liberal pundits who bunker themselves within prescriptive circles of their own devising. Such an approach requires the critic to step outside of their circle, look around, and ask: "Who is allowed to narrate this situation? Whose experiences are obscured by dominant narratives? What forms of connection are being denied by fixed identities? What practices of resistance have been ignored? What futures remain unseen behind the wall of modular solutions?" In the end, this humanist attention to the other reading in your presence – and the contrapuntal critique such attention generates – not only exposes the provincialism of some ideas but also it opens our horizons to the broad possibilities of others.

Conclusion

At the end of the day, a Saidian disposition toward imperialism and politics asks political theorists to do two things at once: resist specific identity narratives that mute polyphony while challenging universal narratives that obscure historical and contemporary forms of domination. For Said, humanism was both a "technique of trouble" that disrupts fixed identities and an instrument for imagining human comity found in our shared capacity to make/interpret/read history and in the fact that Western and non-Western experiences belong together "because they are connected by imperialism."[55] Reading history and politics through Saidian lenses thus demands we restore our analyses of cultural works and political phenomenon to "their place in the global setting" through an appreciation "not of some tiny, defensively constituted corner of the world, but of the large, many-windowed house of human culture as a whole."[56]

This many-windowed disposition, I argue, deserves the enthusiastic attention of political theorists because it both allows us to paint richer accounts of the complex imperial pasts and suggest ways of thinking through that past to the politics of the present. There is nothing, however, straightforward or easy about embracing this disposition. What political theorists will *not* find in the work of Said is either a well-articulated method for deconstruction that ends at the moment of disruption or a conceptual framework providing ideal solutions to political problems. Not only can this unfinished quality be deeply frustrating, the sheer breadth of knowledge necessary for writing contrapuntal history is so overwhelming, but also it's enough to drive even the most interdisciplinary political theorist back into the sheltering arms of Kant or Arendt to mull overwell-contained questions about justice and "the political." Said's "method" is thus neither methodologically complete nor always intellectually coherent and his unremitting insistence on having it all – polyphony and unity, resistance and solidarity, recognition of the victims and the victims' victims – can be exhausting. Even more maddening is Said's insistence that "the task" of humanist, contrapuntal inquiry is "constitutively an unending one" that resists conclusions even as it demands we continue the search for solutions to injustice.[57] Thus, perhaps not surprisingly, Darwish concludes his poetic ode to Said by similarly resisting conclusions, imagining Said's final farewell as both a directive and a puzzle:

> And now, don't forget:
> If I die before you, my will is the impossible.

In the end, it is Said's impossible will – his refusal to abandon or resolve opposed visions and experiences but, rather, to just "hold them together" – that makes this disposition so crucial for approaching the complex, overlapping, ethically charged history and contemporary politics of imperialism. These are the two dreams in one bedroom and as much as they may fight to push each other out, Said wouldn't let either of them go. And neither, I argue, should we.

Notes

1 M. Darwish, "Edward Said: A Contrapuntal Reading," trans. by Mona Anis, *Cultural Critique* 67 (2007), 175–182.

2 Eqbal Ahmad, "Introduction to the 1994 Edition," in *The Pen and the Sword: Conversations with Edward Said*, ed. by David Barsamian (Chicago: Haymarket Press, 2010), p. 7.

3 See, for instance, the recent collection of essays edited by Rosi Braidotti and Paul Gilroy, *Conflicting Humanities* (London: Bloomsbury, 2016), whose contributors include Gayatri Spivak, Akeel Bilgrami, and Judith Butler.

4 See Jennifer Pitts, "Political Theory of Empire and Imperialism," *Annual Review of Political Science* 13 (2010), 211–235.

5 Ibid., p. 212.

6 A welcome exception of a book-length treatment of Said by a political theorist is John Randolph LeBlanc, *Edward Said and the Prospects of Peace in Palestine and Israel* (London: Palgrave MacMillan, 2013).

7 Edward Said, "Permission to Narrate," *The Politics of Dispossession* (New York: Vintage Books, 1995), pp. 247–248.

8 Akeel Bilgrami, "Foreword," Edward Said, *Humanism and Democratic Criticism* (New York: Columbia University Press, 2004), p. ix.

9 See John Gunnell's description of how the history of political thought is predominantly framed by the discipline in, "Dislocated Rhetoric: The Anomaly of Political Theory," *Journal of Politics* 68.4 (2006), 771–782. The normative approach is best captured in the work of John Rawls and Ralwsian liberals since the 1970s.

10 Te-hsing Shan, "An Interview with Edward Said (1997)," *Interviews with Edward W. Said*, ed. by Amritjit Singh and Bruce G. Johnson (Jackson: University Press of Mississippi, 2004), p. 131.

11 Edward Said, "Opponents, Audiences, Constituencies, and Community," *Reflections on Exile and Other Essays* (Cambridge, MA: Harvard University Press, 2000), p. 133.

12 Adel Iskander and Hakem Rustom, "Introduction," *Edward Said: A Legacy of Emancipation and Representation* (Berkeley, CA: University of California Press, 2010), p. 5.

13 See, e.g., R. N. Lebow and S. Reich's argument against American power that refuses to label that power imperial. Lebow and Reich, *Goodbye Hegemony* (Princeton, NJ: Princeton University Press, 2014).

14 Michael W. Doyle, *Empires* (Ithaca, NY: Cornell University Press, 1986), p. 45.

15 Craig Calhoun, Frederick Cooper, Kevin W. Moore, eds. *Lessons of Empire: Imperial Histories and American Power* (New York: New Press, 2006), p. 3.

16 Pitts, "Political Theory of Empire and Imperialism," p. 226.

17 John Tully, "Lineages of Contemporary Imperialism" in *Lineages of Empire*, ed. by Duncan Kelly (London: Oxford University Press, 2009), p. 5.

18 Edward Said, "Intellectuals in the Postcolonial World," *Salmagundi* 70/71 (1986), 44.

19 Edward Said, *Culture and Imperialism* (New York: Vintage, 1994), p. 8, p. 6.

20 Edward Said, *Orientalism* (New York: Vintage, 1979), pp. 49–72.

21 Said, "Intellectuals in the Post-Colonial World," p. 59.

22 Said, "Opponents, Audiences, Constituencies, and Community," p. 119.

23 Said, "Travelling Theory Reconsidered," in *Reflections on Exile and Other Essays*, p. 451.

24 Said, "Opponents, Audiences, Constituencies, and Communities," p. 137.

25 Said, *Culture and Imperialism*, p. 13.

26 Edward Said, "Orientalism 25 Years Later: Worldly Humanism v. the Empire-builders," *Counter Punch*, 2003, www.counterpunch.org/2003/08/05/orientalism/.

27 Edward Said, *Representations of the Intellectual* (New York: Vintage Book, 1996), p. 76.

28 Said, *Culture and Imperialism*, p. 51.

29 Ibid.

30 Said, *The Pen and the Sword*, pp. 77–78.

31 Said, *Culture and Imperialism*, p. 52

32 Ibid., p. xii.

33 Edward Said, "Travelling Theory" (1982), *The Edward Said Reader* (New York: Vintage, 2000), p. 215. Also see Said's critique of Foucault in "Criticism and the Art of Politics," in *Power, Politics, and Culture: Interviews with Edward W. Said*, ed. by Gauri Viswanathan (New York: Vintage, 2002), p. 138.

34 Said, "The Future of Criticism," *Reflections on Exile*, p. 171.

35 Said, *Representations of the Intellectual*, p. 11.

36 Edward Said, "Representing the Colonized: Anthropology's Interlocutors," *Critical Inquiry* 15.2 (1989), 212–213; Said, *Culture and Imperialism*, 55–56.

37 Edward Said, "The Public Role of Writers and Intellectuals," in *Nation, Language, and the Ethics of Translation*, ed. by Sandra Bermann and Michael Woods (Princeton NJ: Princeton University Press, 2005), pp. 23–24.

38 Bradiotti and Gilroy, "The Contested Post-Humanities," *Conflicting Humanities*, 18.

39 Said, "The Politics of Knowledge," *Reflections on Exile*, p. 374.

40 Said, "Intellectuals in the Post-Colonial World," p. 45.

41 Ibid., p. 45.

42 Said, "Criticism, Culture, and Performance," *Power, Politics, and Culture*, p. 99.

43 Edward Said, "Always on Top," *London Review of Books*, March 20, 2002, www.lrb.co.uk/v25/n06/edward-said/always-on-top.

44 Edward Said (with Jean Mohr), *Under the Last Sky: Palestinian Lives* (New York: Columbia University Press, 1998), p. 130.

45 Ibid.

46 Said, "Intellectuals in the Postcolonial World," 54; Said, *Humanism and Democratic Criticism*, p. 68; Edward Said, "The Satanic Verses and Democratic Freedoms," *The Black Scholar* 20.2 (March–April 1989), 17–18 (18).

47 Said, *Humanism and Democratic Criticism*, p. 11.
48 Ibid.
49 Ibid., pp. 142–143.
50 Edward Said, *The Question of Palestine* (New York: Vintage Books, 1992), pp. 13–15.
51 Ibid., p. 15.
52 See, for instance, Said's "Permission to Narrate," pp. 247–248.
53 Edward Said, "The One State Solution," *The New York Times Magazine*, January 10, 1999, www.nytimes.com/1999/01/10/magazine/the-one-state-solution.html?_r=0.
54 Ibid.
55 Said, *Culture and Imperialism*, p. 279.
56 Said, "The Politics of Knowledge," p. 382.
57 Said, *Humanism and Democratic Criticism*, p. 77.

CHAPTER 8

Said, Postcolonial Studies, and World Literature

Joe Cleary

Disturbances and Discontents: Scholarly Formations in a Changing World-System

The emergence of postcolonial studies in the 1980s was one of many indirect products of the 1967 Six-Day War in which the State of Israel defeated several Arab states and seized and occupied the West Bank of Palestine, the Gaza Strip, the Sinai Peninsula, and the Golan Heights. The Arab-Israeli wars and "oil crisis" that followed in the 1970s and the concurrent intensification of the Palestinian resistance contributed to the political radicalization of Edward Said, then a young literature professor at Columbia University in New York, and this in turn to the publication in 1978 of *Orientalism*, one of the most widely read books of cultural criticism written in the late twentieth century. A measured yet devastating critique of the long historical symbiosis between Western imperial power and Western knowledge, *Orientalism* examined the ways in which scholarship and literature had abetted European and American domination of Asia and, more particularly, the Islamic regions of Asia. The study was the most consequential redeployment of the work of Michel Foucault at the time in the United States. American Middle East and Asian specialists responded with a sense of wounded affront or vitriolic backlash, but *Orientalism* was translated into numerous languages and encouraged an enormous array of intellectual projects around the world dedicated to rethinking the relationship between imperial and colonial administration and scholarly and literary discourses. In the Anglo-American academy, the volume was also conscripted as the foundational text of postcolonial studies, which would quickly be recognized as an academic subfield.

World literature emerged as a topic of intellectual interest in Europe in the early nineteenth century and long predated postcolonial studies. Like postcolonial studies, world literature, as most recently formulated at least, is largely, though not exclusively, a mode of scholarship concentrated in the United States, and the field's relationship to American world power is no less intricate than that of postcolonial studies. The al-Qaeda attacks on the World Trade Center in New York in September 2001 represented the deadliest blowback ever visited on an American city as a consequence of American foreign policy in the Middle East and Asia. The subsequent devastation of Iraq led by the Bush and Blair coalition was intended to reassert American global supremacy for the twenty-first century. But the turmoil that war unleashed, combined with the restructuring of the world-system occasioned by the economic "rise of Asia," the 2008 Euro-American financial crisis, and the emergence of China as a more assertive great power, has provoked an ongoing crisis of American hegemony and a wider restructuring of the contemporary capitalist world-system. Cumulatively, these events have ushered in a post–Cold War international system significantly different to the one that existed when postcolonial studies had emerged some decades earlier. In the wake of these events, it was clear that postcolonial studies as a discipline was struggling badly to keep pace with the changing realities of international finance and world power; certainly, few of the most distinguished figures associated with the discipline in its formative stage produced work in this post-9/11 period that matched *Orientalism* in stature, urgency, or capacity to speak to the immediate moment. At the height of his career, Said had displayed an impressive ability to speak to the international exigencies of the current moment, and his last decade, after the Palestinian defeat registered by the Oslo Accords in 1993 and 1995 and in the throes of his own final illness, he continued to produce searing essays that testified to his undiminished abilities as a politically committed thinker. However, in the same period, postcolonial studies generally was settling into a phase of institutional consolidation and had become identified in English literary studies with a fairly predictable canon of modern Anglophone writers largely read in terms of their engagements with British imperialism in the period from early modern European expansion up to the end of the Cold War era. However, the newly emerging field of world literature, inspired initially by the works of Pascale Casanova, Franco Moretti, and David Damrosch, promised to encompass a much-broader range of languages and literatures, and to pay more attention to the extratextual infrastructures and practices that shape the production and consumption of literature – such as translation, circulation, literary consecration, and the uneven distribution of institutional cultural authority – than postcolonial studies had done. Though it may not have realized this ambition, Casanova's Pierre Bourdieu–informed project in particular declared its commitment to exposing the institutional supports and operations that sustained Europe's, and France's, ability to regulate world literature and thus to create the conditions for the "decolonization" of those institutions.[1]

Though the scholarship it provokes has in many ways been much less obviously politically charged than the formative works of postcolonial studies had earlier been, the relationship between world literature and global politics is nevertheless intimate. In its most liberal humanist versions, world literature studies is essentially an expression of a humanist and liberal American cosmopolitanism devoted to establishing a transnational treasury of prestigious "world classics," these associated mainly with former or current empires, that might provide the basis for twenty-first-century transnational intellectual exchange mediated, of course, through English. To this extent, world literature expresses an ambassadorial impetus to check the reputational damage done to the United States by successive generations of Cold War warriors and their academic acolytes. The project is self-consciously motivated by a desire to correct the eurocentrism of traditional comparative literature programs and to situate that discipline's traditional Western canon in a wider repertoire of non-Western literatures; nevertheless, the authority of the elite American university to regulate matters tends to be assumed, and in many ways the project remains largely continuous with the American bid since World War I to consolidate the United States' cultural as well as military and economic ascendancy.[2] However, in its more self-interrogative versions, world literature might equally be grasped as a tacit acknowledgment that the power of Western Europe and the United States is already contracting in the twenty-first century and thus as an anticipatory and tentative recognition of the larger geopolitical realignments already underway in the capitalist world-system. Just as there was never a singular postcolonial studies but rather a congeries of sometimes contradictory, sometimes complementary, intellectual projects that intersected under that umbrella term, so too there is no homogenous world literature project; instead, there are a number of contesting attempts to define a new field of literary and cultural inquiry. Basically, the study of world literature is founded on the idea that while nearly all societies produce literatures of diverse sorts, one cannot properly understand those literatures without also studying the material institutional apparatuses through which they are mediated, circulated, consecrated, transmitted, and structured as a system or field. In the age of the European and American empires, Europe and the United States acquired considerable power to shape the international field of literature to its own requirements. Like other modes of history, modern literary history was conceived in conspicuously Eurocentric terms and European, and more lately American, literary developments were habitually conceived as offering an inevitable lead that the rest of the world was obliged to follow were it to be "modern" as well. Literatures that were not modern in the Western sense might legitimately be studied in Classical, religious, oral, folkloric, or ethnographic terms, but as such they belonged to scholarly specialisms rather marginal to twentieth-century literary critical analysis.

Though he is more commonly identified with postcolonial studies than with world literature, Edward Said's relationship to both projects was intimate and ambivalent. *Orientalism* was, as noted earlier, soon enlisted as a foundational text for postcolonial studies but Said was never more than a wayward recruit to that new discipline. His concept of the intellectual was mercurial and sometimes took its bearings from Noam Chomsky and Alexander Cockburn and a maverick line of American independent radicals; sometimes from Erich Auerbach, Theodor Adorno, and German exilic philologists; and sometimes from Antonio Gramsci, C. L. R. James, or Frantz Fanon and other intellectual-activists from an earlier era. But Said's manner of being an intellectual never comported easily with that of contemporary leading postcolonial theorists such as Gayatri Chavkravorty Spivak, Homi Bhabha, Stuart Hall, Partha Chatterjee, Dipesh Chakrabarty, Walter Mignolo, Edouard Glissant, Hazel Carby, Achille Mbembe, Kwama Anthony Appiah, Paul Gilroy, or others. Differences of temperament and scholarly formation combined with the fact that most postcolonial scholars were either born in the West or else came from already independent postcolonial societies whose dilemmas were therefore quite different to those of the still-colonized Palestinians ensured that Said always remained an awkward fit to the wider academic endeavors with which his name was intrinsically associated. However, world literature's disciplinary origins in the traditions of German philology, its associations with Goethe, Leo Spitzer, Ernest Curtius, and Auerbach, and with the wider history of comparative literature in the United States and Germany, exercised a strong appeal for Said. Though the world literature project in its current formation gathered scholarly momentum only toward the latter end of Said's career, his associations with it are still significant. As early as 1969, Said and his then wife Maire Said, translated Auerbach's famous essay "Philology and *Weltliteratur*" for the *Centennial Review*.[3] Later, several of Said's colleagues and students in the Department of English and Comparative Literature at Columbia University made decisive contributions to the world literature debates (these include David Damrosch, Gayatri Spivak, Franco Moretti, Jonathan Arac, Timothy Brennan, and

Aamir Mufti), and Said wrote an enthusiastic endorsement for Pascale Casanova's *The World Republic of Letters* (1999), which appeared in English translation in his Convergences: Inventories of the Present series at Harvard University Press in 2004. In their different ways, then, the American versions of both postcolonial studies and world literature find paths back to Said and to the Department of English and Comparative Literature in Columbia University where he spent his professional career.

Intellectually, the key to Said's relationship to both of these modes of scholarship is Erich Auerbach. *Mimesis*, famously written in Istanbul during World War II and published in German in 1946 and in English in 1953, is one of the American academy's most venerated texts and a work as foundational to American comparative literature as *Orientalism* would become to postcolonial studies. Said's reverence for Auerbach is well established, but *Orientalism* can profitably be read as a kind of anti-*Mimesis*: It is a work of the *longue durée* nearly comparable in scope to Auerbach's *magnum opus*, though concentrated in Said's case on modern post-Enlightenment French and British cultures. But in direct contrast to *Mimesis*, *Orientalism* stresses the dominative rather than emancipative aspects of European humanism and it highlights Western scholarship's capacity to produce "top-down" fantastically abstract and exotic versions of non-European cultures whereas Auerbach's concern is with the slow evolution and widening scope of "bottom-up" European realism and its fidelity to the minutiae of modern secular everyday life.

Culture and Imperialism, the delayed successor work to *Orientalism* published in 1993, moved away the earlier volume's focus on European intellectual history and situated itself more squarely and forgivingly, in the opening chapters at least, in the domain of literature and the novel. This later study represents a post-Foucauldian return on Said's part to Auerbachian humanism, and while it still stressed the affiliations of literature and power it also declared its faith in the capacity of literature and cultural exchange to disturb settled authority and overcome Manichean civilizational polarities. Like *Mimesis*, *Orientalism* and *Culture and Imperialism* are wartime works flensed by a tormented sense of great power aggression, human waste, international crisis, and intellectual deformation. *Orientalism* was launched on the Western academy as critique of and corrective to Europe's and America's relentless discursive will to global power. *Culture and Imperialism* positioned itself as an appeal to writers and intellectuals everywhere to imagine ways beyond the obdurate legacies of empire and the intensifying "clash of civilizations" after the Cold War. This chapter will consider some of the intellectual trajectories of postcolonial studies and world literature and reflect on Said's Auerbach-inflected relationship to both formations.

Postcolonial Studies from *Orientalism* to 9/11:
Travails and Accomplishments

It is important to remember that postcolonial studies as we now know it did not exist when *Orientalism* was published in 1978. Except for a small number of works such as Jonah Raskin's *The Mythology of Imperialism* (1971) or Benita Parry's *Delusions and Discoveries: Studies on India in the British Imagination* (1972), there were few ambitious academic studies of culture and empire during that period, and *Orientalism* possessed a geo-political scope and a philological and theoretical flair that exceeded any such predecessors. Moreover, Said's monograph touched a raw nerve in contemporary American Middle Eastern studies and area studies in a way that no work of English or British Commonwealth literary scholarship was ever likely to do. Though some of their important articles appeared earlier, the two key scholars who would, alongside Said, become totemic figures for "postcolonial theory" did not publish book-length works for many years after *Orientalism*: Spivak's *In Other Worlds: Essays in Cultural Politics* was published in 1987 and Homi Bhabha's *The Location of Culture* in 1994, a year after *Culture and Imperialism*. In the interim, Said's own career had veered away from the high theoretical and philological modes of *Beginnings: Intention and Method* (1973) and *Orientalism*. After that latter work, he published three books on Palestine and the Middle East – *The Question of Palestine* (1979), *Covering Islam: How the Media and the Experts Determine How We See the Rest of the World* (1981), and *After the Last Sky* (1986) – and a volume of essays, *The World, the Text, and the Critic* (1981). These are all outriders to *Orientalism*, but the works on Palestine and Islam are written in a quite different register to that book, one that suggested a search for a wider general readership, and *The World, the Text, and the Critic*, especially "Reflections on American 'Left' Literary Criti-cism," sounded a sense of alarm with what Said deemed the professionally introspective iterations that theory had taken in the Anglophone academy. In that chapter, Said cautioned that academics were far more invested in insider disputes about the minutiae of favored modes of theory than in the worldly socio-intellectual concerns that had provoked the theories in the first place; he worried that such specialization was effectively diminishing the social role of the cultural intellectual in the name of refining it. In short, during the period in which postcolonial studies was consolidating itself as a disciplinary specialism, Said was shedding his earlier image as a "high theorist" and remaking himself as a "general intellectual" engaged with constituencies and opponents well beyond the university. These were also the years leading up to the Palestinian Declaration of Independence at the Algiers Conference in November 1988 when he was most closely involved with the leadership of the PLO and the Palestinian national struggle.

While Said was thus engaged, two new areas of interest were moving to the center of the field of postcolonial studies. Several major new works on nationalism appeared in the early 1980s that provoked a massive scholarship on the cultural production of nationhood and on the disappointments of postcolonial nationalism more specifically. Benedict Anderson's *Imagined Communities* (1983), Ernest Gellner's *Nations and Nationalism* (1983), Partha Chatterjee's *Nationalist Thought and the Colonial World* (1986), Kumari Jayawardena's *Feminism and Nationalism in the Third World* (1986), Eric Hobsbawm's *Nations and Nationalism Since 1780* (1990), and Homi Bhabha's edited collection, *Nation and Narration* (1990), were formative volumes for this wave of scholarship. In the same period, Ranajit Guha's *A Rule of Property for Bengal* (1981) and *Elementary Aspects of Peasant Insurgency in Colonial India* (1983) appeared, as did volume 1 of *Subaltern Studies: Writings on South Asian History and Society* (1982), edited by Guha. A later volume, *Selected Subaltern Studies* (1988), edited by Guha and Spivak, circulated Indian subaltern historiography more widely in the Western academy. Spivak's introduction to *Selected Subaltern Studies*, "Subaltern Studies: Deconstructing Historiography," and her essay "Can the Subaltern Speak?," published the same year, were also hugely influential interventions and were critically important for feminist postcolonial scholarship especially.[4]

These two bodies of work did not neatly converge: The monographs by Anderson, Gellner, Hobsbawm, and Chatterjee were interested mainly in the material conditions that accounted for the origins and spread of nationalism or in the intellectual histories of the middle- or upper-bourgeois strata most committed to the elaboration of nationalist programs. The works of the Indian and later Latin American subalternists were, however, more concerned with the epistemic systems that regulated the representation or occlusion of the lowest social strata in imperialist and anti-colonial nationalist historiography. Despite these different stresses, both forms of scholarship shared *Orientalism*'s concern with the archives of imperial and anti-imperial discourse and with the styles and politics of knowledge production that underpinned them. And because Indian subaltern studies generally stressed the continuities and complicities that connected British colonial and postindependence nationalist regimes of knowledge, this contributed to a strong emphasis in postcolonial studies generally on the epistemic limitations and oppressiveness of anti-colonial nationalism, a stress compounded by the newly coalescing canons of "postcolonial literature" that were strongly inflected by moods of post-revolutionary disenchantment with nation-building or by an anti-imperialist political liberalism hostile to more militant forms of struggle. Later, a number of scholars on the left would urge the need for a greater discrimination between the more progressive and reactionary forms of anti-colonial nationalism, a topic pressed, for example, in Aijaz Ahmad's *In Theory: Classes, Nations, Literatures* (1992) and Neil Lazarus's *Nationalism and Cultural Practice in the Colonial World* (1999).

An interest in the thematics of exile had always informed Said's work. Intellectually, this was nurtured by his commitments to Joseph Conrad, Auerbach, Adorno, and Georg Lukács; socially, it was charged by his situation as a nonstate Palestinian in the United States and by his helpless awareness of the relentless dispossession of the Palestinian people inflicted by the US-backed Israeli occupation of the West Bank and Gaza. This exilic consciousness found its strongest expression in *After the Last Sky* (1986), *Out of Place: A Memoir* (1999), and *Reflections of Exile and Other Essays* (2000), but it ultimately colored Said's whole conception of the intellectual and artistic vocation in works such as *Representations of the Intellectual* and the posthumously published *On Late Style* (2006). For Said, exile was never simply an existential predicament or a matter of individual ontological distress; it was also a matter, which he deemed fundamental to the profession of the writer and critic, of finding ways to combine intimacy of engagement with critical detachment from the genealogies of the nation, party, profession, or institution to which one nevertheless recognized attachments. In the wider field of postcolonial studies, concerns with globalization and minority discourse were also morphing into new forms of scholarship, which were soon aggregated as diaspora and migration studies, transnationalism, and Black Atlantic studies, these in turn feeding into debates on nationalism, cosmopolitanism, and exilic consciousness that returned to questions of how the intellectual might situate herself culturally and politically in a world where the ties of home or community were being remediated by new global media technologies and information systems. The combined effects of these new technologies and of migration and globalization were arguably creating new deterritorialized "imagined communities" hard to reconcile with the territorial nation-state and often seemingly at odds with earlier twentieth-century conceptions of class solidarity or proletarian internationalism. The weaker forms of this scholarship may have fetishized the sorrows of an elite exilic consciousness, but the stronger versions contributed significantly to an awareness of those histories of imperialism and colonialism – including the slave trade, indentured labor, population transfer, and forced migration – that were never seriously accommodated under the rubrics of national liberation struggles dedicated to state seizure. The wider preoccupation with exile, migrancy, and diaspora in this quarter of postcolonial studies sometimes tipped into a facile consensus that assumed the obsolescence of the nation-state or national class struggles; more commonly, it led to a stress on the articulation of new social movements, albeit often of a rather culturalist kind.[5]

Though sometimes traduced on both the right and the left as nothing more than a faddish "Third Worldist" version of poststructuralism favored by a self-promoting migrant intellectual elite in the Western academy, postcolonial studies in these formative phases displayed an energetic capacity to reconfigure many disciplines across the humanities. The work it enabled reshaped teaching and research practices in many language and literature, anthropology, history, and geography departments especially. Intellectually, postcolonial studies posed serious questions to modes of knowledge production favored not only by the European and American imperial great powers but also by post-independence nation-states and contemporary experts in counterinsurgency, foreign policy, area studies, political administration, and human rights studies. Though always a rather sprawling, centrifugal intellectual formation, postcolonial studies also allowed scholars from different parts of the world to establish a modest solidarity with each other within the Western university and to channel new kinds of intellectual exchange between the Western universities and literary and intellectual currents originating in Latin America, the Caribbean, Africa, and Asia. It would be a gross exaggeration to claim that all this activity cumulatively amounted to some kind of "provincialization of Europe" because the global reach of the American and Western European media, culture industries, university systems, and awards systems remains enormous, but postcolonial studies at the very least signposted the possibilities of such change.

This begs the question as to why postcolonial studies was held by so many in its own ranks to have become an exhausted intellectual constellation after 9/11.[6] There were probably multiple factors at play. First, postcolonial studies came into being as a corrective to the economistic conceptions of imperialism advanced from the classical Marxism of Lenin and Luxemburg to the dependency and world-systems theories of Waller- stein, Andre Gunder Frank, Giovanni Arrighi, and others. In Said's work, and in the new modes of postcolonial theory and subalternist historiog- raphy that followed, the epistemic and cultural dimensions of imperialism and anti-imperial struggle were treated with an unprecedented scholarly seriousness and sophistication. Ultimately, though, this necessary correct- ive to overwhelmingly economistic forms of thinking about imperialism detached itself altogether from Marxist political economy, and this soon proved to be intellectually damaging in its own right as well as disabling analysis of the rampaging new neoliberal imperialisms unleashed after 1989. As a Palestinian Arab, Said remained to the end a staunch and unintimidated critic of this latest phase of American imperialism, but his scholarly lack of interest in political economy and his tendency to dissoci- ate the problematics of imperialism and capitalism compounded this wider culturalist turn. Second, postcolonial studies represented a critique of the constitutive limitations of Western Enlightenment and humanist epi- stemic regimes and of their redeployments by national bourgeoisies in the developing nations. Its focus on these epistemes seems to have blinded most postcolonial scholars to the role of religion in many anti-imperial struggles, to the resurgence of Christian and Jewish fundamentalism in the United States and Israel, and, finally, to an Islamic fundamentalism that proffered itself as both an anti-imperialist insurgency and a resurrected supranational caliphate. As neoliberal and various forms of religious and right-wing fundamentalism flared toward the end of the Cold War, post- colonial studies faltered, the field's fundamentally liberal multiculturalist premises and practices increasingly showing through its theoretical radic- alism. However, exhaustion or professional caution were never the whole story even then; new modes of postcolonial scholarship committed to the study of the intersection of racial, sexual, and biopolitical discourses and to environmental degradation have emerged in recent decades as have some significant materialist studies of the ways in which "postcolonial literature" has been converted into marketable commodities.[7] Nevertheless, as an older generation of intellectuals including Said and others who had direct contact with the last wave of secular nationalist anti-imperial liberation struggles faded, and as the new neoliberal and religious fundamentalisms pitted themselves against each other in a vast theater of war stretching from Turkey and Iraq to Afghanistan and Pakistan, it was clear that postcolonial studies as institutionalized in the decades after *Orientalism* had run up against many of its own constitutive limitations.

Specters of Anglo-Globalization: World Literature from *Mimesis* to *The World Republic of Letters*

The idea of *Weltliteratur* was broached by nineteenth-century German thinkers such as Goethe and Marx in an excited, even prophetic, spirit of anticipation and possibility. Goethe's sense of Enlightenment discovery and Romantic fascination with otherness fired his enthusiasm for a high-minded cosmopolitan intellectual community capable of reading (in translation) the principle classicisms of Europe and Asia, thereby quickening the creation of a "universal world literature" already in the process of formation.[8] In Marx's case, the stress falls more on how the creation of a capitalist world market facilitates the emergence of a new "world literature" mediated by forms of international literary circulation that will challenge self-regarding national literatures.[9] However, the problem of world litera-ture was reformulated in very different circumstances after World War II by another generation of German intellectuals – now, the accent shifted from emancipatory possibility to imminent crisis: comparativist classics such as Auerbach's *Mimesis* (1946) and Curtius's *European Literature and the Latin Middle* Ages (1948) resonate with a shocked sense of European civilization in terminal crisis, and the note was also somber when Auerbach wrote his "The Philology of World Literature" essay published in 1952. For Auerbach, the messy profusion of the world's cultures is a *felix culpa*, but what intellectuals should be bracing themselves for now, he contends, "is a homogenization of human life the world over," this brought about by a standardized modernity divided between "the Euro-American or the Soviet-Bolshevist patterns," though the distinctions between these were, in his view, "relatively minor when they are compared, in their current forms, with the patterns that underlie the Muslim, South Asian or Chinese traditions."[10] The decisive reality of the Cold War era for Auerbach, then, is not diversity but its eradication: "It may even happen that, within a comparatively short period of time, only a limited number of literary languages will continue to exist, soon perhaps only one. If this were to come to pass, the idea of world literature would simultaneously be realized and destroyed."[11]

Auerbach's anticipation of what is now called "Anglo-globalization" was certainly prescient and the world literature debates that have gathered pace in the 1990s and early twenty-first century reflect the domination of "a limited number of literary languages," and the primacy of one, English, that Auerbach had anxiously forecast. However, it is also fair to say that those debates have allowed more critical thinkers a forum at least within which to discuss the terms and mechanisms of Euro-American and Anglo-phone domination. Postcolonial studies as it had earlier developed ought in theory to have enabled meaningful exchange on the subject of culture and imperialism across all the languages of European imperial globalization, but in practice the scholarship involved thrived mainly in monolingual departments of English literature and the take-up in French, Spanish, Portuguese, Dutch, German, Turkish, or Russian departments was fitful and uneven. Moreover, by the end of the twentieth century English had already become the premier language of global commerce and the crucial language of literary-theoretical mediation among educated readerships across the world. This was true not just in Europe or the United States where English enjoyed a status above all other languages but also in Africa or South Asia where literatures written in non-European languages (Tamil, Kannada, Urdu, Hindi, Xhosa, Yoruba, etc.) can often be read by non-speakers of those languages only when translated into English. The more mainstream versions of world literature as it has developed in the United States reflects the impetus in Said's work to challenge the eurocentrism of the European humanist heritage, but they have nevertheless reasserted the primacy of "literature" and "exchange" in ways that have depoliticized literary studies and oftentimes returned them to the modes of uncritical liberal humanism that predated *Orientalism*. In these versions of world literature, there is, in other words, a commendable attempt to widen the category of "literature" historically, linguistically, and culturally to challenge the inherited narrowness of Western comparative literature departments constructed around the Greek and Roman classics and a few core modern European Romance literatures. But this impulse to remake comparative literature for a new post–Cold War century has gone hand in hand with a distinct lack of critical scrutiny about the ways in which an American-sponsored "world literature" might be affiliated to wider projects of American global supremacy, a subject that troubles Auerbach's essay, however discreetly, and that Said had kept throughout his career to the forefront of his scholarship.

The works of Pasacale Casanova and Franco Moretti, two key figures in the development of world literature, have been widely censured for the eurocentrism ascribed to world literature more generally.[12] These are legitimate critiques up to a point, but they usually fail to allow for the fact that what Casanova and Moretti have attempted to track is the means by which Europe attained its ability to become the crucial curator and mediator of modern "world literature" and to uncover the mechanisms by which its control and regulation of that system is sustained. For Moretti, the European novel as fashioned from the eighteenth century in England and France, and then disseminated across Europe and the wider world, eventually reconstructed what counted almost everywhere as "modern literature," and in so doing allowed England and France to establish themselves as the metropolitan cores of a modern literary world-system. In Casanova's work, the stress is shifted from the evolution and dissemination of genres and forms to the respective functions of literary capitals and their peripheries. Paris, Casanova contends, managed to become the literary capital of capitals in Europe from the eighteenth century onward; thereafter, she argues, it was the European city that had greater capacity than any other to determine what counted as literary modernity and non-modernity, to consecrate the great modern "world writers," and to regulate circuits of literary exchange and translation between the core nations of the system, those with the greatest accumulations of literary tradition and capital, and the peripheral nations, those whose national literatures wanted for international recognition or prestige and were therefore deemed only imperfectly modern. For Casanova, the cultural power of Western Europe, and more recently the United States, to regulate the literary world-system rests not just on the economic supremacy of these core states but also on their capacity to concentrate, skim, and monopolize literary capital. Thus, if Paris was the capital city of world literature until recent times, this was grounded in something more than French "universalism" or *amour propre.* The city's role as literary arbiter was secured by the exceptional prestige and reach of the French language and French national literature; by the capacity of postrevolutionary Paris to attract literary and political migrants from all quarters of the globe; by the accumulated strength of French academies, universities, and salon cultures; by the industry and brio of French intellectuals, critics, and translators; and by the receptiveness of French publishing houses to writers and trends emerging far outside of France. This mix of institutional and intellectual assets, Casanova infers, fertilized an unrivaled sense of Parisian *élan mondiale* in literary matters, something that provoked a mixture of cultural envy and anxious deference or rivalry nearly everywhere. Though her account of the matter is tentative, Casanova allows that Paris's role of mediator of the literary world-system may have declined in recent decades, that role now appropriated by New York or perhaps by New York working in concert with London.

To read Said against Casanova or Moretti is to note several things. The latter two position themselves as critics of the European-dominated literary world-system (not as its champions), but in their works the "literary" is separated in Kantian fashion as a wholly distinctive category of writing whereas in *Orientalism* it was one mode of discourse woven through a skein of other discourses including travel, ethnographic, philosophical, philological, and administrative writings. In the opening section of *Culture and Imperialism* Said had reverted to a conception of the relative autonomy of the literary, but in the later sections of that work he attended more to radical anti-imperial activist-intellectuals such as Frantz Fanon, Aimé Cesaire, C. L. R. James, George Antonious, or Ranajit Guha than to "Third World" writers. (Curiously, he seldom dwelled on such writers.) Whereas Said's major works typically took the forms of genealogies of the present, studies starting with the constitutive limits of knowledge in the contemporary moment and then working back across the various trans-formations in the subjects and objects of knowledge that have taken us into the contemporary episteme, Casanova and Moretti practice a more traditional literary historiography. That is to say, their works on "world literature" start by explaining the origins and evolution of the modern European realist novel or of Paris as a dominant literary center and then try to identify the forces that enabled and sustain this Europe-centered literary system. Because their stress is habitually on how Europe came to dominate the modern literary world, their studies typically tail off as they approach the present moment with vague intimations of European decline, this leaving the question of contemporary European or American power to one side. As a consequence, Moretti and Casanova lose some of the politically motivated urgency of investigating the present order of things that animates Said and the more radical versions of postcolonial studies. In the "world literature" debates, the term *the world* more commonly refers to questions of how to manage contemporary scholarship on a planetary scale than to the kinds of "worldliness" Said had stressed.

That acknowledged, though, this deficit is offset by a cultural material-ist and sociological underpinning to Moretti's and Casanova's writings, something usually missing from Said's and from most subsequent literary scholarship in postcolonial studies. In Said's writings and in those of most postcolonial literary critics, the metropolitan authority of Western litera-ture and the peripherality of "Third World" or "postcolonial literature" is simply accepted as an unexamined given, the critic typically identifying with the marginalized writer or with the subaltern communities eclipsed in this system to protest the asymmetries of power involved to a presum-ably wider international readership. In contrast, the works of Moretti and Casanova are supported, to a degree at least, by sociologies of culture that try to explain how these asymmetries took the shape they did. In Moretti's work, this sociology of culture is modeled loosely on Immanuel

Wallerstein's world-systems analysis; in Casanova's, it is based on a combination of the work by Ferdinand Braudel and Pierre Bourdieu, especially on the latter's conceptions of social and cultural capital and modes of distinction. Both postcolonial studies and world literature assume the combined and uneven nature of the literary world-system; only in the more materialist versions of the latter mode of scholarship have the institutional systems that sustain that unevenness been highlighted as theoretical and historical objects of scholarship in their own right.

While Casanova and Moretti work in their different fashions to historicize the contemporary European-dominated literary world-system, both might be said to overstress the regulative authority of France and England and to downplay the extent to which the European-centered system always coexisted alongside a plurality of other competing world-systems. The Soviet attempt to create a communist "world literature," with Moscow as a world literary capital able to rival Paris, is completely ignored by both of these scholars. Maxim Gorky's 1919 lecture, "*Weltliteratur*," attempted to rewrite Goethe's earlier conception in accordance with Soviet ideals, and Gorky stressed popular education and mass literacy rather than intellectual traffic among refined cosmopolitan elites. The Gorky Institute of World Literature, founded in 1932 (and named after Gorky following his death in 1936), is only one instance of the Soviet institutionalization of such ambition; in 1983 the institute started to publish a nine-volume *History of World Literatures*, one of its stated ambitions being to challenge the eurocentrism of Western literary history.[13] The fact that the Soviet Union imploded before the nine volumes were completed might be taken as a vivid instance of the hubris of such totalizing ambitions or else perhaps as testimony to the fact that "world literature" is, as Franco Moretti has argued, not an object but a problem – a problem, it might be added, that comes most clearly into view when the domination of some great world power or the coherence of a particular literary world-system reaches a stage of terminal crisis.[14] Jing Tsu, a Taiwanese scholar of Chinese literatures, argues that the term *world literature* was introduced in China in 1898, the concept motivated at the time by a sense of indignation at Europe's failure to acknowledge the millennial literary achievements of the Chinese Empire. In 1909, Tsu continues, the Chinese writer, Lu Xun, and his brother, Zhou Zuoren, compiled *A Collection of Fiction from Abroad*; this project spurred, however, not by a sense of nostalgia for an endangered Chinese imperial grandeur but by a socially progressive vision linking those oppressed by the Chinese imperial system with other oppressed peoples under Western colonialism.[15] Here, too, the concept of "world literature" gained traction in a particular conjuncture of national crisis and turbulent world capitalist restructuring, that turbulence stimulating reactionary and progressive literary projects of great ambition in both the old and new centers and peripheries of the world-system. Even if extremely old literary world literary centers in China or new twentieth-century ones in the Soviet Union could never match or surpass the power of Paris, London, or New York in the modern era, the very fact that they existed suggests a more polycentric, intersecting, and contested literary universe than that for which Casanova's or Moretti's works allow.

What will become of "world literature" as a field in coming decades? Will it simply swallow up postcolonial studies to become a new institutional space for comparative literary scholarship in the twenty-first-century university? Will it be fashioned in ways that reflect a determined new assertion of American cultural power for the twenty-first century or is the term's currency a symptom rather of the current distress of American and European cultural hegemony and a signal of the beginning of a new and more multipolar world of great power politics and cultural interchange as "the American century" wanes? These questions cannot be answered with any certainty at present. But it is certain that something more than humanist exchange conditions the scholarly field changes provoked by both postcolonial studies and world literature, and it seems likely that the kinds of "world literature" that will prevail in the decades to come will depend to large degree on the outcome of wider social struggles that are still far from decided. It can only be hoped that intellectuals in the future can contemplate the possibilities of "world literature" in conditions less desperate than those that distressed the later careers and motivated the scholarship of both Auerbach and Said.

Notes

1 See Pascale Casanova, *The World Republic of Letters*, trans. M. B. DeBevoise (Cambridge, MA: Harvard University Press, [1999] 2004). See also Franco Moretti "Conjectures on World Literature," *New Left Review* II.1 (January–February 2000), 54–68 and "More Conjectures on World Literature," *New Left Review* 20 (March–April 2003), 73–81. These and related essays were later collected in Franco Moretti, *Distant Reading* (London: Verso, 2013). The literature on world literature is now extensive and growing exponentially in many languages, but for some key Anglophone contributions, see David Damrosch, *What Is World Literature?* (Princeton, NJ: Princeton University Press, 2003); Gayatri Chakravorty Spivak, *Death of a Discipline* (New York: Columbia University Press, 2003); Emily Apter, *Against World Literature:*

On the Politics of Untranslatability (London: Verso, 2013); Andrew Beecroft, *An Ecology of World Literature: From Antiquity to the Present Day* (London: Verso, 2015); Pheng Cheah, *What Is a World? On Postcolonial Literatures as World Literature* (Durham, NC: Duke University Press, 2016); and Aamir R. Mufti, *Forget English! Orientalisms and World Literatures* (Cambridge, MA: Harvard University Press, 2016). Other important interventions with a post-colonial studies inflection include Timothy Brennan, *At Home in the World: Cosmopolitanism Now* (Cambridge, MA: Harvard University Press 1997); Michael Denning, *Culture in the Age of Three Worlds* (London: Verso, 2004); and Sarah Brouillette, *Postcolonial Writers in the Global Literary Marketplace* (Basingstoke, UK: Palgrave Macmillan, 2007). The appearance of works by Spivak, Damrosch, and Moretti in 2003 and the English translation of Casanova in 2004 clearly mark a moment of intellectual convergence and recall the simultaneous appearance twenty years earlier in 1983 of a now-famous cluster of works on nationalism by Benedict Anderson, Ernest Gellner, and Eric Hobsbawm. The shift of concern from nation to "world" over that twenty-year interval is indicative.

2 On American intellectual and cultural self-assertion in twentieth-century Europe, see Volker R. Berghahn, *America and the Intellectual Cold Wars in Europe* (Princeton, NJ: Princeton University Press, 2001).

3 Edward Said (with Maire Said), translator and introduction to Erich Auerbach's "Philology and *Weltliteratur*," *Centennial Review* 13.1 (Winter 1969), 1–17.

4 Gayatri Chakravorty Spivak, "Subaltern Studies: Deconstructing Historiography" in *Selected Subaltern Studies*, ed. by Ranajit Guha and Gayatri Chakravorty Spivak (Oxford: Oxford University Press, 1988), pp. 3–32, and "Can the Subaltern Speak?" in *Marxism and the Interpretation of Culture*, ed. by Cary Nelson and Lawrence Grossberg (Urbana and Chicago: University of Illinois Press, 1988), pp. 271–313.

5 The body of work involved here is far too large to summarize, but for a few influential works of various kinds, see Paul Gilroy, *The Black Atlantic: Modernity and Double Consciousness* (Cambridge, MA: Harvard University Press, 1993); Arjun Appadurai, *Modernity at Large: Cultural Dimensions of Globalization* (Minneapolis: University of Minnesota Pres, 1996); Edward Said, *Reflections on Exile and Other Essays* (Cambridge, MA: Harvard University Press, 2000); and Ato Quayson and Girish Daswani, eds., *A Companion to Diaspora and Transnationalism* (Hoboken, NJ: Wiley-Blackwell, 2013).

6 For a symptomatic example of this climate of disciplinary demoralization, see Sunil Agnani et al., "Editor's Column: The End of Postcolonial Theory? A Roundtable with Sunil Agnani, Fernando Coronil, Gaurav Desai, Mamadou Diouf, Simon Gikandi, Susie Tharu, and Jennfier Wenzel," *PMLA* 122.3 (May 2007), 633–651.

7 The literatures here are again too vast to cite. On feminism, gender, sexuality, and empire, see the work usefully anthologized in Reina Lewis and Sara Mills, eds., *Feminist Postcolonial Theory: A Reader* (London: Routledge, 2004) and

Philippa Levine, ed., *Gender and Empire* (Oxford: Oxford University Press, 2004); on environmental degradation, see Rob Nixon, *Slow Violence and the Environmentalism of the Poor* (Cambridge, MA: Harvard University Press, 2011); Dispesh Chakrabarty, "Postcolonial Studies and the Challenge of Climate Change," *New Literary History* 43.1 (Winter 2012), 1–18; and Amitav Ghosh, *The Great Derangement: Climate Change and the Unthinkable* (Chicago: University of Chicago Press, 2016); on postcolonial writing and the capitalist marketplace, see Brouillette's *Postcolonial Writers and the Global Literary Marketplace*, op. cit., Graham Huggan, *The Postcolonial Exotic: Marketing the Margins* (London: Routledge, 2001) and Robert Fraser, *Book History through Postcolonial Eyes: Rewriting the Script* (New York: Routledge, 2008).

8 See Fritz Strich, *Goethe and World Literature*, trans. C. A. M. Sym (New York: Hafner Publishing Company, 1949), p. 350.

9 Karl Marx and Friedrich Engels, *Manifesto of the Communist Party* (Beijing: Foreign Languages Press, 1990), p. 38.

10 Erich Auerbach, *Time, History, and Literature: Selected Essays of Erich Auerbach*, edited with an introduction by James I. Porter, trans. Jane O. Newman (Princeton, NJ: Princeton University Press, 2014), pp. 253–265, p. 253, p. 254.

11 Ibid., 254.

12 For particularly sharp critiques of world literature as it is institutionally emerging in the US academy, see the works by Apter and Mufti cited previously.

13 Maxim Gorky, *"Weltliteratur," Maxim Gorki: Über Weltlieratur* (Leipzig: Philipp Reclam 1969 [1919]), pp. 31–40. Cited in Theo D'haen, *The Routledge Concise History of World Literature* (London: Routledge, 2012), p. 24.

14 Moretti, *Distant Reading*, op. cit., p. 46.

15 I owe the Soviet and Chinese examples cited here to Theo D'haen's *The Routledge Concise History of World Literature* (London: Routledge, 2012), pp. 24–25 and pp. 169–170. For a wider study of Soviet conceptions of world literature see also Katerina Clark, *Moscow, the Fourth Rome: Stalinism, Cosmopolitanism, and the Evolution of Soviet Culture, 1931–1941* (Cambridge, MA: Harvard University Press, 2011). For Chinese conceptions, see Jing Tsu co-edited with David Der-wei Wang, *Global Chinese Literature: Critical Essays* (Leiden, The Netherlands: Brill, 2010) and Zhang Longxi, *From Comparison to World Literature* (Albany: State University of New York Press, 2015).

CHAPTER 9

Postcolonial and Transnational Modernism

Dougal McNeill

Modernist literature framed Edward Said's career. His first book, *Joseph Conrad and the Fiction of Autobiography* (1966), initiated a decades-long investigation into the possibilities opened by modernist style. This formal fascination had political consequences: for Said, it was the "hybrid text[s]" of modernism, born out of "the issues of exile and immigration" that constituted "one of the major contributions of late twentieth-century culture."[1] Modernism's characteristic features – aesthetic self-consciousness, an obsession with vision, the celebration of the fragment, and Eliot's "heap of broken images" over the delusions of linearity – travel, in Said's account, from their putative origins in the often-told story of 1922 and the crises of Western culture only to be rediscovered elsewhere and in a new political, dissident, resisting register. The "search in the metropolis for a newly invigorated, reclaimed tradition follows the exhaustion of modernism" but, "simultaneously, modernism is rediscovered in the formerly colonized, peripheral world, where resistance, the logic of daring, and various investigations of age-old tradition . . . together set the tone."[2] For the oppressed of the Arab world, Said told an interviewer in the year of the "Palestinian Versailles," the Oslo Accord, modernism was "the issue of the moment": "[T]he crisis of 'modernism' and 'modernity' is a crisis over authority, and the right of the individual . . . to express himself or herself."[3] Said fuses here the three major concerns of his intellectual and activist career – the struggle against imperialism, the intellectual's vocation, and the inheritance of early-twentieth-century Anglophone literature – into one issue. "Modernism," in this account, carries intertwined political, pedagogical, and literary possibilities. This intertwining remained implicit across much of Said's writing but became, in his late works, an explicit and guiding method. In *Humanism and Democratic Criticism* (2003) he challenges the critic to imagine a distinctly modernist critical-creative political practice:

> Would it be possible to introduce a *modernist* theory and practice of reading
> and interpreting the part to the whole in such a way as neither to deny the
> specificity of the individual experience in and of an aesthetic work nor to
> rule out the validity of a projected, putative or implied sense of the whole?[4]

The "return to philology" Said advocated as part of this "modernist"
introduction – connecting formal readings of modernist literature with
accounts of the social whole – has been taken up in the decade and a half
since his premature death as one of the most vital parts of his legacy. The
crucial links that Said, and, following him, contemporary postcolonial
theory, makes between modernism, anti-colonial thinking, and post- or
anti-nationalist politics inform a whole new field of literary scholarship
recommending modernism as a new form of dissenting art and subjectivity. Transnational modernism is seen as post-national, cosmopolitan,
boundary slipping and border shattering: *the* literary style, then, for Said's
own unhoused, boundary-crossing intellectual vision. Modernism after
Said involves institutional shifts, as teaching practices change under pressure from new disciplinary-political figurations; political projects, as modernism is held up as the exemplary literary form; and particular analytical
groundings, as these accounts of modernism's status rely on ways of
understanding contemporary capitalism informed by Said's work. During
Said's own lifetime the critical controversies enlivening the literary field
were to do with *post*modernism and the contested inheritance of what
many assumed was modernism's enervation. In the twenty-first century,
however, and as part of Said's own influence, the confluence of postcolonial studies and a newly energized modernism has set out a quite different
political-literary encounter. But what might be occluded and lost in this
inflation and expansion of modernism? What politics undergird this new
remobilization of modernist aesthetics?

Transnational Bull Markets

The intellectual and institutional stocks of modernism have never been
higher. In the world of academic fashion and research grant–endowed
projects, all institutional signs point to a bull market. There have been
significant edited volumes from major publishers, *The Oxford Handbook of
Modernisms* (2010), *The Oxford Handbook of Global Modernisms* (2012),
the three-volume *Oxford Critical and Cultural History of Modernist Maga-
zines* (2009–2016); and two important new journals – *Modernism/modern-
ity* and *Modernist Cultures* – were established in the last two decades, as was
the Modernist Studies Association. Surveying the field in *PMLA* in 2008,

Douglas Mao and Rebecca L. Walkowitz noted the "expansive tendency" in what they called the New Modernist Studies. This is not just the expansion of a growing field but also the "temporal and spatial expansions" of what counts as modernism and a "vertical" expansion, as older distinctions between high and low cultures have been knocked away by new contextualizing work. Modernist studies, above all, has been marked by what Mao and Walkowitz call "a transnational turn," as older national literary canons have been supplanted by critics interested in building canons framed around the border-crossing, nationally uncertain work of writers such as Mina Loy – English, American, Jewish – or Claude McKay. The emergence of the New Modernist Studies, Mao and Walkowitz suggest, has "coincided with a powerful revival of modernist sensibilities" in contemporary arts. Literary theory and critical practice converge in this revived modernism, its reshaped canon and expanded reach underpinned, Susan Stanford Friedman remarks, by "the pervasive influence of postcolonial studies."[5]

As with all bull markets in a capitalist economy, speculative growth is followed always by a bear market. The publication of Susan Stanford Friedman's *Planetary Modernisms* (2015), with her claim that there should now be a "planetary turn" in modernist studies and that modernism could be defined as "the aesthetic dimension of any given modernity," suggests, to me at least, the moment of a kind of "peak modernism," after which returns on intellectual investments begin rapidly to fall. A planetary turn may be so capacious it ends up encompassing nothing much at all.[6]

But the shift, viewed against work from even a few decades past, is striking. The very nature of modernism seems to have changed beyond recognition. Said's influence here is pervasive. It was he who called for "a kind of globalism in the study of texts,"[7] he who developed the case for combining celebrations of modernist art's "state of ecstatic freedom"[8] with political hostility toward nationalism and a cosmopolitan vision of art provoking "a transformation of social consciousness beyond national consciousness."[9] Said's emphasis on the productive value of exile and liminality, his stress on spatial analysis over historical accounts, his advocacy of modernist aesthetics, and his suspicion of totalizing, systematic political theories and projects (whether historical materialism or Communist movements) are all echoed and reverberate in the chambers of the New Modernist Studies. Jahan Ramazani adopts what he calls Said's "early paradigm for trans-hemispheric studies" while arguing criticism needs to push further the "boundary-traversing power of poetry" to "complicate identitarian boundaries."[10] His own *Transnational Poetics* based itself on

"Said's insights into the transnational affiliations that form the basis . . . for anticolonial poetic solidarities," while his term "travelling poetry" consciously echoes and evokes Said's "travelling theory."[11] Simon Gikandi goes further still, arguing that "a convergence of political and literary ideologies mark a significant part of the history of modernism and postcolonialism" and that "it was *primarily* . . . in the language and structure of modernism that a postcolonial experience came to be articulated and imagined in literary form."[12] Whereas once the Third World "project" was seen as combining political commitment to national liberation with a realist aesthetic of demystification and ideological emancipation, the emphasis in New Modernist Studies is on *anti*-nationalist combinations of modernist "boundary-traversing" poetic form and cosmopolitan "postcolonial experience."[13]

What assumptions inform this association of modernist aesthetics with postcolonial, transnational politics? The pedagogical benefit, whatever else is at stake, is an uncomplicated good. Any student exposed to C. L. R. as well as Henry James is bound to have a richer experience of modernist aesthetics, as well as a fuller life. But the slippages between terms in Gikandi's claim, from ideology to modernism to postcolonial "experience" show up disturbing imprecisions in the new modernist case. Is modernism a dissenting art? The connection is carried, by Said and those after him, more often by allusion and association than by sustained argument. If Conrad's awareness that words could be "the great foes of reality" became accessible to Said by way of the "affinities" provided from his Palestinian experience to this "radical exilic vision,"[14] it is unclear what is to be made of these affinities. Modernism's politics are notoriously contradictory, with similar formal innovations being aligned to diverging political projects. For every socialist of Brecht's stature there is a reactionary monarchist such as Eliot, a quietist liberal Christian in Auden, or a flamboyantly fascistic and anti-Semitic ideologue in Pound. The New Modernist Studies' "expansive" tendencies merely stretch the definitional problematic in their key term rather than resolving modernism's core features. Modernism's political lineaments – contested, contradictory, often unclear – pose for critics the problem of the relationship between literary form, political possibility, and social alignment: Modernism after Said, however, refuses these very problems in its celebration of a particular mode of writing and its assumption that an anti-nationalist, boundary-crossing view is uncritically to be celebrated. The *strategic* dilemmas of the nation-state, national liberation and national oppression – dilemmas imposed upon writers by their historical and geographical location much more than by any choice of outlook, do not interrupt the rhetoric of contemporary modernist criticism. But if critics following Said can extol the value of exile for the critic and the "navigating"[15] role of exilic writing, the stubborn persistence of national boundaries elsewhere forces writers and critics into much more precise accounting. The agonizing complexity of Lebanese politics, for instance, with the particular "transnational" vision of Ba'athism a presence through the Syrian regime's long dominance a factor alongside colonial-era sectarian divisions and US-sponsored threats from Israel, produces a social formation in which national *immobility*, constriction, and bounded experience – in refugee camps for Palestinians or long-term displaced Syrians as much as for Lebanese citizens – has been the focus of intellectual life. Samir Kassir's denunciation of "the Arab malaise" ends with a call to "force destiny's hand" by acknowledging these difficulties,[16] while Elias Khoury's epic novel *Gate of the Sun* (1998) takes the Palestinian experience of defeat as an opportunity to reconstruct the promise and betrayal of Arab nationalism generally. Khoury's novel is unthinkable without the national spaces its characters inhabit and fight over, from the state of Israel to Jordan to Lebanon. The crossings represented are unimaginable without these particular, historically determinate boundaries. Academic celebrations of transnationalism offer no critical tools with which to encounter works of this kind.

Said, for all that his journalistic work for the Palestinian cause was rigorous, detailed, and precise, never developed any critical account of nationalism or, more surprisingly, colonialism or imperialism. His political response was always more liberationist, awakened as he was by the Palestinian revolution from the late 1960s, than to do with demands for statehood. Like Fanon, Said's nationalism was of a self-canceling kind, a revolutionary project hoping for a nationalism *aufgehoben*, cancelled in its own victory and transformed into a humanism. Always contemptuous of the organized left in the Popular Front for the Liberation of Palestine and elsewhere, Said's affiliation, before Oslo at least, was with Fatah's elite, but his national outlook was, like Mahmoud Darwish's, for a homeland imaginable only as "a place that gives people the opportunity to grow."[17] This outlook was, in other words, much more an aesthetic sensibility than the result of a detailed political strategy. With these two parts of his intellectual life kept, for the most part, separate from one another, the weaknesses in one did not lead to weaknesses in the other; New Modernist Studies, without Said's grounding in a concrete anti-colonial situation and lived struggle, collapses both accounts together. Said persistently *culturalized* colonialism and imperialism, rarely distinguishing between the two – and thus applying analyses developed from literature produced in periods of formal European colonial administration to the very different

post-1945 era of decolonization and inter-imperialist rivalry. Half-formed
definitions flowed in his discursive wake. Imperialism is thus both "the
export of identity" and "an act of geographical violence through which
virtually every space in the world is explored, charted, and finally brought
under control."[18] Literary figures are introduced as substitutes for any real
engagement with scholarly, and especially Marxist, debates on the political
economy of imperialism, as with the way T. S. Eliot is used to open
Culture and Imperialism (1994) while Lenin, Luxemburg, and Bukharin,
all whom produced major theoretical works on imperialism, are not
mentioned at all. The specificities of contemporary struggles, such as the
Eritrean-Ethiopian conflict, in which Haile Selassie's Ethiopia claimed
Eritrea with US support following Italian defeat in World War II, cannot
be analyzed using Said's vocabulary: with formal colonialism finished after
the war's conclusion, the geopolitical machinations shaping the nation's
future from there require materialist analysis more detailed than metaphorical evocations of exploration. Alongside his own studied vagueness, however, Said culturalizes others' attempts at such analysis. Lukács's *History
and Class Consciousness* and Adorno's philosophical work are thus described
by him as "Modernist," both "desperate attempt[s] to reconstruct whole-
ness out of fragments."[19] Lukács's work may well be this, but it is also,
among other things, an attempt to solve the "*intellectual* problems in the
history of revolution";[20] in other words, a guide to revolutionary action. In
place of Lukács's concern with strategy, tactics, and intervention, Said's
interests are in states of being, in exile as "unlike nationalism . . . fundamentally a discontinuous state of being."[21] If his biographical and ethical
affiliation to the Palestinian cause prevented him from making statements
as politically empty as Homi Bhabha's that "the postcolonial perspective
resists the attempt at holistic forms of social explanation" or his advocacy
of the "transnational as the translational" against "those nationalist or
'nativist' pedagogies that set up the relation of Third World and First
World in a binary opposition," Said could still praise this work as produced by "a reader of enormous subtlety and wit, a theorist of uncommon
power."[22] The New Modernist Studies after Said takes this commitment
to the transnational and shears off any residual coating from early anti-
imperialist debates.

Exile and Solidarity

"I will try to express myself in some mode of life or art as freely as I can
and as wholly as I can, using for my defence the only arms I allow myself
to use – silence, exile, and cunning": Joyce's much-quoted lines from

A Portrait of the Artist as a Young Man link modernist aesthetic dislocation and disruption ("cunning") with geographical dislocation ("exile") in ways critics have associated with the wider modernist project for many decades now. Said takes this familiar association and inflates its political reach considerably. "The emergent voices and currents of the present" are, for Said, in their most important expressions, "exilic, extraterritorial, and unhoused."[23] "The critical task for the exile" is "to remain somehow sceptical and always on guard," productively askance from settled communities and their ideologies.[24] The exile is, for Said, an exemplary figure, their human experience joining them to the most important social-political dynamics of the current period, while their social location opens up epistemological, expressive, and creative possibilities unavailable to more settled figures. "The huge waves of migrants, expatriates, and refugees . . . have become the single most important human reality of our time the world over"[25] and modernism, with its blending and clashing registers of different national material and multilingual, code-switching poetics, is the aesthetic of this important human reality. The exile, in Said's account, becomes a kind of modernist "fit reader." The exile knows "that in a secular and contingent world . . . borders and barriers, which enclose us within the safety of familiar territory, can also become prisons . . . . Exiles cross borders, break barriers of thought and experience."[26] Just as the modernist artist slips between fixed representations, so too the exilic intellectual, filled with "unhoused, decentred . . . energies" can pursue a project of liberation by remaining a figure "between domains, between forms, between homes, and between languages."[27] A whole political project and subjectivity is here conjured through association with modernist sensibility. But Said's list of "migrants, expatriates, and refugees," usefully capacious, connects through rhetorical imprecision three very different human realities. Migrants are, after all, as easily part of projects of *settlement* as they are disruptive agents: The great waves of postwar migration after 1945 to Australia, New Zealand, and Israel as part of the last phase of white settler colonialism reinforced not "decentred and exilic energies" but the political projects of White Australia and Zionism. Expatriates are a more diffuse grouping still, and the presence of British retirees in the Spanish state may indicate no "human reality" more profound than our species' enjoyment of warm weather. Said's desire to lash together modernist aesthetics with the lived experience of contemporary politics leads him to flatten out real social differences and divisions.

Refugees, the third group in Said's trinity, may be further still from his vision of modernist subjectivity. Exile, Said suggests, "far from being the fate of nearly forgotten unfortunates . . . becomes something closer to a norm, an experience of crossing boundaries and charting new territories in defiance of the classical canonical enclosures, however much its loss and sadness should be acknowledged and registered."[28] Boundaries often enclose refugees to a claustrophobic degree, however, and, far from opening "new territories" to investigation, the refugee experience is often one of *immobility*, permanent stasis, and constriction – as in the Australian state's "offshore detention facilities" in the Pacific – as it is border crossing. Many Palestinian refugees – at least 1.5 million in UNRWA camps – live in camps in the Levant: their reality, for more than seventy years now, remains in difficult linguistic, cultural, and political proximity to the lands of historic Palestine. If there is a modernism here it is Samuel Beckett's variations on trapped, damaged, and immobile figures – "I say to myself that the earth is extinguished, though I never saw it lit"[29] – more than it is the border crossing of contemporary transnationalism.[30]

Said was a critic too alive to the "loss and sadness" of exile for his own writing ever fully to forget this sense of possibilities limited: the sadness of his own memoir's description of living in New York "with a sense of provisionality" underlines the "disorientation" of the exile's life, as does his meditation on the "broken narratives, fragmentary compositions, and self-consciously staged testimonials" of Palestinian existence in *After the Last Sky* (1986).[31] The modernist *form* of these two texts, both moving in their registration of the damage done to a life of exile, is in tension with the modernist *content* of Said's writing, with its celebration of the exilic intellectual as a model political subjectivity. After Said, however, this tension is loosened by less politically engaged critics. Bridget Chalk thus writes that Gertrude Stein offers a political model "for new modes of community and affiliation that transcend either the national or bureaucratically defined nationality," while Rebecca L. Walkowitz, arguing for a "critical cosmopolitanism" impossible "without modernist practices," suggests that "transnational thought" can be brought into being through an encounter with "the salient features of modernist narrative" all in the service of "a critical cosmopolitanism . . . thinking beyond the nation."[32] Neither prescription is specific enough to be wrong: Walkowitz's list of formal techniques never queries what might be "beyond" the nation for those not yet in control of a distinct nation-state, while Chalk's chosen example, a writer reliant for her transnational status on collaboration with the Vichy regime sustained by Nazi-occupied France, hardly seems, whatever her formal brilliance, a promising model for any democratic criticism or humanist subjectivity.

Absent from the New Modernist Studies is any sense of modernist practice being the result of writers' responses to social *dilemmas* and representational strategies. Anxieties about the reliability of our representational apparatus, feelings of isolation, restlessness about art's status, the sense that, as Conrad's Marlow muses, "it is impossible to convey the life-sensation of any given epoch of one's existence":[33] All this presses on readers and writers in particular historical-political conjunctures, and modernism stands as the symptom, and attempted solution, to these conjunctures. Modernism's claims and conventions are both historically grounded and responsive to particular political situations but Said domesticates these by making them a set of relatively free-floating individual choices. By reading Lukács and Adorno as themselves modernists, and thereby reducing their own works to answers to the question of "what to read and what to do with that reading,"[34] Said evacuates the terms of the contest from modernist discourse, and those reading after Said acknowledge that contest barely at all. Said and others quote, approvingly, Adorno's dictum that "the whole is the false," and yet this comes from an account, in *Minima Moralia*, of the state of society as much as any aesthetic modeling. Adorno saw "what the philosophers once knew as life" as now "mere consumption, dragged along as an appendage of the process of material production, without autonomy or substance of its own."[35] Adorno's defense of modernism is, in other words, inseparable from his analysis of contemporary capitalism as a wholly administered society in which opportunities for collective resistance or expression have been extinguished. "The reactionary nature of any realist aesthetic today is inseparable," for Adorno, from its "commodity character. Tending to reinforce, affirmatively, the phenomenal surface of society, realism dismissed any attempt to penetrate that surface as a romantic endeavour."[36] This is, in an ironic twist, an argument for modernism's *realism*, an analysis of its negative capacities to "penetrate that surface" of society and produce reliable information about its workings. Adorno thus shares Lukács's belief that if "works are important it is almost always because they achieve a form which can render the conflicts of their times at their fullest range within the given historical reality."[37] The two theorists' debate is over the *nature* of that "given historical reality"[38] and their differing literary prescriptions – Lukács's condemnation of modernism's "basically static approach to reality" against Adorno's valorization of the autonomous possibilities of Beckett's unassimilable art – are to do with their sense of the political possibilities of their moment much more than with any particular literary technique or narrative form. Said's description of Palestinian literature written just before the First Intifada, and so at that moment when the "given historical reality" of Palestine seemed more hopelessly inaccessible than ever, follows this Adornian pattern: "[T]he striking thing about Palestinian prose and prose fiction is its formal instability: our literature in a certain very narrow sense *is* the elusive, resistant reality it tries so often to represent."[39] Mahmoud Darwish's later poetry registers and works with this modernist frustrated sense of lost agency:

> I never said goodbye to the ruins.
> Only once had I been what I was.
> But it was enough to know how time
> collapses like a Bedouin tent in the north wind,
> how places rupture, how the past
> becomes the ghost of a deserted temple.[40]

The poetry of Darwish's earlier period, when the energies of the Arab anti-imperialist revolutions and the emerging Palestinian liberation movement led him to works such as "Identity Card" ("beware of my hunger / & of my anger"),[41] is not so easily located within this Adornian aesthetic, however, and can be read alongside Lukács's account of realism as a form "bound up with that minimal hope of a change for the better" as the writer portrays "history as a process" in creative motion.[42]

Realism is, however, the missing term in Said's aesthetic and in the works of the theorists of the New Modernist Studies. For all that Said admired Lukács, he paid little attention to his work on realism and was content, in *Orientalism* and elsewhere, to make a very general critique of realism:

> The realistic novel ... organizes reality and knowledge in such a way as to make them susceptible to systematic verbal reincarnation. The novel's realistic bodying forth of a world is to provide representational or representative norms selected from among many possibilities. Thus the novel acts to include, state, affirm, normalize and naturalise some things, values, and ideas, but not others ... the novel ... is not only selective and affirmative but centralizing and powerful.[43]

Which values, and whose ideas? Said's Foucauldian vocabulary here obscures the *class* dynamics at work in realism's attempts to "select and affirm" particular views of the world and the dynamics shaping the world. These have, in the historical record, proven as much of an inspiration for anti-colonial literature as any modernist experiment. As Michael Denning has shown, there are continuities in aesthetic projects linking proletarian and socialist realist works of the 1930s with more recent innovations in "magical realism": The "vital elements of a global culture comes out of this internationalism as it intersected with the national-popular hopes of the anticolonial movements." The "emerging canon of the world novel" – Naguib Mahfouz, Gabriel Garcia Marquez, Pramoedya Ananta Toer – was composed by writers in creative dialog with the socialist tradition and realist aesthetics.[44] Hone Tuwhare, the first Māori poet to publish a book of verse in English, drew on his experiences in the Communist Party and on its officially sanctioned realist writing. Albert Wendt, in *Leaves of the Banyan Tree* (1979), produced an epic, inter-generational narrative of Sāmoan colonization and independence following the Lukácsian demands of the realist novel.

This rich, varied, multiple realist legacy is inaccessible to Said and the modernist critics following him. If that absence is aesthetically impoverishing, it is also politically disabling. Said's refusal to distinguish between imperialism and historical colonialism renders many aesthetic-political situations in the twenty-first century illegible for modernist criticism. The "division system" in the Korean peninsula, for instance, formally independent for seventy years but with a continuous presence of US military forces throughout that time and an ongoing civil war the reminder of a colonial past, forces its writers to make choices between modernism and realism as they assess the representability of their social formation. Hwang Sok-yong has called for realism to be "dismantled drastically and recomposed with more richness," and his *The Guest* (2000) fragments its historical narrative of the Korean War and Sincheon Massacre by modeling itself after traditional exorcism practices to act as an aesthetic exorcism for its readers, bringing repressed historical material back into view.[45] Young-Ha Kim's *Your Republic Is Calling You* (2010), by contrast, pursues modernist strategies of indirection, its narrative limited to a single day in the life of Seoul in the tradition of Joyce's *Ulysses*, its textual allusions to Japanese commodities offering reminders of half-forgotten colonial histories obscured by the "indiscriminate weariness" of life in the hyperreality of contemporary Seoul.[46] The Korean American poet Suji Kwock Kim, meanwhile, negotiates the impossible demands of an historical inheritance demanding "may you never remember & may you never forget," her own verses drawing on international modernism to register the ways of remembering a "forgotten war."[47]

Realism after Said

Said offers no guide for us to account for these strategic divisions because of his twin disavowals. The specifically imperialist and contemporary nature of the "division system" in Korea cannot be analyzed following the model of "the West" as a culturally monolithic bloc as proposed in

Orientalism and *Culture and Imperialism*, and the turn to realism cannot be read using the torn half of the realism-modernism debate Said has bequeathed to modernist studies. His metaphor of "global contrapuntal analysis" gives no guide to understanding the *contradictory unity* of a particular situation,[48] and his claim that "the intellectual's provisional home is the domain of an exigent, resistant, intransigent art into which, alas, one can neither retreat nor search for solutions"[49] deprives criticism of any political-strategic orientation. The force of Said's own personal history and example obscured that deprivation in his own lifetime; its absence is even more pronounced in the more comfortable critics of our own day.

The Korean example points to another problem of Said's transnational modernist inheritance. The "Korean wave," a transnational phenomenon across East Asia and, more recently, the Anglophone world, has seen a great boom in Korean popular music, soap operas, movies, and dramas with international audiences. Commodity culture from the south of Korea is now a major part of the global entertainment industry, and a component of the regional "soft power" strategy of the Republic's increasingly assertive political class. The coordinates of this political-cultural situation, into which both Hwang's realism and Kim's modernism can be seen as interventions, are shaped by the US presence in the region, certainly, but cannot be limited to this particular imperialist force. Tellingly, as the Anglophone novelists of the Korean diaspora come to try and understand the ways the ongoing tragedy on the Korean Peninsula distorts individual lives – and shapes collective destinies in the region and in the United States – it is to the generic conventions of realism that they have turned. Min Jin Lee's *Pachinko* (2017) uses the classic device of the intergenerational family epic to narrate Korean displacement and transnational colonial experience the US sphere of influence and Japan. Chang-Rae Lee's *A Gesture Life* (1999) similarly uses realism's resources to represent the unsettled legacies of the Pacific War and Japanese colonialism in Korea and its subsequent willed forgetting in the United States. Korea, Korean literature, and the literature of the Korean diaspora all point to political and cultural difficulties and struggles that cannot be mapped onto the coordinates offered by either *Orientalism* or the new modernist exultation of border crossing. The ongoing military division of the peninsula, mutating now as part of the growing rivalry between the United States and China, co-exists with a boom in cultural production and dissemination abroad. As Vivek Chibber observes:

> As capitalism spreads across the globe, it does not inevitably turn every subculture into a replica of what has been observed in the West. The

universalisation of capital is perfectly compatible with the persistence of social, culture and political differentiation between East and West. Capital does not have to obliterate difference in order to universalise itself. It merely has to subordinate those dimensions of social reproduction that are essential to its own functioning. These dimensions are the ones directly involved in the production and distribution of use-values.[50]

Chibber's Marxist analysis challenges critics to provide satisfactory explanations for the *relationships* between given historical moments, particular literary-cultural forms, and the process of the "production and distribution of use-values." The first debate between realism and modernism, forged in the anxious interwar years as Marxist critics such as Adorno, Lukács, Bloch, and Benjamin attempted to chart a path between aesthetics and politics during the triumph of fascism, offered us one set of competing explanation and advocacy. Said, because he never engaged with the Marxism of that tradition, offers no conceptual frame in which to organize the debate for today. The problem is not, of course, that Said was not a Marxist. But his own position, and its borrowing from the specifically Marxist framework of Adorno and Lukács's debate over modernism, carried over the terms without properly contesting their conceptual location. Stylistic eclecticism can produce theoretical confusion. The breadth and anti-colonial generosity of Said's reading remains an inspiration for contemporary materialist criticism, but his terms, and their uncritical elaboration in the field of New Modernist Studies, do not provide us with the tools for a proper encounter with modernism in the era of the universalization of capital. If "survival is about the connections between things"[51] then a truly transnational modernist art will be possible only when it is connected to an understanding of transnational modern capital. That task, a political project as much as an analytical research program, remains unfinished.

Notes

1 Gauri Viswanathan, ed., *Power, Politics and Culture: Interviews with Edward Said* (New York: Vintage, 2001), p. 148.
2 Edward Said, *Culture and Imperialism* (London: Vintage, 1994), pp. 67–68.
3 Viswanathan, *Power, Politics and Culture*, p. 259.
4 Edward Said, *Humanism and Democratic Criticism* (New York: Columbia University Press, 2003), pp. 55–56.
5 Douglas Mao and Rebecca L. Walkowitz, "The New Modernist Studies," *PMLA* 123.3 (2008), 737–748 (737); Douglas Mao and Rebecca L. Walkowitz, "Introduction," in *Bad Modernisms* (Durham, NC: Duke University Press, 2006), p. 1; Susan Stanford Friedman, *Planetary Modernisms: Provocations on Modernity Across Time* (New York: Columbia University Press, 2015), p. 6.
6 Stanford Friedman, *Planetary Modernisms*, pp. ix, x.

7 Viswanathan, *Power, Politics, and Culture*, p. 140.

8 Edward Said, *On Late Style: Music and Literature Against the Grain* (London: Bloomsbury, 2008), p. 124.

9 Edward Said, "Yeats and Decolonization," in *Nationalism, Colonialism and Literature* (Minneapolis: University of Minnesota Press, 1990), p. 83.

10 Jahan Ramazani, "Poetry, Modernist and Globalisation," in *The Oxford Handbook of Global Modernisms*, ed. by Mark Wollaeger and Matt Eatough (Oxford University Press, 2012), p. 296.

11 Jahan Ramazani, *A Transnational Poetics* (Chicago: University of Chicago Press, 2009), p. 141, p. 60.

12 Simon Gikandi, "Preface: Modernism and the World," *Modernism/modernity* 13. 3 (2006), 419–424 (420).

13 See Vijay Prashad, *The Darker Nations: A People's History of the Third World* (New York: New Press, 2007).

14 Joseph Conrad, *Under Western Eyes* (Cambridge: Cambridge University Press, 2013 [1911]), p. 22; Edward Said, *Reflections on Exile and Other Literary and Cultural Essays* (London: Granta, 2001), p. xxxiv.

15 Robert T. Tally Jr., "*Mundus Totus Exilium Est*: Reflections on the Critic in Exile," in *The Geocritical Legacies of Edward W. Said*, ed. by Robert T. Tally Jr. (London: Palgrave, 2015), p. 211.

16 Samir Kassir, *Being Arab*, trans. Will Hobson (London: Verso, 2006), p. 1, p. 92. Kassir's assassination, most likely the work of Syrian security agents active in Lebanon, is a tragic reminder that, outside the rhetoric of academic criticism, border crossing is a neutral activity and can bring with it disaster as much as delivery.

17 "Exile Is So Strong Within Me, I May Bring It To the Land: A Landmark 1996 Interview with Mahmoud Darwish," *Journal of Palestine Studies* 42.1 (2012–2013), 46–70.

18 Said, *On Late Style*, p. 85; *Culture and Imperialism*, p. 271.

19 Said, *Reflections on Exile*, p. 482.

20 Georg Lukács, *History and Class Consciousness: Studies in Marxist Dialectics*, trans. Rodney Livingstone (London: Merlin, 1971), p. 320.

21 Said, *Reflections on Exile*, p. 177.

22 Homi K. Bhabha, *The Location of Culture* (London: Routledge, 1994), p. 173. Said's endorsement appears on the book's blurb.

23 Said, *Humanism and Democratic Criticism*, p. 11.

24 Said, *Reflections on Exile*, p. xxxiii.

25 Said, *Humanism and Democratic Criticism*, p. 47.

26 Said, *Reflections on Exile*, p. 170.

27 Said, *Culture and Imperialism*, p. 403.

28 Ibid., p. 407.

29 Samuel Beckett, *Endgame*, in *The Complete Dramatic Works* (London: Faber, 1990), p. 132.

30 Darko Suvin's "Displaced Persons," *New Left Review* II.31 (January–February 2005), 107–123, is an excellent, and critical, exploration of these questions in Said's work and elsewhere.

31 Edward Said, *Out of Place: A Memoir* (London: Granta, 1999), p. 222; Edward Said, *After the Last Sky: Palestinian Lives* (New York: Pantheon, 1986), p. 38.

32 Bridget Chalk, *Modernism and Mobility: The Passport and Cosmopolitan Experience* (New York: Palgrave, 2014), p. 13; Rebecca L. Walkowitz, *Cosmopolitan Style: Modernism Beyond the Nation* (New York: Columbia University Press, 2006), p. 18, p. 2.

33 Joseph Conrad, *Heart of Darkness* (Mineola, NY: Dover, 1990 [1902]), p. 24.

34 Said, *Culture and Imperialism*, p. 70.

35 Theodor Adorno, Minima Moralia: *Reflections from Damaged Life*, trans. E. F. N. Jephcott (London: NLB, 1974), p. 50, p. 15.

36 Theodor Adorno, *The Culture Industry: Selected Essays on Mass Culture* (London: Routledge, 2001), p. 182. I draw here on the important work of the Warwick Research Collective, *Combined and Uneven Development: Towards a New Theory of World Literature* (Liverpool, UK: Liverpool University Press, 2015).

37 Georg Lukács, *Essays on Thomas Mann*, trans. Stanley Mitchell (New York: Grosset and Dunlop, 1964), p. 16.

38 Georg Lukács, *The Meaning of Contemporary Realism* (London: Merlin, 1963), p. 34.

39 Said, *After the Last Sky*, p. 138.

40 Mahmoud Darwish, *Mural* (2000), trans. Munir Akash and Carolyn Forché, in *Unfortunately, It Was Paradise: Selected Poems* (Los Angeles: University of California Press, 2013), p. 135.

41 Mahmoud Darwish, *Selected Poems*, trans. Ian Wedde and Fawwaz Tuqan (Manchester, UK: Carcanet, 1973), p. 24.

42 Lukács, *The Meaning of Contemporary Realism*, p. 68, Lukács, *The Historical Novel*, trans. Hannah and Stanley Mitchell (London: Penguin, 1969), p. 18.

43 Edward Said, *The World, the Text, and the Critic* (London: Faber, 1984), p. 176.

44 Michael Denning, *Culture in the Age of Three Worlds* (London: Verso, 2004), p. 32.

45 Hwang, "Writers in a Region of Conflict," in *Writing Across Boundaries*, ed. by Uchang Kim (Seoul: Hollym, 2002), p. 333; Hwang Sok-Yong, *The Guest*, trans. Kyung-Ja Chung and Maya West (New York: Seven Stories, 2005), p. 7, p. 9.

46 Young-Ha Kim, *Your Republic Is Calling You*, trans. Chi-Young Kim (Boston: Mariner, 2010), p. 59.

47 Suji Kwock Kim, *Notes from the Divided Country* (Baton Rouge: Louisiana State University Press, 2003), p. 37, p. 30.

48 Said, *Culture and Imperialism*, p. 386.

49 Said, *Humanism and Democratic Criticism*, p. 144.

50 Vivek Chibber, *Postcolonial Theory and the Spectre of Capital* (New York: Verso, 2013), pp. 150–151.

51 Said, *Culture and Imperialism*, p. 408.

CHAPTER 10

Political Predicaments of Exile

Joan Cocks

The only homeland, foreigner, is the world we live in; a single Chaos
has given birth to all mortals.[1]

– Meleager of Gadara, first century BC

Introduction

In an autobiographical portrait, Sigmund Freud recalls certain "appre-
ciable disappointments" that beset him when he entered medical school
in 1873.

> Above all, I found that I was expected to feel myself inferior and an alien
> because I was a Jew. I refused absolutely to do the first of these things.
> I have never been able to see why I should feel ashamed of my descent or, as
> people were beginning to say, of my "race." I put up, without much regret,
> with my non-acceptance into the community; for it seemed to me that in
> spite of this exclusion an active fellow-worker could not fail to find some
> nook or cranny in the framework of humanity. These first impressions at
> the University, however, had one consequence . . . at an early age I was
> made familiar with the fate of being in the Opposition and of being put
> under the ban of the "compact majority". The foundations were thus laid
> for a certain degree of independence of judgment.[2]

It is hard for any discerning reader not to be struck by a family resem-
blance between Sigmund Freud's fleeting passage and Edward Said's
extensive meditations on the amalgam of deprivations and advantages that
exile offers its sufferers. There is, at the heart of both Freud's condensed
and Said's elaborated accounts, the plight of those accused of belonging to
some racially distinct and inferior group, and their status as alien in the
eyes of a national or so-called civilizational majority. There is the prickly
repudiation of the attribute of inferiority but proud affirmation of the
posture of the outsider, and the belief in a link between imposed exclusion
and critical intelligence. Finally, there is the implicit hope for a humanity

that delights in, without reifying, its own variations; that is inviting to mavericks and hybrids; and that is less sharply divided into legally and militarily fortified identity camps than the humanity history has had to offer until now.

It is true that the contexts pressing Freud and Said to ponder the ambiguities of exile are chronologically and geographically distinct, even while they are historically related in the sense that the Zionist solution for transcending, once and for all, the exilic predicament of Jews in Europe by forging them into a majority people was predicated on transferring the exilic predicament to Palestinian Arabs. These two men's contexts differ not just in time and space but also in key circumstantial details as a result of the settler colonial dimensions of that transfer. Freud is responding to the persecution of a diasporic minority by various native majorities, not living quite long enough to see persecution metastasize into mass extermination. The touchstone for Said's reflections is instead a native majority whose members have been forced by outsiders into one of three differently estranged positions: to live on remnants of their land as second-class citizens in a state created by and for another people, to live as sequestered noncitizens in occupied territory under the tyrannical control of that same state, or to disperse to find a new life in other nation-states.

What George Lamming once dubbed the pleasures of exile are fully available only to members of this third, dispersed group, to which Said belonged. The elective affinity between marginality and critical thought that Freud uncovered can be enjoyed (if *enjoyment* is the right word) by external and internal exiles alike. But the ability to breathe freely after escaping a claustrophobic atmosphere, to which Lamming referred while portraying fellow writers who fled the postcolonial but still psychoculturally colonized Caribbean; the contrapuntal sensibility; and the worldly as opposed to parochial perspective that Said applauded in many of his works are more readily available to border-crossing strangers abroad than to populations estranged and immobilized at home. In the pages that follow, I will focus less on the pleasures of exile than on political conundrums that exile poses for natives and strangers alike.[3] Nevertheless, the line of argument I pursue pertains most centrally to people migrating across nation-state borders to become strangers elsewhere, with only indirect implications for those who have been exiled by strangers in their native place.

Perhaps Said's most explosive essay, when it first came out more than thirty-five years ago, was "Zionism from the Standpoint of Its Victims." That essay has been extended by contemporary scholars to incorporate the injustices to Zionism's victims that have been mounting up since then. What I wish to do here instead is to mull over a formally analogous issue that Said's legacy also encourages us to address, now that millions of Syrians, Afghans, Iraqis, Sudanese, Indians, Filipinos, Bangladeshis, Rohingyas, Nigerians, Guatemalans, Mexicans, and so forth have been catapulted by economic misery, political violence, and ecological disasters across an inhospitable globe. What is citizenship from the standpoint of the exile? And if citizenship has been, from that standpoint, an exclusionary rather than a protective or an emancipatory good, how might exiles find a home in a world of nation-states without being required or tempted to meld into a particularistic and encapsulated whole? More precisely, how can outcasts from their places of departure become the accepted equals of compatriots in their places of arrival without forfeiting the critical acuity, contrapuntal sensibility, and enlarged vision that the exilic condition, for all its melancholic torments, has bequeathed especially to them?

Let me tackle these questions first by remarking on the citizen/stranger distinction in traditional Western political theory, second by examining Freud's and Said's complementary insights into that distinction, and third by confronting, in the spirit of both men, current structures of feeling at odds with exile-friendly cosmopolitan ideals, before suggesting how those structures might be at least partly shifted for the sake of strangers and citizens alike.

The Stranger in Western Political Thought

The figure of the stranger has been of compelling interest for many modern novelists, philosophers, religious thinkers, and travel writers, as well as for psychoanalysts, who, whether they share Freud's ethnic marginal status, are in the business of ferreting out the unconscious wishes and anxieties that make every self at some deep level a stranger to itself. In contrast, traditional political theorists have treated this figure as tangential to the drama of political life. Within the canonical texts of Western political thought, the citizen and the sovereign have been, until recently, the two protagonists starring on the political stage. Foreigners who remain at home as citizens or sovereigns in their own nation-states have played supporting roles that demonstrate the plurality of political societies in the world and the primacy in each of the citizen/sovereign couplet. Meanwhile, individuals or groups who have moved from their place of origin to places in which they are received as outsiders, or who have been treated, inside, as if they *were* outsiders, have been awarded at best only bit parts in the typical political theoretical story as anomalies extraneous to the project of authorizing and constituting legitimate government, and delineating and defending the rights of citizens with respect to it. The noteworthy exceptions to the general rule of stranger inconsequentiality are glory-seeking leaders, despotic monarchs, and colonial administrators who travel from distant places to conquer and rule over other peoples, such as those who make respective guest appearances in Niccolò Machiavelli's *The Prince*, Thomas Hobbes's *Leviathan*, and John Stuart Mill's *On Representative Government*. Still, imperial rulers are mostly subplot actors in those texts, which focus largely on subjects and sovereigns who "belong" to one another, whether by ethno-racial descent, contractual consent, or shared culture and history. Even Jean-Jacques Rousseau's "Legislator" – who arrives from elsewhere to constitute a polity in such a way that its citizens can become, from then on, simultaneously sovereign and subject – enjoys center stage in *The Social Contract* only for a moment, bowing out of the picture as soon as he has accomplished his foundational task.

The marginalization of the stranger in the political theory canon goes at least as far back as Aristotle's passing references to resident aliens in *The Politics*. In the modern period, in addition to typifying liberal social contract theories, it is reprised in such disparate texts as *Reflections on the Revolution in France*, where Edmund Burke represents politics and culture as the entailed inheritance of Englishmen (not to speak of insinuating the Jewish-and-hence-not-truly-English identity of nonconforming English radicals), and *Reason in History*, where G. W. F. Hegel conceives of the state as the unity of individual subjectivities and objective institutions in a single national cultural totality. Such marginalization is very faintly ameliorated in Alexis de Tocqueville's chapter in *Democracy in America* on "The Three Races in the United States" (European settlers, enslaved descendants of Africans, and Indian natives who have been turned by Europeans into strangers in their own land) and in John Stuart Mill's chapter on intermixed, minority, and subjugated majority nationalities in *On Representative Government* – although both chapters have the quality of being parenthetical. The inconsequentiality of the stranger in the Western tradition only comes to a halt in the mid-twentieth century, after Hannah Arendt turned her spotlight on stateless peoples, refugees, and self-conscious pariahs in *The Origins of Totalitarianism*. Since then, a cascading series of stranger-multiplying empirical conditions and events has disrupted political theory's conventional sovereign-and-citizen storyline.

To the extent that they had mused on the citizen/stranger distinction at all, canonical theorists tended to view both figures as unambiguous identities and the citizen/stranger relation as purely external. Admittedly, the notion that every native of political society has a stranger deep inside him (and later, her) was not completely unimaginable to pessimists or "realists" such as St. Augustine and Thomas Hobbes, who saw natural drives and desires lurking beneath the surface of civilized life as threats to civic peace and consequently as appropriate targets of sovereign laws and prohibitions. Indeed, such realists not only anticipated but also outdid Freud in viewing animalistic or egoistic human passions as ever-present "aliens" in the soul or psyche of all members of political society that required constant cultural and political repression.

Nevertheless, most realist *and* idealist political thinkers ignored a host of other perplexing citizen/stranger entanglements to which, once again, Freud was exquisitely alert. Augustine perhaps came closest to acknowledging such entanglements when he remarked that the birth of political society per se and the birth of every new political society after that must be counted as acts of fratricide – suggesting that those whom conationals now see as foreigners, and as strangers on that account, they once had seen as "brothers," and that characteristics currently parceled out between collective self and other that have come to count as telltale signs of their essential difference from one another were once family resemblances shared by self and other alike. But Augustine's denial of any intrinsic truth to the line dividing one politically organized people from another was rooted in his religious belief that the only division between human beings that mattered was the one between those who loved things of the spirit and those who loved things of the flesh; that the only two cities that were intrinsically opposed were the City of God and the City of Man; that the only significant type of strangers were citizens of the heavenly city during their temporary sojourn on earth, where they lived among citizens of earthly cities whose sinfulness required political law and order to keep them in check; and, finally, that the only true exiles were the sinful, as they had deserted their own hearts, where God's voice spoke.

The Freud/Said Nexus

In contrast, Freud's skepticism toward essential collective identities and differences was profoundly secular. This secularism meant that any meaningful prescription for treating animosities on the terrain of national identities and differences, where the modern citizen/stranger distinction is most prominently located, would have to be "earthly" rather than "heavenly." Said clearly was drawn to Freud, on whom he wrote on multiple occasions, because the two shared a sensitivity to the plight of the ethnic (or racial or religious) stranger, a grasp of the psychological dynamics fueling divisions both within and between national groups, and a recognition of the historical contingency of those divisions, however much the groups might see their distinctiveness and mutual antagonisms as etched into a cosmic order of things. But Said also found Freud sympathetic for insisting, contra Augustine, that the transcendence of sociopolitical ills such as national persecution and exclusion requires, as its elemental prerequisite, not divine grace or otherworldly salvation but rather an understanding by human beings of how they came, often eagerly, to initiate and perpetuate those ills. In turn, that critical self-understanding hinges on the refusal of human beings to swallow national bromides about the superiority of their own identity group or to harbor notions of identity in general as something internally harmonious, without contradictions, fractures, and ruptures.

While noting, in *Freud and the Non-European*, the Eurocentric blinders that Freud's time and place produced for him,[4] Said represents Freud's commitment to critique as exemplary. In a piece he wrote for *Al-Ahram Weekly* after visiting a Freud exhibition in Vienna, Said associates an image of Freud "with his pen, ink and paper" with "a heroic unwillingness to rest in the consolidation of previously existing attitudes" and a determination to plumb and expose subterranean floors of "the house of human existence" and to submit "the turbulent actualities of human life … to the rational processes of judgement and criticism."[5] Likewise, in *Freud and the Non-European*, Said praises the father of psychoanalysis as a "remarkable instance of a thinker for whom scientific work was, as he often said, a kind of archeological excavation of the buried, forgotten, repressed and denied past … an explorer of the mind, of course, but also, in the philosophical sense, an overturner and a re-mapper of accepted or settled geographies and genealogies."[6] This is an especially generous tribute in light of Said's signature insistence on the culturally situated and interest-saturated character of all forms of knowledge, for Freud, in contrast, had an antiseptic view of scientific reason as a universal key that could be used to unlock human beings from their individual and collective delusions, if only they had the desire to *be* unlocked.

As much as he admired Freud's "stubborn" conviction that the struggle to understand "is not yet, is never, over,"[7] Said was far more preoccupied than Freud with the occasions on which intellectual struggles had a political impetus and/or political reverberations. Moreover, although neither a naïf nor a romantic, Said believed in the positive potentialities of the political, perhaps because he had seen what collective anti-colonial struggles had been able to achieve, even if he was by temperament, as he often put it, not a joiner of political movements and parties but a gadfly. Said's abiding faith that political action, informed by intellectual critique, could wring, even from the oppressive conditions fueling the Israeli/ Palestinian conflict, greater social justice as a necessary stepping-stone toward peace and reconciliation was at odds with Freud's bleak allusions to the recalcitrance of self/other oppositions. At times, these allusions seem absolutely defeatist, as when Freud suggests that any set of strangers who find themselves inhabiting the same railway compartment will unite as a little community against other strangers who later try to get in; or when he declares that a society can bind together any number of people in relations of love to reproduce the unity of the family on a broader scale, as long as there remain people outside that unity against whom the pent-up aggressive instincts of insiders can be redirected. It is thus against the grain of Freud's pessimism about negativities seemingly cemented into human nature that Said draws out the promising implications of Freud's person and his work for restaging the relationship between citizen and stranger (in Freud's terminology, between compact majority and alien minority, and in Said's, between native and exile).

In a nutshell, Said presents Freud as an "irremediably diasporic, unhoused character" who is fruitfully alienated both from the general tendency of groups to "resolve identity into some of the nationalist or religious herds in which so many people want so desperately to run" and from "the orthodoxy of his own community," with whom he had an "uneasy relationship."[8] Freud had good reason to despair, in the 1920s and 1930s, of the animus prompting a vindictive national majority to go after a vulnerable ethnic minority, but to Said's mind, the man was living proof that individuals have the capacity to refuse to comply with the demands of rigid collective identification on which such animus feeds. In addition, Freud conceived of identity as being, at both the individual and group level, non-self-identical, metamorphosing through a series of relationships with other identities. Both Freud's personal nonconformity and his identity concept are on display, Said argues, in Freud's depiction of Moses, the founder of the Jewish people, as "a non-European Egyptian."[9] In showing how being Jewish "did not begin with itself but, rather, with other identities (Egyptian and Arabian)," Freud challenges the self-complete identity of his own community – an always unpopular move, but especially so when one's community is as beleaguered as Freud's was.[10] At the same time, he extrapolates the general rule that identity is always a composite. Said echoes Isaac Deutscher in seeing such challenges and extrapolations as supporting the cosmopolitan principle of "the ultimate solidarity of man."[11] As such, they provide an optimistic counterweight to Freud's accent on the heritage of antagonisms between citizens and strangers that modern history has bequeathed to us, as well as to his gloomy proposal that an aggressive instinct that seeks outward discharge against others is as much a part of the psychic bedrock of humanity as the erotic instinct to bond or fuse with others (and, indeed, obtains certain of its satisfactions by erotic means).

Let me make three summary points about Freud, the crisscrossing ties between Freud and Said, and their shared sensibility on the question of the stranger. First, a concern for the stranger may be foreign to much of the tradition of Western political thought, but, as Freud illustrates, it has not been foreign to Western thought per se, although of course it could be argued that Freud was attuned to the position of the stranger precisely because other Westerners did not see him as really one of their own and made sure to let him know it. Second, as we have seen, Said reads Freud as denying the truth of essentially opposed collective identities both in his theory and in his relationship to his own identity group, a phrase that we consequently must always put in quotation marks. Similarly, Said can be read, in his reading of Freud, as denying, in both *his* ideas and person, an ontological opposition between Arabs and Jews, in distinction from a political opposition that has emerged out of, and so can be amended by, historical circumstances, decisions, and events. Said does not merely draw on Freud as a fellow archeologist to uncover intimacies between seemingly essentially estranged identities; he also displays, for all to see, his own intimate ties to this "non-Jewish Jew." By underlining his affinities with Freud on theoretical questions of identity, exile, and secularism, and by highlighting Freud's revelation of an Arab contribution to the birth of the Jews, Said presents himself and Freud, despite the current conflicts between their respective ethnic communities, as not aliens to one another but affiliates of one another – intellectually, temperamentally, and genealogically.

My third point is that Freud and Said can be congratulated for standing on the side of the stranger at the same time that they contest the hard-and-fast citizen/stranger divide. However, that posture, which is just as urgent to adopt today as it was in Freud's period, is doomed to political impotence unless the sensibility that informs it percolates through the world's popular majorities so that it can be democratically institutionalized in the admission and membership rules and practices of what we still conceive of as nation-states. Until then, visions of a culturally homogeneous and territorially self-enclosed national body, trumpeted by government officials, right-wing populists, and demagogues, and resonating with many ordinary hearts and minds, are likely to continue to appeal to a subsegment of citizens watching strangers massed at the borders of their home countries. In turn, strangers repudiated en masse by such citizens will be tempted to dream of a sheltering political entity of their own that can save them from all future repudiations.

Natives, Exiles, and the Politics of Loss

If I were to limit these reflections to the question of how strangers ought to be received by the countries on the shores of which they wash up, I might next turn to designs for improving that reception that have been sketched out over the last few decades, including designs by political theorists who have taken their cues from Arendt rather than from Aristotle and others. Suggested improvements include recognizing that "We the People" is always a project-in-the-making in which those barred from the "We" yesterday help to reconstitute "the People" today; increasing the porosity of national borders and extending civil and social rights to aliens while easing their path to citizenship; elasticizing the rules of membership in national bodies to conform as much as possible with universal moral principles, without denying the inescapable contradiction between national particularism and moral universalism; offering unconditional hospitality to foreigners, migrants, refugees, and internal strangers on the part of those at home in their own countries; awarding the right to stay to aliens on the grounds of their physical presence in a place where they have developed place-specificities and obligations; creating states without nations; opening the borders of rich countries to all peaceable migrants who wish to enter, after redistributing wealth across the globe; challenging the "entire architecture of sovereignty, all its borders, locks and doors, and internal hierarchies" and elevating the human right to free movement above the border-controlling right of sovereign states; and devising an international system in which individuals carry their rights to political voice, sustenance, and security wherever they go.[12]

While some scholars offer empirical accounts of how aliens are claiming the prerogatives of citizenship without asking the permission of sovereign states,[13] most make normative arguments or ideal proposals for supplying migrants, refugees, and exiles with rights in strange lands, or at least in strange lands that supply those rights to their own citizens. Such normative arguments and ideals conflict with one aspect of exilic reality and another aspect of native reality that may be incongruous politically but are related at the psychological level. First, however advantageous they may be in other ways, legal/political improvements to the status of exiles abroad cannot provide an antidote for the exile's longings for the texture of life as it was lived at home and the debilitating traumas of dislocation that can be set off by the sudden disappearance of that texture. As Said notes in his most poignant reflections on the subject, the exilic condition, for all its enhancing qualities – its "eccentric angles of vision," its "double perspective," its firsthand grasp of the contingency of situations[14] – is also synonymous with a "terminal loss," an "unhealable rift," and a set of anguished "mutilations."[15] That synonymy threatens to condemn the exile to the experience of being "perpetually haunted and alone in an uncomprehending society," even when that society has relatively open entry and membership rules.[16] What is the solution to this sickness of the heart, which no law or state policy can properly treat? Exilic nationalism declares that the only cure for such isolation and desolation is the restoration of exiles to their rightful place as members of a national people in "communal habitation" in their native homeland, where they can be reconnected to "their roots, their land, their past." However, as Said rightly reminds us, every national restoration project promises to reinstate the citizen/stranger distinction in inverted form. To the extent that it succeeds in turning exiles into natives inhabiting their own country, it opens "the perilous territory of not-belonging" in that country to someone else – not because every national restoration project is exclusionist in intent, but because of the intrinsic logic of the nation-state, ethnic or civic.[17]

Second, as Freud reminds us in his more jaundiced way, natives are even more likely than exiles to identify with their own life world as a magnification and confirmation of their own egos and to see everything outside their world as unnervingly alien. One might reject the psychoanalytic claim that natives will balk at extending their love to an even broader swath of humanity than an exclusivist national identity requires them to do because they would have to repress their aggressive instincts toward the same broader swath. Nevertheless, the attachment of many ordinary people everywhere to lineaments of their own life worlds and their unease with those who are physically inside those life worlds but culturally outside those lineaments make it dubious that all natives will embrace the citizenship reforms that cosmopolitan theorists urge on them. Furthermore, native unease with the stranger has a habit of metastasizing into overt hostility when the native's familiar patterns of existence have been subjected to stress by other forces beyond their comprehension and control, economic forces first and foremost. It is not only that natives are prone to misrecognizing strangers in their midst, who are also beyond their comprehension and control, as the source of those other problems. In addition, they are likely to see those strangers as competitors for scarce resources. As the right-wing Zionist Vladimir Jabotinsky once quipped in reference to the Eastern European antagonism toward the Jewish stranger, "[I]t's either my son or the Jew's son, for there's only one loaf."[18] Or, in the reverse context of Israeli Jewish antagonism toward Palestinian Arabs (reverse because here it is the stranger who presses the point against the native), "[I]t's either my son or the Palestinian's son, for there's only one sliver of land."

By now the reader may have deduced that the exile's longing for home is not entirely dissimilar to the resistance of natives to the stranger who, in Georg Simmel's words, "comes today and stays tomorrow" (as opposed to the wanderer who briefly appears and then disappears).[19] Thus, for example, we see a sense of loss that resembles the exilic sense, although in the form of a phantasmic anticipation rather than an accomplished fact, in the protests of European right-wing populists against "too many" Syrian and African exiles being forced on them, as well as of American right-wing populists against immigrants who "destroy our way of life." This is not to deny the paranoid fears, racist hatreds, and sadistic impulses in nativism that beg as much for psychiatric as for political treatment. It is rather to suggest a point of human contact between the exile's and the native's desire for the company of others who are, in their linguistic associations, social habits, everyday routines, and ways of shaping and inhabiting a landscape, more like than unlike themselves. It is also to suggest that unless the emotional impact of actual and imagined loss is ameliorated respectively for the exile and the native, reconfiguring citizenship in the direction of what Said would have called an enlarged humanity is fated to remain a thought experiment. This is not only because, in liberal democratic societies, more generous entry rules and more equal rights for citizens and strangers inside the borders of those societies hinge on legislative and juridical changes dependent in some way on popular votes. It is also because liberalizing legal rules and rights is insufficient to defuse a hostile social environment for strangers and even may exacerbate such hostility, as both Arendt and Jabotinsky noted with respect to the increase in majority resentment toward legally emancipated European Jews.

What prevents critics of exclusive citizenship from addressing the gap between cosmopolitan ideals and practical politics where, despite or perhaps because of the many pressures of globalization, parochial structures of feeling prevail that can verge on or at times explode into xenophobia? One answer to this question, when those critics are normative political theorists, is that inhabiting the pristine realm of the "ought," not the recalcitrant realm of the "is," is what political theorists professionally do. A second answer is that many intellectuals are flummoxed by parochial structures of feeling because their own structures of feeling are quite different. After all, academics, journalists, artists, technocrats, and policy makers from New York to New Delhi tend to be more metropolitan in outlook and habits than the general population in their own countries, more at ease in multiple geographical locations and hybrid cultural settings, more secure in knowledge economies, and better acquainted with the pleasures of globe-trotting than the pains of coerced homelessness. In these respects, they have little in common with the less physically mobile and more economically precarious segments of their own societies. They also have little in common with exiles – unless they happen to be, like Said and (metaphorically and ultimately literally) Freud, intellectuals who have been exiled themselves, and even then they are likely to have greater resources at their disposal than most others who share that plight. But there is, in addition to these two reasons for a disjuncture between the sensibility of intellectuals and the sensibility of native and exilic masses, a third reason that pertains specifically to intellectuals trained in the Western political theoretical tradition.

If we return for a moment to that tradition, we will find another failing relevant to our topic in addition to a lack of interest in the stranger in political society. This failing does not afflict every Western canonical thinker. Edmund Burke, for example, is not guilty of it, nor is Rousseau or Hegel, even though each of them can be found guilty of other things. However, the classical fathers of liberal individualism – Thomas Hobbes, John Locke, and J. S. Mill – can be charged (as Uday Mehta *has* charged them in *Liberalism and Empire*) with being impervious to the qualitative aspects of place – the physical landscape, sights and smells, linguistic sensibilities, and habits of sociability – that make the country of departure more resonant for the exile than the country of arrival, regardless of the difficulties that drove the exile out. As I have suggested, the same qualitative specificities of people and place make the country of arrival resonant enough for many segments of its own native population that they may hesitate to welcome strangers en masse with open arms, a hesitance that can only increase the exile's sense of dislocation and isolation. While particular attachments may be felt and expressed at the level of the village or city neighborhood or subregion of a country, they are most ominous for the stranger when they are mobilized at the level of the sovereign nation-state.

If we may use the term *style of thought* to indicate a set of abstract ideas that hang together, as distinct from thinkers who may exhibit that style without endorsing every one of those ideas, we can say that liberal individualism as a style of thought is free from the nativist prejudices against the stranger described previously. At the same time, it is free for the same reason that it is more obtuse than communitarian philosophies to the longings for home that can destroy the stranger's chances for happiness and as well as to the nightmares of intrusion that disturb the native's sleep. Both that freedom and that obtuseness can be traced to liberal individualism's tendency to view places as physical containers of accumulated utilities and resources that serve as means to personal ends, and persons as identical in their abstract individuality, for whom particular social fabrics and historical contexts operate solely as external constraints on, rather than constitutive frames for, thought and action. On the one side, classical liberal individualism, and even more so neoliberal individualism, views the productive potentialities of places as important, and it is capable of welcoming the stranger to enhance those potentialities or rejecting the stranger for being likely to deplete them, depending on the circumstances. But the sensuous, meaning-laden, and social-historical particularities of places, and their contribution to a collectively enjoyed (or suffered) life world, are, to a mentality that can barely digest the idea of collectivities, inconsequential. Whatever risk the stranger might be thought to bring to the perpetuation of the native's life world is also, then, inconsequential. Indeed, perpetuation per se is looked down on from this angle as something retrograde.

On the other side, liberal individualism views all developed human beings as rational choosers of the best means to satisfy their diverse and ever-multiplying wants, as individuals whose highest value is their own autonomy to pursue the good as they individually see it, and as citizens who see political societies as a means to protect their private liberty, property, and lives from the incursions of others. Their instrumentalist view of places and atomistic view of persons help explain why many neoliberal individualists are avid enthusiasts of mobility inside and across nation-states. These same views about places and persons also explain why liberal individualists who nonetheless object to the arrival of strangers in their own countries do not do so because they fear the unsettling effects of outsiders on familiar collective life patterns. They object instead because they fear that those strangers will bring with them a collectivist ethos at odds with an individualist one and because of the opposite fear (which right-wing populists also share) that all the world's poor, spurred by the calculative self-interest that is supposedly the bedrock motivation of all individuals, will flock to rich countries for a share of the material resources that the natives of those countries have corralled for themselves.

Conclusion

In *Modernity and Ambivalence*, Zygmunt Bauman asserts that the stranger rattles the modern polity by failing to fall neatly within the category of either the citizen or the foreigner. The stranger's undecidability in being neither fully inside nor fully outside the national society disturbs the sovereign state, which seeks to maintain control over its people and territory by strictly distinguishing between friends *in here* and enemies *out there*. That same ambiguity also disturbs members of the native population who are discomforted whenever boundary lines dividing one thing from another are blurred, whenever anomalies and incongruities appear, and whenever otherness emerges that is near to instead of far away from them.[20]

Perhaps one of the most unsettling yet enriching incongruities in the context of the modern nation-state is the stranger's potentiality for combining worldliness, an existentially significant rather than touristic tie to his or her newly adopted society, and a deep reservoir of feelings toward an absent life world. Although not every stranger straddles or even wants to straddle these antinomies, Said clearly did. More generally, he had the complexity of mind to realize that, in human affairs, A and not-A can hold true at the same time. In his memoir and many of his interviews, he describes his fraught relationships with his father, with British-inflected Egypt and Israeli-controlled Palestine, and with his country of work and residence, the United States. His tango with undecidability, as evidenced in his simultaneous affirmation of universalism and particularism, detachment and engagement, solitude and solidarity, the emancipatory promise of knowledge and the always-compromised conditions of knowledge-formation can be seen as the positive product of this series of connections and estrangements. In turn, the understanding that it is possible and indeed preferable to be alert to the connected histories of all the world's places and to the specificities of *this* history in *this* place, to be contrapuntal in perspective rather than either myopically chauvinistic or cosmopolitan in the blasé sense, and to be equally insistent on a shared humanity and the need to win justice for a particular people is one of the gifts in intellectual and emotional acuity that Said (along with other strangers) has bequeathed to us.

As a tribute to this gift, let me conclude with an A and not-A that has yet to be fully grasped by those who contest the exclusivity of modern nation-states. At this dangerous moment in world politics, when the conflict between the native in the West and the exile to the West is fast reaching a boiling point, two disparate social interests must, I think, be melded into a new political synthesis to stave off greater catastrophes for the stranger and the citizen alike. More than a century ago, Jabotinsky learned the bitter lesson that economic distress exacerbates the resistance of natives to strangers in their midst. In light of that lesson, but also to ward off the kind of national restoration project that Jabotinsky championed in response to it, anti-exclusionist movements today must shoulder a double task. They must fight for the exile's right to have rights, *and* they must fight for the economic security of unemployed, working-class, and sinking middle-class natives – even natives who think their problems would be solved by barring exiles from their countries and throwing immigrants out.

There are limits to what can be accomplished through a political movement on behalf of both immigrants and economically distressed natives, including immigrants yesterday who have become economically distressed natives today. Such a movement cannot, by itself, eradicate either native racism or class inequality. It cannot directly assuage the stranger's longings for home and so is not sufficient to counter the self-image of exilic nationalism as the best cure for those longings. However, it does target one serious obstacle to the native's openness to the exile and thus to the exile's freedom to refashion elements of its familiar mode of life in a new setting, where those elements optimally will contribute to a broader cultural mélange. While Said's interest in socioeconomic issues may have been less than energetic, he would, I think, appreciate the value in materially ameliorating native class anxieties to ease the way for that openness and that freedom. In turn, as both Freud's and Said's lives and life works attest, the syncretic amalgam of native and stranger influences *on* society is the truest meaning of the exile's integration *into* society, in the West and probably everywhere on earth.

Notes

1 This quotation appears in Julia Kristeva, *Strangers to Ourselves*, trans. Leon S. Roudiez (New York: Columbia University Press, 1991), p. 56.
2 Sigmund Freud, "An Autobiographical Study" (1924), in *The Freud Reader*, ed. by Peter Gay (New York: W. W. Norton, 1989), p. 4.

3 I would like to note the complication that in all settler colonial states, populations that today claim that status of natives for themselves, and to whom the phrase "nativist politics" now applies, either descend from strangers who originally displaced native peoples or owe their native status today to that displacement. In this chapter, I use the term *native* to register the subjective self-understanding of contemporary citizens, not objective historical realities.

4 Edward W. Said, *Freud and the Non-European* (London: Verso, 2004), pp. 14–16.

5 Edward Said, "Heroism and Humanism," *Al-Ahram Weekly* 463 (January 2000), 6–12 (9).

6 Said, *Freud and the Non-European*, p. 27.

7 Said, "Heroism and Humanism," p. 9.

8 Said, *Freud and the Non-European*, p. 53.

9 Ibid., p. 54.

10 Ibid., p. 44.

11 Ibid., p. 52. Said here quotes from Isaac Deutscher's *The Non-Jewish Jew and Other Essays* (New York: Hill and Wang, 1968), p. 35, p. 40.

12 See, respectively: Jason Frank, *Constituent Moments: Enacting the People in Postrevolutionary America* (Durham, NC: Duke University Press, 2010); Seyla Benhabib, *The Rights of Others: Aliens, Residents and Citizens* (Cambridge: Cambridge University Press, 2004); Linda Bosniak, *The Citizen and the Alien: Dilemmas of Contemporary Membership* (Princeton, NJ: Princeton University Press, 2006); Jacques Derrida, "Avowing – The Impossible: 'Returns,' Repentance, and Reconciliation," trans. Gil Anidjar, in Elizabeth Weber, ed., *Living Together: Jacques Derrida's Communities of Violence and Peace* (New York: Fordham University Press, 2013), pp. 18–41, as well as the critical response to Derrida in Priya Kumar, "Beyond Tolerance and Hospitality: Muslims as Strangers and Minor Subjects in Hindu Nationalist and Indian Nationalist Discourse," in ibid., pp. 80–103; Paulina Ochoa Espejo, "Taking Place Seriously: Territorial Presence and the Rights of Immigrants," *The Journal of Political Philosophy* (Online. DOI: 10.1111)(2015), 2–21; Jacqueline Stevens, *States Without Nations: Citizenship for Mortals* (New York: Columbia University Press, 2010); Joseph H. Carens, *The Ethics of Immigration* (Oxford: Oxford University Press, 2013); Peter Nyers, "Abject Cosmopolitanism: The Politics of Protection in the Anti-Deportation Movement," in *The Deportation Regime: Sovereignty, Space, and the Freedom of Movement*, ed. by Nicholas De Genova and Nathalie Peutz (Durham, NC: Duke University Press, 2010), pp. 413–441, quotation from p. 439; Nicholas De Genova, "The Deportation Regime: Sovereignty, Space and the Freedom of Movement," in ibid., pp. 33–65.

13 See, e.g., Kamal Sadiq, *Paper Citizens: How Illegal Immigrants Acquire Citizenship in Developing Countries* (Oxford and New York: Oxford University Press, 2009); Ayten Gündoğdu, *Rightlessness in an Age of Rights: Hannah Arendt and the Contemporary Struggles of Immigrants* (New York: Oxford University Press, 2015); and Nyers, "Abject Cosmopolitanism."

14 Edward Said, "Intellectual Exile: Expatriates and Marginals" (1993), in *The Edward Said Reader*, ed. by Moustafa Bayoumi and Andres Rubin (New York: Vintage, 2000), pp. 377–378.

15 Edward W. Said, "Reflections on Exile," in *Reflections on Exile and Other Essays* (Cambridge, MA: Harvard University Press, 2000), pp. 173–174.

16 Ibid., p. 180.

17 Ibid., p. 177.

18 Vladimir Jabotinsky, *The Jewish War Front* (London: George Allen and Unwin, 1940), p. 62. Today such economic anxieties can be found not just among older generations of workers with antiquated skills who will die off soon enough but also among younger workers ill-equipped to meet the demands of the global knowledge economy, as well as among members of the sinking working and lower-middle classes. Many analyses of Brexit voters, Donald Trump supporters, and anti-immigrant sentiment in Eastern Europe support this point. See, for just one example, John Curtice, "Brexit: Behind the Referendum," *Political Insight* 7.2 (September 2016), 4–7.

19 Georg Simmel, "The Stranger," in *The Sociology of Georg Simmel*, ed. by Kurt H. Wolff (New York: Free Press, 1950), p. 402.

20 Zygmunt Bauman, *Modernity and Ambivalence* (Cambridge: Polity Press, 1991), p. 61.

CHAPTER II

Orientalism Today

Saree Makdisi

The publication of Edward Said's *Orientalism* in 1978 dramatically altered the nature of literary and sociocultural scholarship. The book drew together and amplified the arguments of what had been until then a variety of disparate critiques of the hegemonic culture of "the West" (including the works of feminist, Marxist, post-structuralist, and anti-colonial writers). But it also made people more aware of the highly contingent nature of such categories as "the West" and "the East" (or the "Orient") in the first place – and of the ways in which such categories must be actively produced by scholars, artists, poets, and historians, rather than being taken for granted as natural or inevitable essences.

In demonstrating the extent to which scholars and writers, far from being merely innocent and detached "observers," are complicit in the production of the very worldly reality that they claim to be merely re-presenting, the book pays particular attention to the relationship between Orientalist art, writing, and scholarship and the invention of the Orient, not only in the classical Orientalism of the eighteenth and nineteenth centuries but in the practice of contemporary Orientalism as well. According to Said, Orientalism today is no longer primarily the provenance of learned scholars (such as Sir William Jones, the greatest British Orientalist of the eighteenth century), but rather of intellectually clumsy media hacks and think-tank "experts," such as Martin Kramer and Daniel Pipes, whose work is as intimately bound up with the foreign policy apparatus of a neocolonial United States as Jones's work was with the East India Company administration in colonial India.

Lord Byron famously referred to the Orient as one of the "isle[s] of my imagination," a claim that allows us to address one of the main points made in *Orientalism*. Said argues that the Orient is the product of what he calls the "imaginative geography" of Orientalists like Byron and Jones. Drawing on the work of Foucault and other theorists, Said distinguishes this "imaginative geography" from what he calls "positive geography."[1]

He argues that we can think of imaginative geography as something that goes beyond, or gets added to, positive knowledge, by which he means concrete knowledge of actual realities. Thus, for example, imaginative geography provides "the lenses through which the Orient is experienced,"[2] and it allows Said to distinguish "the East itself" from "the East made known,"[3] or, in other words, the "actual Orient," to which positive knowledge pertains, from the fictive Orient generated through imaginative geography.

This is obviously a problematic distinction – for how are we to separate the "positive" from the "imaginative"? By what criteria are we to decide where the one ends and the other begins? How do we distinguish the "representations" from the "realities"? Said chooses not to resolve this dilemma: "We need not decide here," he writes, "whether this kind of imaginative knowledge infuses history and geography or whether in some way it overrides them. Let us just say for the time being that it is there as something *more* than what appears to be merely positive knowledge."[4] This is one of the most difficult moments in Said's argument, but it is also one of the most productive because much of the force of *Orientalism* emerges from this point. And it is no surprise that much of the criticism directed at Said's book is focused on just this crucial issue – which remains problematic for many readers.

Some critics have picked up where Said left off, elaborating his arguments, amplifying and adding detail to strokes he sometimes (and often of necessity) painted with a broad brush. Said, for example, sometimes makes both the Orient and even Orientalism too monolithic – as though there could be no way for a Westerner to view the East other than through the one set of lenses provided by Orientalism; as though, in other words, there has been only one Western way of seeing the East, and as though that way has not changed over the past 2,000 years (thus Said sometimes moves too quickly between and hence collapses together, say, Aeschylus and Jones, Herodotus and Goethe, Napoleon and Henry Kissinger, "Monk" Lewis and Bernard Lewis). It should be pointed out, however, that he also specified very clearly that his primary interest is in the specifically *modern* form of Orientalism that emerged at the end of the eighteenth century at around the time of Napoleon's invasion of Egypt.

Said's approach pushes us to see the extent to which all knowledge is situated in – and participates in the making of – the worldly realities that we inhabit. Such a proposition makes it much more difficult, or even impossible, to locate a single "objective" standpoint from which to accumulate knowledge and evaluate a golden Truth. This approach thus contests and undermines the authority of coercive systems of knowledge such as Orientalism – whose very claims to validity depend on the privileging of one particular standpoint, that of the West – by bringing to the surface a previously repressed, silenced, or ignored plurality of voices and perspectives. Reality should be seen no longer as a level field that can be known and dominated from one particular standpoint, but rather as an uneven and heterogeneous terrain, in which the project to locate a common ground takes on momentous political importance. Reality can now be seen not as an inert given that we inherit from the past without being able to question it, but rather as a common or shared possession in which all participate. In making this claim, Said reaffirms the point made earlier by Marx and Vico: Human beings make their own history. The reality that we inhabit and the futures that we contemplate should no longer be seen as the provenance of licensed experts and certified authorities to whom all knowledge and decision-making should be left – but rather as something in whose making all can take part.

Scholars following in the wake of Said have deepened many of his claims, filling in some of his broad strokes with fine details, allowing us to see a variety of Orientalisms that have over the decades produced a number of different and sometimes conflicting Orients, and allowing us to see some of the ways in which the production of the "Orient" was variously modified, accepted, challenged, or altered by Orientals. Indeed, most of what is today recognized in the American and European academy as the fields of colonial and postcolonial studies emerged directly from engagements with and elaborations of Said's influential book, though over the past two or three decades these fields have taken on identities of their own as scholars have diverged from the set of initial studies provoked by *Orientalism*.

A great many critics, however, have been all too willing to reify Said's highly provisional distinction between "positive" and "imaginative" knowledge, but they ask how we can get access to the concrete realities whose true nature is obscured by the imaginative categories through which we approach them. If the representations of Orientalism mask the realities, how, they ask, can we acquire genuine knowledge of the Other – how can we get at the "real" Orient, if not to dominate it, then at least to learn about its cultures and peoples? Hence, one criticism that is often leveled at Said is that, although he does an admirable job of demonstrating the ways in which Orientalism has historically mythicized the Orient – a task he continued long after the book in his confrontation with Zionist mythography, and in his criticism of the work of such pseudo-authorities as

Thomas Friedman, he does not provide a set of tools with which to analyze and interpret the underlying reality in a more "objective" way. As recently as March 2005, Daniel Lazare protests in a really quite vicious review in *The Nation* that *Orientalism* is "rife with contradictions that over the years have become more difficult to ignore." Lazare attacks what he claims is Said's "badly made argument," claiming that "in Said's hands, Orientalism becomes a metaphysical force, over and above history and politics and other such mundane factors."[5]

Contradictions can sometimes be productive, however, and such critics are, for the most part, either unable or unwilling to grasp the enormous potential offered by the various ambiguities that Said leaves open: a potential that Said put to use in much of his other work. For it is precisely by *not* cleanly resolving the ambiguous distinction between "positive" and "imaginative" knowledge, or the distinction between reality and representation, that the most powerful component of Said's argument is preserved. To say that the Orient does not exist *as such* is not to say that the complex realities gathered under the designation of "the Orient" do not exist, but rather that they do not exist as specifically or essentially Oriental realities and, moreover, that there is ultimately no way to achieve pure or genuinely "positive" knowledge of them, which is precisely the sort of knowledge that the proponents of Orientalism have claimed – and still do claim – to produce. For Said, all forms of knowledge are contingent rather than absolute.

Perhaps the best way to grasp Said's argument on this point is, in effect, to invert it and to see that what he is warning us about are the claims to absolute knowledge, or the claims to a real, literal, actual distinction between what some consider to be real, literal actual entities called, respectively, "The West" and "The East," if not "The West" and "The Rest." Such claims are essential not merely to various forms of Orientalism but also to such derivative arguments as, for example, Samuel Huntington's absurd notion of a clash of supposedly impermeable, watertight, hermetically sealed, and internally homogeneous "civilizations," where what is at stake is not merely a set of claims about a degenerate, violent, despotic, sexually repressed, and religiously crazed Islam but also the opposite claim, about a secular, modern, and of course morally virtuous West.[6]

Indeed, given the popularity of Huntington's thesis as well as the contemporary resurgence of full-blown Orientalism among policy makers, it would be folly to understate the extent to which Orientalism continues – to this day – to claim an absolute certainty of and a monopoly on knowledge, both of the Eastern other and of the narrating, representing,

Western self. Sadly, perhaps the best way to assess the enduring value of Said's book is to reflect on some of the lessons *not learned* from it by considering the role of Orientalism in contemporary cultural and political discourse in the United States. Here, unfortunately, we are presented with an embarrassment of riches, from which I will only have time to select one – albeit arguably the central – example, Bernard Lewis.

Having essentially demolished the epistemological and ideological basis of the bulk of Lewis's work in *Orientalism*, Edward Said felt able to dismiss him in the book's 1994 afterword as "almost comically persistent."[7] Lewis's verbosity, Said argues in that text,

> scarcely conceals both the ideological underpinnings of his position and his extraordinary capacity for getting nearly everything wrong. Of course, these are familiar attributes of the Orientalists' breed, some of whom have at least had the courage to be honest in their active denigration of Islamic, as well as other non-European peoples. Not Lewis. He proceeds by distorting the truth, by making false analogies, and by innuendo, methods to which he adds that veneer of omniscient tranquil authority which he supposes is the way scholars talk.[8]

Not having modified any of his essential arguments in fifty years, Bernard Lewis may indeed be thought of as persistent, but the comic nature of that persistence is probably overshadowed by the tragedy that in the wake of the September 11 attacks his strand of Orientalism has come to provide a central element in the worldview of the current US administration. In a laudatory assessment of his work in the *Slate* in November 2001, Emily Yoffe describes how Lewis suddenly found himself at the center of the Bush administration's thinking of how to deal with the new threat from the Orient, namely, Osama bin Laden and so-called militant Islam. Dismissing Said's critiques of Lewis out of hand, Yoffe claims that Lewis offers "one-stop shopping for baffled Westerners needing a coherent worldview to explain our current situation."[9]

And what do we find if we turn to Professor Lewis for some explanation as to why "they hate us"? On Lewis's view, it turns out that Islam (by which he means the Arab world in general) is something like a record that's been stuck for a thousand years. "It should by now be clear," Lewis wrote in a 1990 article in *The Atlantic* called "The Roots of Muslim Rage," from which Huntington would derive the concept that would make him famous in turn, "that [in confronting Islam] we are facing a mood and a movement far transcending the level of issues and policies and the governments that pursue them. This is no less than a clash of civilizations – the perhaps irrational but surely historic reaction of an ancient rival against our

Judeo-Christian heritage, our secular present, and the worldwide expansion of both."[10] The point here is not merely that the Muslim world is basically full of rage at a Judeo-Christian secularity (and note the self-contradiction), but that Lewis authorizes himself to speak of a Muslim world that he supposes is not only absolutely homogeneous but also, like some spoiled child, has remained essentially the same for more than a thousand years of seething bitterness and jealousy at Western "success" and modernization. The core problem, in other words, is that the Muslim world has failed to modernize because there is something inherent in Islam that makes it resistant to modernity – something that Lewis, in a *New Yorker* article meant to explain the September 11 attacks, argues is Islam's wholesale "rejection of modernity."[11]

Western culture, Lewis argues in his triumphal, "I told you so," post–September 11 book, *What Went Wrong: The Clash between Islam and Modernity in the Middle East*, is inherently harmonic and peaceful. "A distinguishing characteristic of Western music," he asserts confidently, in a passage that I am sure that the participants in this conference will find particularly intriguing,

> is polyphony or counterpoint. This begins in its simplest form with the choir, in which matched voices sing different notes in a planned sequence to produce a combined effect; then comes the keyboard instrument, matching the ten fingers of the two hands, following different routes in a common purpose; and finally the musical ensemble, from duets and trios to the full orchestra. Different performers play together, from different scores, producing a result that is greater than the sum of its parts.[12]

Having revealed his talents as a music critic, Lewis then goes on to address the entire ensemble of Western culture:

> [W]ith a little imagination one may discern the same feature in other aspects of Western culture – in democratic politics and in team games, both of which require the cooperation, in harmony if not in unison, of different performers playing different parts in a common purpose ... One may also detect the same feature in two distinctly Western literary creations – the novel, and still more the theater ... The same qualities may be seen, ... [Lewis adds, without so much as a trace of modesty,] ... in a more obvious form, in the work of the historian, and indeed distinguishes his writing from that of the chronicler or analyst.

And there's one final feature of this sweeping argument: "Polyphony, in whatever form, requires exact synchronization. The ability to synchronize, to match times exactly, is an essential feature of modernity and therefore a requirement of modernization."[13]

By now, of course, it's obvious where Lewis is going with this line of argument (if that's what it is). Muslims and Arabs are incapable of telling the time, or at least of doing anything in a timely and synchronized manner (clearly he's forgotten that the attacks of September 11 involved a finely choreographed and highly technical ballet of murder and destruction); their music is cacophonic rather than harmonic; their histories are all really chronicles; their novels – well, perhaps they don't even have novels (Lewis never says); their poetry, religion, values, in sum, their entire culture is inherently, essentially, nonharmonic, nondemocratic, non- or even anti-modern.

Never mind that Lewis's grotesque celebration of the inherent superiority of Western culture has no way to account for the work of William Blake, or T. S. Eliot, or Ezra Pound, or, come to think of it, poetry in general, not even love sonnets and limericks, or – shifting media – the art of Pablo Picasso or Vincent van Gogh or Edvard Munch, or – shifting media again – the music of Arnold Schoenberg or Igor Stravinsky, much less John Coltrane or Ornette Coleman. Never mind that the novels not merely of Franz Kafka and James Joyce and David Jones and Joseph Conrad and Thomas Hardy and Thomas Pynchon and Jean Genet and William S. Burroughs but also, in many cases, those of Charles Dickens (*Bleak House*, e.g.) or William Godwin (*Caleb Williams*) or, for that matter, most of the great eighteenth-century novelists (Fielding, Smollett, Swift, Defoe) don't work in the way that Lewis wants them to. For the point isn't that by Lewis's definition harmonic Western culture is something that – if it can be said to have existed – emerged sometime after Romanticism in the 1830s and was blasted to pieces on the first day of the Battle of the Somme in 1916, though signs of its impending doom are already there to see in the work of Hardy, Conrad, and H. G. Wells years before that. The point is that Lewis's account of a fatally flawed Islamic culture is equally, if not even more, mendacious than his absurd mischaracterization of so-called Western culture. This mindless juxtaposition of a West founded in a culture that inherently leads to freedom, democracy, women's rights, modernity, and the free market, and a Muslim East that is inherently unfree, undemocratic, and anti-modern is something that permeates Lewis's work through and through.

And yet Lewis's simple-minded account of the supposed clash of civilizations has come to define the ideological core of a violently interventionist American foreign policy. "Call it the Lewis Doctrine," writes a staff reporter for the *Wall Street Journal*; "Though never debated in Congress or sanctified by presidential decree, Mr Lewis's diagnosis of the Muslim world's malaise, and his call for a US military invasion to seed democracy in the Mideast, have helped define the boldest shift in US foreign policy in 50 years."[14] Shortly after the September 11 attacks, Lewis appeared on television. "The question people are asking is why they hate us. That's the wrong question," he said,

> in a sense, they've been hating us for centuries, and it's very natural that they should. You have this millennial rivalry between two world religions, and now from their point of view, the wrong one seems to be winning ... More generally, you can't be rich, strong, successful and loved, particularly by those who are not rich, not strong and not successful. So the hatred is something almost axiomatic. The question which we should be asking is why do they neither respect nor fear us?[15]

It was shortly after this that presidential advisor Karl Rove summoned the octogenarian Lewis to the White House to address the National Security Council. According to the *Wall Street Journal* account, "The historian recited the modern failures of Arab and Muslim societies and argued that anti-Americanism stemmed from their own inadequacies, not America's. Mr Lewis also met privately with Mr Bush's national security adviser, Condoleezza Rice," and, soon afterward, Mr. Bush was spotted "carrying a marked-up article by Mr Lewis among his briefing papers." White House staffer David Frum says that "Bernard comes with a very powerful explanation for why 9/11 happened. Once you understand it, the policy presents itself afterward." Talking with Lewis, according to Richard Perle, is "like going to Delphi to see the oracle." Bernard Lewis, says Paul Wolfowitz, has taught us "how to understand the complex and important history of the Middle East, and use it to guide us where we will go next to build a better world for generations to come."

Sadly, we now all know where the policies of the so-called Lewis Doctrine have led the people of the United States, and – much more forcefully and immediately of course – the people of Afghanistan and Iraq.

And even more sadly we also know that there is as yet no sustained scholarly, let alone public, movement to reveal the Orientalism of Lewis for what it is, much less to abandon it. For one thing, Lewis is far from the only person proclaiming the inherent incompatibility between "Islam" and "The West," which has taken hold even among otherwise quite distinguished scholars. Here is my colleague Anthony Pagden, professor of history at UCLA, in the epilogue to his book *Peoples and Empires*:

> The struggle between Islam and the West is now ... no longer one between competing religions, between peoples each of whom look upon the other as

deluded and aberrant, yet all of whom belong to worlds that are mutually intelligible ... [Thus, Pagden concludes,] ... [T]he struggle is between two mutually unintelligible worlds. In one world are the Muslim militants who still cling to beliefs that correspond very closely to those Saladin's soldiers might have shared ... [and] ... in the other world is the modernized West (which now includes most of Southeast Asia), overwhelmingly secular as regards all matters of policy and almost all of its social and domestic life as well. Between the two [worlds] any dialogue on almost anything of real significance is virtually impossible. They may be able to tolerate each other when they do not conflict, but they can never assimilate with each other. All the other great religions of the world – Hinduism, Buddhism, Taoism, Confucianism – have succeeded in accommodating themselves to modernity, and in some cases have hasted its progress. Islam, by contrast, at least in its dominant form, remains resolutely opposed.[16]

This is the assessment not of a media hack but of a respected scholar at a major research university. Similar sentiments abound. "To come bearing modernism to those who want it but who rail against it at the same time," proclaims Fouad Ajami (and I don't have time here to go into the distinction between *modernity*, which I think he means, and *modernism*, as in the work of Pound and Eliot and Picasso, which I think he doesn't mean in this instance, though finally he may not know the difference), "to represent and embody so much of what the world yearns for and fears – that is the American burden ... Today, the United States carries the disturbance of the modern to older places – to the East and intermediate zones in Europe."[17] "We are eager to come out well from this expedition to Iraq, and the transfer of authority marks the beginning of a new relationship between Iraqis and their American liberators ... [Even if] it would have been easier and more comforting had we not redeemed their liberty with such heartbreaking American losses." "Our writ," "Our mission," "Our time," "Our stewardship," "Our soldiers": Ajami, a Lebanese American with a thick Lebanese accent in English, is desperate to let his readers know that he too is one of "us."

Perhaps it would be best to close this brief survey of a resurgent Orientalism with even a passing mention of the abuse scandal at Abu Ghraib Prison near Baghdad. According to Seymour Hersh, the US army's interrogators had discovered that Arab men have a particular complex about sexuality, and would be particularly vulnerable to sexual humiliation, like being stacked in pyramids without any clothes on.[18] In his coverage of this event, neither Hersh nor any of the journalists who picked up on his story bothers to ask whether, say, German, French, or American men would particularly enjoy being stacked in pyramids or forced to

masturbate, or whether this is something that only Arab men are likely to
be bothered by. In any case, it turns out that the source of this brilliant
discovery is a book called *The Arab Mind*, originally published by the
Israeli Orientalist Rafael Patai in the 1970s; although it has been steadily
republished ever since, including in a 2002 edition that was required
reading for US army officers heading to Iraq.[19] The profound insights of
Patai's deep and meticulous scholarship include the claim that Arab
mothers ignore their baby daughters while fondling the penises of their
male children (p. 36); that Arabic is a notoriously "illogical" language
(p. 47) and one that is prone to "exaggeration and overemphasis" (p. 55);
that Arabs are pathologically obsessed with self-esteem (p. 102); that
there is "an all-encompassing preoccupation with sex in the Arab mind"
(p. 133), which explains the "sexual repression-frustration-aggression syn-
drome of the Arab personality" (p. 137); and that "loss of self control and
outbursts of temper" are normal for Arabs "because in the Arab view of
human nature no person is supposed to be able to maintain incessant,
uninterrupted control over himself" (p. 169); and finally, that "once
aroused, Arab hostility will vent itself indiscriminately on any and all
outsiders" (p. 171). What we are to gather from all this, explains the
sagacious and learned Mr. Patai, "is the picture of a human type which
readily and frequently throws off the restraints of discipline and, especially
in mass situations, is likely to go on a rampage." (And this from the man
who proclaims in the very first sentence of his book, "[W]hen it comes to
the Arabs, I must admit an incurable romanticism; nay, more than that, to
having had a lifelong attachment to Araby!").

As I said, this book was required reading at the US Army Staff College.
It has also been hailed by a number of American reviewers, writing as late
as 2002. "*The Arab Mind* is not for those wanting a short briefing on the
Middle East," writes the book reviewer for the Congressional Institute in
Washington. "[B]ut for those wanting a deep and sophisticated understanding ... of a people and culture that are affecting the future of the
world, look no further than *The Arab Mind*." Patai's book was first
published in 1973, admits Ken Ringle in *The Washington Post*, in October
2001, "but its truths would appear to live on."[20]

I must admit that I can't readily imagine a way to climb out from these
slippery depths back to the level of analysis where Said had taken us in
Orientalism. Perhaps the best thing would be simply to state the obvious,
which is that Orientalism has indeed returned in a full-blown form and
that, strangely enough, the most appropriate thing, the surest antidote to
this outbreak, would be to read Edward Said all over again, as though for
the very first time.

Notes

1 Edward Said, *Orientalism* (New York: Pantheon, 1978), p. 55.
2 Ibid., p. 58.
3 Ibid., p. 59.
4 Ibid., p. 55.
5 Daniel Lazare, "Jews without Borders," *The Nation*, March 9, 2005.
6 See Samuel Huntington, *The Clash of Civilizations and the Remaking of World Order* (New York: Simon and Schuster, 2009).
7 Edward Said, *Orientalism* (New York: Vintage, 1994), p. 337.
8 Ibid., p. 343.
9 Emily Yoffe, "Bernard Lewis: The Islam Scholar US Politicians Listen To," *Slate*, November 13, 2001.
10 Bernard Lewis, "The Roots of Muslim Rage," *The Atlantic*, September 1990.
11 Bernard Lewis, "The Revolt of Islam," *New Yorker*, November 19, 2001.
12 Bernard Lewis, *What Went Wrong?* (Oxford: Oxford University Press, 2002), p. 129.
13 Ibid., pp. 129–131.
14 Peter Waldman, "A Historian's Take on Islam Steers US in Terrorism Fight," *Wall Street Journal*, February 3, 2004.
15 Quoted in ibid.
16 Anthony Pagden, *Peoples and Empires* (New York: Modern Library, 2004), p. 173.
17 Fouad Ajami, "The Falseness of Anti-Americanism," *Foreign Policy*, October 30, 2009.
18 See Seymour Hersh, "Torture at Abu Ghraib," *New Yorker*, May 10, 2004.
19 See Rafael Patai, *The Arab Mind* (New York: Heatherleigh Press, 2002).
20 Ken Ringle, "The Crusaders' Giant Footprints," *Washington Post*, October 23, 2001.

CHAPTER 12

Political Economy and the Iraq War
Said and Arrighi

Robert Spencer

In a trenchant 1992 critique of the then emergent discipline of postcolonial studies, Aijaz Ahmad bemoaned the displacement of "an activist culture with a textual culture."[1] One particularly urgent question still facing postcolonialists is: How do we combine textual analysis, which is after all our specialism and an essential aspect of any worthwhile progressive project, with effective activism aimed ultimately at political and economic transformation? There are practical implications here, of course, but I want to focus on the methodological ones. It is, in my view, unarguable that, for all its methodological eclecticism, the one disciplinary weapon that has been largely absent from the arsenal of postcolonial criticism has been political economy. My argument is that Edward Said urges us to take up that particular cudgel, especially in his late commentaries on the buildup to the invasion of Iraq and its immediate aftermath in 2003, though others are better at showing us how to use it.

Among the great strengths of Said's work is its insistence on the historical continuities of imperialist ideology and practice. Another strength is Said's occasional willingness to point out the connections between imperialism and the accumulation of capital. But Said's work does not go into detail on that latter question. He does not define the phenomenon of neoliberalism or explain in detail the links between the resurgent imperialism of the United States since the end of the Vietnam War and the immediate as well as strategic goals of US capital. By contrast Giovanni Arrighi, the late Italian political economist, presents neoliberalism as a "US-led capitalist counter-offensive" against the social democratic aspirations of labor movements in the First World, against the very existence of the nominally socialist Second World, and against the revolutionary ideals of national liberation in the Third World.[2] Arrighi presents neoliberalism as a largely, though only temporarily, successful as well as concerted campaign waged by the owners and representatives of capital to counteract a serious crisis of profitability that afflicted world capitalism by the end of the 1960s.³ It is vital to remember that this period represented a profound and systemic as well as potentially existential political and economic crisis for capital, one brought about by the profit-squeezing aspiration of workers for full employment and high wages in the First World and in the postcolonial world by the real prospect that revolutionary regimes would cease to play the role of suppliers of cheap labor and primary commodities and instead seize control over their own resources. In Arrighi's *The Long Twentieth Century* (1994) and *Adam Smith in Beijing* (2007), neoliberalism stands unveiled as part of the longer-term campaign by the political and economic establishments in the United States and other leading nations to prolong and extend their supremacy. The war in Iraq was a gambit essayed in this larger strategy. One does not have to concur with Arrighi's speculative conclusion that we are currently witnessing the advent of a Sinocentric or multipolar world-system to sympathize with his broader argument that the American defeat in Iraq marks both the end of its decades-long drive to preside over the profitable expansion of the capitalist world economy and, therefore, the opening up of a variety of political and economic alternatives.⁴

As Said presents the matter, however, the war was motivated by a combination of cupidity and stupidity, by a barefaced greed for profit unconvincingly "justified" at the level of discourse in the corporate media and elsewhere by centuries-old Orientalist dogma about the altruism of Western power and the backwardness and passivity of the Middle East. An administration made up of cynical "oil men" and of functionaries of a political party totally and corruptly subordinated to the demands of US corporations saw the invasion as a chance to make a killing from oil revenue and reconstruction contracts. Arrighi demonstrates something that this account overlooks. The invasion was also seen by US political elites as a chance to forestall the long-term decline of US economic and political hegemony. The invasion was a predominantly strategic decision or rather a failed gamble made by a US political establishment that is relatively autonomous from vulgar considerations of immediate profit. The goal was ultimately to uphold the political and military authority of the United States and its regional allies by either cornering Iraqi oil or by deterring an independent Iraq as well as the United States' global and regional rivals from controlling that indispensable resource. Said's writings on the war in Iraq do not elucidate the connections between the immediate requirements of capital accumulation and the mediation of those requirements by the wide-angle strategic calculations of the US political establishment. For that kind of elucidation, we will have to examine the work of Arrighi.

In the process I hope to demonstrate the vital usefulness for postcolonial scholarship of political economy. I will define *political economy* here, after Arrighi, as the discipline that seeks to understand in various situations the relationship between "capitalist" and "territorialist" "modes of rule or logics of power," the interconnections between the control and accumulation of capital and the control and expansion of territory (*LTC*, 34).

Arrighi's argument is that the assertion of expansionist military power in Iraq was a bold but ultimately unsuccessful attempt to break out of the long-term relative stagnation of the US-centered world economy. Said was no Marxist, or at least he frequently expressed his skepticism about the political record of existing Communist regimes.[5] But my aim is to show that his public or journalistic writings emphatically *are* consistent with, though they neither explore in detail nor even directly state, the distinguishing Marxist proposition that, in Lenin's words, "[i]mperialism emerged as the development and direct continuation of the fundamental attributes of capitalism in general."[6] So what prevented Said from identifying the precise link between the imperialist occupation of Iraq and the specific requirements of American capital and of the wider capitalist system over which the United States presides? The answer is that Said rightly associated political economy with Marxism but wrongly refused Marxism for being crude and doctrinaire. Despite his admiration for individual Marxist thinkers whose interests were predominantly aesthetic or philosophical, such as Theodor Adorno, Georg Lukács, and C. L. R. James, Said dismissed Marx as an accessory of British imperialism and the intellectual and political tradition of Marx*ism* for being characterized largely by orthodoxy, "limitations and drawbacks," "failures," and "lack of reach."[7] This is despite the fact, as Ahmad observes, that "the vast majority of the socially enlightened and politically progressive critiques of colonialism had been affiliated with either Marxism or, at least, with the general cultural anti-imperialism which Marxism, and the communist movement generally, had helped to bring about."[8] It is the criticality and sheer range of the Marxist tradition that Said underrates, as Benita Parry has pointed out, plus its capacity to "explain modern colonialism and imperialism as integral to capitalism's beginnings, expansion, and ultimate global entrenchment" as well as "the ethics of solidarity that has marked the internationalist traditions of the radical left, traces of which are visible all the same in [Said's] urging professional criticism to engage with matters of inequality, injustice, and oppression at large."[9]

Despite his conviction that criticism, in the words of his mentor R. P. Blackmur, is "the formal discourse of an amateur," the ideal critic roving freely between disciplines to track down the various "worldly" origins and implications of texts, one discipline into which Said very rarely ventured was political economy.[10] Said shows us that the critical analysis of the discourses and ideologies of imperialism, which is obviously the very *raison d'être* of postcolonial studies, includes the probing of the pious homilies of Bush Jr. with the same critical acuity as one might dissect the poetry of Rudyard Kipling. We also need to make plain what Said, because of his unwarranted suspicion of Marxism, usually soft-pedaled: the inseparability of empire from capital and the susceptibility of both to critique and practical transformation. If we miss that fact then we miss understanding *why* the world is as it is and *what* prevents it from becoming *post*colonial.

In the months leading up to the war, Said argued again and again that the very discourse of "regime change," with its "fantasies about surgical strikes, clean war, high-technology battlefields, changing the entire map, creating democracy, and the like, all of it giving rise to ideas of omnipotence" and "wiping the slate clean," entailed an Orientalist-style ignorance of the obvious fact that Iraq is a place with a history and a population that cannot be made to conform passively to US expectations. Absent from the simplistic opposition between Western "freedom" and Arab tyranny was any sense of the real preferences and aspirations of a sophisticated and heterogeneous, albeit long-suffering, population. With the Bush administration listening only to exiles' reassurances that US troops would be greeted with open arms and bouquets of flowers, "the image of Iraq as in fact a large, prosperous, and diverse Arab country has disappeared; the image that has circulated both in media and policy discourse is of a desert land peopled by brutal gangs headed by Saddam."[11] The corporate media had by and large surrendered its obligation to elucidate the history and the complex social and ethnic makeup of the nation that military planners and Reaganite ideologues were preparing to overhaul. Nor did the media make much of an effort to interrogate the US or British governments' moral claim or right to make such consequential decisions about the destiny of an entire people whom they had condemned for years to poverty, malnutrition, and death by first arming and sponsoring Saddam's odious regime, waging war against it and then cack-handedly shoring it up with the murderous sanctions regime. Iraq's people simply "dropped out of sight," US policy toward the Middle East being based not on saintly altruism or the promotion of democracy but "on two mighty pillars, the security of Israel and plentiful supplies of inexpensive oil" (*FOIRM*, 216). The discourse of Orientalism had served over centuries to obscure the disparate histories and cultures of the Middle East with the aid of insistently repeated and self-serving clichés about Arab backwardness. Said's Palestinian compatriots' accounts of their history and aspirations had similarly been drowned out for a time by the strident legends of Zionism and Israeli nationalism. In almost the same way that the US news media had managed since the late 1970s to portray Islam not as a religion (with all of a religion's historical complexities and its differences of observation and interpretation) but a fundamentalist cult of violence. Said also argued that the unfortunate people of Iraq were being prepared for a violently imperialist "intervention" by a sustained campaign of misrepresentation: "An immense carpet of mystification and abstraction has therefore been laid down all over the Arab world by this effort at systematic dehumanization" (*FOIRM*, 218).

The long historical continuities between imperialisms past and present are forcefully emphasized in Said's commentaries. Precisely *why* the television news was so easily corralled into accepting the Bush administration's fantasies about "freedom promotion" and its lies about Saddam's links with al-Qaeda receives less attention from these essays, alas, but perhaps inevitably, in the succinct format of articles written for *Al-Ahram*, *Al-Hayat*, *The Guardian*, and the *London Review of Books*. In Said's *Covering Islam*, however, first published in 1981 in the wake of the Iranian hostage crisis, the media's submissiveness before the prevailing political and economic consensus was given a much lengthier and more detailed elucidation than the precise links between "colonial discourse" and French and British capitalism ever received in *Orientalism*. The overwhelming consensus about the benignity of American power, Said argues, "sets limits and maintains pressures" on individual reporters and organizations not because they dutifully reproduce government propaganda or because the media "mechanically reflect a certain class or economic group's interests,"[12] but because, quite simply, "the media are profit-seeking corporations and therefore, quite understandably, have an interest in promoting some images of reality rather than others."[13]

There is a great deal in *Covering Islam* to complement the careful exposition in Edward Herman and Noam Chomsky's *Manufacturing Consent* of the way in which a self-censoring media internalizes the priorities of political and economic power due to the reliance on advertising, the dependence on government and business "experts" for information, concentrated structures of ownership, and the transformation of news into entertainment in a saturated media market.[14] Similarly, Said's articles on the buildup to the war in Iraq are sensitive to the near disappearance of dissenting voices "from a mainstream media swollen with a surfeit of ex-generals and ex-intelligence agents, sprinkled with recent terrorism and security experts drawn from the Washington right-wing think tanks" in addition to reporters and news readers who had become "all-too-embedded sentinels of America's war" (*FOIRM*, 268). To have demonstrated the repetitive consistency of the corporate media's belligerent xenophobia is achievement enough, one might think, and to have reiterated the point once more in the context of the Iraq War is certainly a commendable feat. But how much more enabling is it to have not only demonstrated and censured that discourse but also explained it in relation to the interests and priorities of political and corporate "elites," in short, to have construed it not as a discourse at all, properly speaking, but as an ideology?

Said excoriates the hacks, pseudo-scholars, and biddable "experts" like Fouad Ajami and Kanan Makiya who were hired by the government and the news channels to sing reassuring ditties about the docility of Iraq's people and their keenness for a US-style "free market" democracy. He also castigates "the cynical anti-Arab hawks (like Richard Perle, Paul Wolfowitz, and Donald Rumsfeld) who dot the Bush administration like flies on a cake" (*FOIRM*, 237). Noble ideals like democracy, liberation, and human rights had been cheapened by these scoundrels and evacuated of any substantive meaning. "What seems so monumentally criminal is that good, useful words like *democracy* and *freedom* have been hijacked, pressed into service as a mask for pillaging, muscling in on territory, and settling scores" (*FOIRM*, 270–271, emphasis in the original). Rather than viewing them as universal principles by which the United States' own far from perfect social, political, and economic arrangements might be evaluated, such words had been twisted into hypocritical synonyms for American power. Yet who could plausibly believe that the United States could not bear to see continue in Iraq the very same abuses it had encouraged unconditionally for decades in the occupied territories and elsewhere, from torture and illegal detention to mass killing and the annexation of territory? And who could tolerate the cynical manipulation of terms like *democracy* and *freedom* by leaders who do everything in their power to prevent their own societies from realizing them? "Who," in short, in Said's prescient words, "asked the United States to take over the Arab world allegedly on behalf of its citizens and bring it something called 'democracy,' especially at a time when the school system, the health care system, and the whole economy in America are degenerating into the worst levels since the 1929 Depression?" (*FOIRM*, 294). In the "American formula," "democracy" is just "a euphemism for the free market" (*FOIRM*, 277).

The "war on terror" was "a cover for a preemptive oil and hegemony war" that would supposedly lead to "a triumph of democratic nation-building, regime change, and forcible modernization *à l'américain*." This was "a purifying war whose goal is to throw out Saddam and his men and replace them with a redrawn map of the whole region" in the manner of the Balfour Declaration and the Sykes-Picot Agreement that partitioned the Ottoman Empire at the end of World War I (*FOIRM*, 246). Once again, Said insists on the continuities in imperialist policy and practice. The reasons for this particular colonial mission are slightly harder to fathom from Said's writings on Iraq, however, for it is not discourse that generates imperialist war but the material interests of the owners and representatives of capital. As one might expect, Said stresses time and again the links between "the Bush administration's semireligious belligerency" (*FOIRM*, 224) toward Iraq and its uncritical support for the tyranny exerted by Israel over Palestinian territory and national life. Here Said blames that domination on the power of the "Israel lobby" in the US Congress and on Israel's role in furthering the US elite's interests in the region. Said rightly (if vaguely) refers to oil supplies and reminds us that support for Israeli colonialism and the elimination of regional threats and competitors is an essential part of US policy in the Middle East. But there is much more to say, of course.

Said died in September 2003. He therefore did not live to see the devastating consequences of what Naomi Klein has called the "experiment in free-market utopianism" undertaken by the Coalition Provisional Authority (CPA), including the protracted insurgency as well as the abominable regime of incarceration and torture imposed on Iraq by the occupying forces.[15] But Said's last articles, from spring of that year, did note the quickly unfolding consequences of the occupation and of Britain's and the United States' total disregard for the obligation imposed on occupying powers by the Fourth Geneva Convention to safeguard a nation's laws and assets until sovereignty might be restored. Said deplores "the coldly calculated destruction of [Iraq's] modern infrastructure," "the looting and burning of one of the world's richest civilizations," and "the totally cynical American attempt to engage a band of motley 'exiles' plus various large corporations in the supposed rebuilding of the country and the appropriation not only of its oil but also of its modern destiny" (*FOIRM*, 269). Said's premonition was subsequently proved correct.

As Klein shows, Iraq was the latest victim to disintegrate under the pressure of a form of violent social and economic "shock therapy."

After the fall of Saddam, the CPA under Iraq's new viceroy Paul Bremer rapidly set about selling state-owned enterprises, sacking half a million state employees, deregulating the labor market, opening borders, and reducing subsidies, taxes, tariffs, and ownership restrictions. "All that remained of Saddam Hussein's economic policies," in the aftermath of this neoliberal "Year Zero," "was a law restricting trade unions and collective bargaining."[16] For Peter McPherson, the CPA's Director of Economic Policy, even the looting of state property was a form of spontaneous private enterprise and therefore, in his view, "just fine."[17] Tom Foley, the Director of Private Sector Development, told a contractor who pointed out that the auctioning off of Iraqi state assets to foreign firms was illegal: "I don't give a shit about international law. I made a commitment to the president that I'd privatize Iraq's businesses."[18] But, of course, Iraq was emphatically not what the CPA ignorantly assumed it to be: "a quiescent terrarium in which to cultivate democracy and a free market," in Rajiv Chandrasekaran's words.[19] As unemployment hit nearly 70 percent the militias in the Shia slums began to assume some of the basic functions of a state that had fled behind the green zone's concrete blast walls. When the military began rounding people up and torturing them, a full-blown civil war broke out. Far from becoming a war that would rapidly pay for itself, a neoliberal utopia that would reap vast profits for US firms and secure strategic control of energy reserves, Iraq became a lawless neoliberal *dys*topia, a land without a functioning state in which, in Klein's words, a simple journey to a business meeting could get you beheaded or burned alive.[20] The plan to remodel Iraq and the entire West Asian region as well as the dreams of a New American Century went up in acrid black smoke. Yet how exactly are we to account for this catastrophe? Said reads the war as the result of greedy corporations and of the discursive and military domination of the Middle East by Western imperialism. That much is now beyond all doubt. A more precise answer to the crucial question about why the invasion was launched, to which Said offers only brief and rather approximate responses, requires that we turn to political economy.

The fact of the matter is that the invasion and occupation of Iraq is literally incomprehensible without an accurate conceptualization of the necessary connection between empire and capital. Imperialism takes different forms, though its violence and cupidity as well as its racist contempt for its victims never change. Said was always at his strongest when identifying and denouncing the long-term continuities between the American imperium and its European predecessors, as he does at length in the final chapters of both *Orientalism* and *Culture and Imperialism*.[21] Said is at his weakest and a world-systems theorist like Arrighi at his strongest in elucidating specific connections between empire and capital. Said does not elucidate the ways in which the invasion of Iraq and the wider war on terror were in fact an effort by the Bush administration to reverse what Arrighi has characterized as the protracted crisis of US political, economic, and military hegemony since the early 1970s. Systemic problems of capital accumulation have bedeviled the US-centered regime of accumulation since then. Arrighi shows that an ingenious redefinition of the United States' central role in the world economy, plus the crushing of organized labor, financialization, and finally the recklessly expansionist "war on terror" have all been failed palliatives to those problems. It was not just oil or American imperial prestige that was at stake in "Operation Iraqi Freedom," Arrighi shows, but the ability of American imperial power to control the profitable expansion of the capitalist world economy. The catastrophe in Iraq is an essential aspect of the long-term relative stagnation of world capitalism. It is one of the many "morbid symptoms" occurring during the "interregnum" between the old order of US hegemony and the potential emergence of a new, more egalitarian, and multipolar order.

Arrighi's wider argument in *The Long Twentieth Century* and *Adam Smith in Beijing* is that the development and expansion of the capitalist world economy has been undertaken since the fifteenth century at the behest of a succession of militarily powerful hegemons, from Italian city-states in alliance with the armed power of Spain and Portugal to the Netherlands, Great Britain, and latterly the United States. The tendency for the accumulation of capital to outstrip what can be reinvested profitably within existing territorial systems results in idle liquidity and productive capacity (*ASB*, 217). New outlets for the profitable investment of surplus capital are found either through imperial expansion or through financialization. Until now, when the limits of existing territorial systems have been reached new hegemons have always come into being with the financial and military capacity to preside over a further period of expansion. That is, of course, an extremely unlikely eventuality at the moment given the overwhelming military supremacy of the United States. Arrighi's model sounds deterministic, but his basic point is that there are intrinsic structural and systemic limits to the long phases or cycles of accumulation in the history of world capitalism. When those limits are approached, the system is faced with political choices, or rather struggles, over the military and financial supremacy of hegemonic power.

Arrighi traces the first challenges to the supremacy of the United States to the profound crisis of profitability that set in around the late 1960s. That crisis was caused mainly by the increasing unsustainability (in the United States and elsewhere) of the postwar compromise between capital and labor, whereby social programs, civil rights struggles, strong trades unions, and historically high wages were squeezing the profits of US businesses (*ASB*, 134). The result was declining profitability in addition to a ballooning trade deficit. A vastly expanded federal budget deficit was brought about by the gigantic costs of the war in Vietnam. The United States was no longer in a position to play the role it had discharged in the years after World War II when it had exported its surplus capital in the form of direct investment to its allies and protégés, not least Japan and West Germany, whose debts it forgave and who also benefited from lavish Marshall Plan aid. From being the world economy's main creditor in the years after the war and thus the main engine of global expansion American political elites took the audacious decision in the early 1970s to turn the United States into the world's main debtor. Previously the United States had recycled its surplus capital in Europe and Asia. That surplus had now disappeared, so it proceeded to massively expand its deficits (aided by Nixon's decision to ditch the gold standard in 1971 and the consequent collapse of the Bretton Woods regime of fixed exchange rates). The United States paid for those deficits by sucking in capital from the surplus economies of Japan, West Germany, South Korea, the Gulf States, and later China. This inflow of capital was used to buy US Treasury bonds and was also turned into investments in US corporations and funneled toward Wall Street where it was turned into dubious new financial instruments as well as the loans to US consumers that kept the mutually beneficial demand for imported commodities so high. This ingenious ruse, effectively to use Wall Street as well as US government debt and consumer demand to recycle the surplus capital of the manufacturing economies in Europe and South and East Asia, has ensured the United States' continuing financial centrality and military supremacy during this period. Those countries that were well-positioned to compete for a share of expanding US demand, like Japan and West Germany and later China, prospered, while others, like most of Africa, did not (*ASB*, 147).

So, the period of world history between the early 1970s and 2008 ought to be seen as part of a "capitalist counter-offensive," as Arrighi calls it, intended partly to counteract relative long-term stagnation and to extend and prolong US control over the world economy (*LTC*, 328). There were three main fronts in that counteroffensive. The first was the massive reversal in the direction of global capital flows analyzed by Arrighi: the funneling of surplus capital into US government debt, household debt, and financial speculation.[22] The second front was a sustained and varyingly successful effort across the globe to free capital from the constraints imposed by the political-economic organization of working classes: from, for example, "burdensome" taxation, employment regulations, legislation protecting the environment, and political and state "interference" in the right of "entrepreneurs" to get a quick return on their investments.[23] The third front witnessed a campaign "to contain, through the use of force, the joint challenge of nationalism and communism in the Third World" (*ASB*, 134) and in so doing frustrate the desire of previously colonized peoples to control their own resources. We are also talking about an imperialist counteroffensive. The generalized war of capital against labor ended both the compromise formations of "democratic capitalism," as Wolfgang Streeck shows,[24] as well as the world-altering aspirations of decolonization. Streeck refers to "a demobilization along the broadest possible front of the entire post-war machinery of democratic participation and redistribution."[25] Imperialist domination had been a key feature of US hegemony after World War II, when the unprecedented expansion of the world economy was combined with a long list of subversions and "police actions" in the Philippines, Korea, Iran, Guatemala, Cuba, Indonesia, and, of course, Vietnam, the ostensible purpose of which was to "contain" the threat of communism but the real purpose of which was to pursue global power and prevent newly independent regimes from taking control of their own resources.[26] The "threat" of communism and revolutionary nationalism has now largely been vanquished. But the sclerosis and later the defeat of the Soviet Union did not diminish the number of punitive "interventions." That list now contains, among others, the names of Chile, Libya, Nicaragua, El Salvador, Haiti, Grenada, and now Afghanistan and Iraq. Imperialism remains an essential attribute of US world hegemony.

Arrighi's work presents the invasion of Iraq in the longer context of the effort by US economic and political elites to counteract a crisis of profitability and defeat the challenges posed by domestic and international opponents. His interpretation of the war is therefore different to Said's in a crucial respect. *Cui bono?*, Said asks. But Arrighi does not present the war as just an opportunistic grab for profits by the oil industry and the military-industrial complex. The war was not the automatic effect of capital, in some crude and deterministic sense. It was instead, as Vivek Chibber also argues, a politically mediated decision, a calculated (albeit doomed) strategic ploy by influential policy makers to prolong US control of the world economy. The Project for the New American Century outlined in the late 1990s by Cheney, Wolfowitz, and Rumsfeld as well as the invasion of Iraq launched when those worthies found themselves in government under Bush Jr. was nothing less than a desperate and unavailing effort to prolong the US-centered phase of world history. The invasion and occupation of Iraq were an "attempt of the declining hegemonic power to resist decline by turning itself into a world state" (ASB, 253) with the geopolitical reach to recycle surplus capital, control the supply and price of oil, deter competitors, and discipline recalcitrant regimes. The president told a cabinet meeting on September 12, 2001 that the bombing of the World Trade Center was a "great opportunity" to extend US control over the strategically important energy reserves of the Middle East and Central Asia under the guise of a "war on terror."[27] The plan for "full-spectrum dominance" was thus a "neoconservative project to counter the economic decline of the United States" (*ASB*, 178), a failed gamble or "tactical move in a longer-term strategy aimed at using military might to establish US control over the global oil spigot, and thus over the global economy, for another fifty years or more" (*ASB*, 190).

But it is possible to exaggerate the influence of the neocons. The invasion of Iraq was not a conspiracy hatched in secret by a motley band of ex-Trotskyist intellectuals and Leo Strauss acolytes. The policy of regime change was vigorously backed by virtually the entire US political establishment, as Chibber shows, the only quibbles being about the timing and the manner of the invasion. The war in Iraq was entirely consistent with elite thinking and policy in the United States. Indeed, the United States has been expanding its power through a global network of military bases since the end of the Cold War. It has assiduously marginalized the institutions of the United Nations at least since its horrified reaction to the adoption by the General Assembly in 1974 of the program for a "New International Economic Order" that sought to aid development in the Global South by stabilizing commodity prices, canceling debts, setting up a system of preferential tariffs that would give Third World manufactures competitive access to First World markets, legitimizing protectionist trade policies, and expanding foreign assistance as a form of reparation for European colonialism.[28] The Clinton administration bombed Iraq in 1998 and Serbia a year later without the approval of the Security Council.[29] The idea that there was anything new about the

Bush administration's militarism, expansionism, contempt for the United Nations and for international law, or even its willingness to countenance torture does not stand up to the slightest scrutiny.

What *was* new, as Chibber observes, and what undoubtedly focused the attention of policy makers in the latter years of the Clinton administration and the early years of Bush's incumbency was the fact that by 2000 increases in the global supply of oil were no longer keeping up with the rate at which demand was increasing. Iraq and the wider region of the Middle East and Central Asia were, therefore, more strategically important than ever. We need to look closely, as Arrighi does, at such long-term political questions of strategy and not only at short-term economic questions of investment and profit. If considerations of profit alone determined US policy then the logical solution would have been to lift the sanctions and permit foreign investment again in Iraq. This was not done because of the obvious and prohibitive "*political* cost – a steady decline in power and leverage for the US in the region."[30] No country, let alone Iraq, a potential rival to the United States' regional allies and the oil producer with the greatest spare capacity, could be seen to emerge from more than a decade of siege and strangulation, especially once Iraq had started to make deals with non-US energy companies and to invoice its oil exports under the United Nations' oil-for-food program in euros. The war in Iraq was, quite simply, a strategic decision by policy makers to extend US control of the world economy. The transformation of the United States into "the biggest debtor nation in world history"[31] had permitted US elites to retain and enlarge their wealth but had also made US financial and military power increasingly dependent on a flow of money and credit from its competitors and even potential victims (*ASB*, 191). In Iraq the United States behaved like a cornered gunslinger, desperately seeking to escape from the constraints placed by economic globalization on its power.

Arrighi sees the Vietnam War as the signal crisis of US hegemony and the war in Iraq as its terminal crisis (*ASB*, 185). The United States had already surrendered much of its moral and political hegemony in the hecatombs and napalmed forests of South East Asia. Its economic hegemony, that is, its claim to be able to lead the world economy in the direction of more prosperity, was forfeited at about the same time. Since then that economic hegemony has rested precariously on dollar seigniorage, the American market of heavily indebted consumers for the manufacturing industries of foreign powers, and Wall Street's ability to direct surplus capital into speculative profits. These are all privileges that the United States is gradually losing. All that is left is the United States' dwindling military hegemony, which is not really a form of hegemony at all but of dominance, one that other powers may soon no longer think it is in their interests to bankroll (*ASB*, 260). Military hegemony is in any case a long-term hindrance as much as it is an advantage because, as Immanuel Wallerstein argues, spending on weapons "diverts capital and innovation away from productive enterprises."[32] The war in Iraq should be seen as an economic attempt to secure new outlets for the profitable investment of surplus capital *and* as a political attempt to use the United States' sole remaining competitive advantage, military force, to ward off threats to its hegemony by securing control of the Gulf oil reserves on which its European and East and Southeast Asian competitors rely.

The murderous fiasco in Iraq was an "abysmal failure" (*ASB*, 7) even in its own terms. It has potentially brought about the breakup of the Iraqi state and enhanced the regional power of Iran. It has further reduced the United States' global standing and exposed the limitations of its military strength. The occupation of Iraq revealed the costly stupidity of the US military machine, its trademark combination of extraordinary destructive force and strategic impotence. Able to inflict mass murder with cluster bombs and phosphorus grenades or, increasingly, with remotely piloted drones that machine is nonetheless totally incapable of holding territory, let alone of building sustainable nation-states. The war and the disastrous occupation announced the beginning of the slow but sure and chaotic collapse of the United States' grand plan to "initiate a new phase of accumulation by dispossession" (*ASB*, 227).

> In sum: far from laying the foundations of a second American century, the occupation of Iraq has jeopardized the credibility of US military might, further undermined the centrality of the US and its currency in the global political economy, and strengthened the tendency towards the emergence of China as an alternative to US leadership in East Asia and beyond (*ASB*, 209).

In short, the defeat in Iraq announced the rout of US plans to extend and consolidate its control of the world economy: "[T]he new imperialism of the Project for a New American Century probably marks the inglorious end of the sixty-year long struggle of the United States to become the organizing center of a world state" (*ASB*, 261).

What Said's vivid commentaries indicate but do not fully elucidate are the connections between capital and empire in the specific context of the

invasion of Iraq. It is undoubtedly true that corporations coveted the
bonanza of oil revenue as well as supply, reconstruction, and security
contracts. US political elites, however, which despite the deeply corrupt
nature of the American political system are by no means identical with US
economic elites, lifted their eyes beyond such immediate concerns to the
even weightier matter of the long-term prospects of a US-centered capitalist world economy. If we are to understand the war in Iraq then we need to
do more than deconstruct the pronouncements of Bush Jr., more than
analyze the consent manufactured by the corporate media, more than
detail the murderous results of the war, more even than heed the advice
that Deep Throat gave to Woodward and Bernstein (to "follow the
money" and so identify the oil men, arms manufacturers, and private
security contractors who had the most to gain from the invasion in the
short term) and to start thinking, as Arrighi and Chibber implore us to do,
about the wider strategic agenda assumed by the United States as the self-
appointed guarantor of the world capitalist system. We need, as David
Harvey has argued, to analyze "capitalist imperialism in terms of the
intersection of these two distinctive but intertwined logics of power," the
economic *and* the political, the logic of capitalists' individual decisions
about the investment and accumulation of capital alongside the territorial
logic of decisions made by relatively autonomous states about strategy and
war.[33] Only political economy, or rather only political economy allied with
Said's characteristic aptitudes for ideology critique and textual analysis, is
capable of answering questions about how and why the invasion of Iraq
took place and what its various implications and consequences might be.
Because the aim of postcolonial studies is to understand imperialism and
thus assist in its overthrow, the discipline cannot afford to neglect those
resources. We need not be restricted by Said's disciplinary loyalties.
Without political economy postcolonial studies will be starved of a worthwhile cause in the twenty-first century. A crisis-stricken political and economic system, not to mention the advancing catastrophe of climate change
and the perennial threat of imperialist war, will not be counteracted by a
sort of ethical or merely text-focused project.

   The invasion of Iraq was wholly consistent with the principal aim of US
foreign policy since World War II of maintaining US control of the world
economy. This has been done by binding defeated foes and emerging
competitors into the US-centered world-system, by skulduggery and military force, the financial centrality of Wall Street, and the attempted "shock
and awe" remodeling of the entire Middle East. Has US hegemony now
been definitively exposed by the rout in Iraq? Has it collapsed along with

the credit pyramid on which the relative prosperity of the 1990s and 2000s relied? Neoliberalism has brought low growth, stagnating living standards, gigantic inequalities within and between states, the transformation of national states in the periphery and now in the center into massively indebted engines of permanent "austerity," epidemics of un- and under-employment especially in the so-called developing world, unsustainable booms and catastrophic crashes, the gutting of public services, not to mention the ongoing annihilation of the ecosphere and the looming mass extinction of species. Everywhere ruling groups hoard power and strip assets under cover of "austerity." Exoduses of peoples from lands laid waste by war, climate change, and extremes of wilfully imposed destitution are forced up against the fortifications erected by a fretful and directionless First World. In the overdeveloped world, a stubbornly unregulated inter-national financial system is blithely inflating new asset bubbles, even as the developing world's self-styled powerhouse economies succumb to political crisis and economic stagnation. As ever, the underdeveloped world endures its perennial agonies of debt and impoverishment. This is the state to which we have regressed, the one depicted by Thomas Piketty's *Capital in the Twenty-First Century*, an "inegalitarian spiral"[34] of low growth and concentrating private wealth, to which the only conceivable solution is a campaign of global redistribution and the herculean imaginative and political effort required to undertake it.

Capital and empire are inseparable, which is not to say that they are impregnable. Untransformed, the faltering US-centered world-system por-tends more aggression and more structural inequality. These are political questions ultimately, not just scholarly ones. Time and again, Arrighi stresses the reality of political and economic struggle. Neoliberalism, for example, was in part, he argues, a reaction to the labor militancy of the 1960s and 1970s that was squeezing profits by driving up wages. "Class war conservatism" managed through violence and other means to push societies across the globe in the direction of more inequality. But political and economic struggle might have propelled those societies in the other direction. The persistent stagnation of the long downturn of 1873–1896, Arrighi notes, appears "to have been due, not just to the intensification of inter-capitalist competition, but also to the effective resistance of workers against attempts to make them bear the costs of that competition, and to the difficulties which capitalists encountered in outflanking that resistance" (*ASB*, 124). Imperialist expansion was the result. The prolonged profit squeeze of those years initiated, as Arrighi notes, the Global North's greatest territorial conquest of the Global South. It is no accident that the later downturn of the 1960s and 1970s "occurred at the tail-end of the greatest wave of decolonization in world history" (*ASB*, 136). We are talking here about economic crises that were also political crises. They unfolded and were fought out and ultimately decided on a global scale. The war in Iraq was the result of a political decision taken by elites to try and prolong US hegemony. So, it is political struggle that is required if we are to countermand that system and replace it.

For all we know, the United States, which spends more on weaponry than the rest of the world, might resort to new forms of imperialist domination and might even convert its massive foreign indebtedness into a kind of protection racket. "There are no credible aggressive new powers that can provoke the breakdown of the US-centred world system," as Arrighi and Beverley Silver note, "but the United States has even greater capabilities than Britain did a century ago to convert its declining hegemony into an exploitative domination."[35] Then again, political struggle might accomplish a very different outcome: "a fundamental departure from the socially and ecologically unsustainable path of Western development . . . This is an imposing task whose trajectory will in large part be shaped by pressure from movements of protest and self-protection from below" (*LTC*, 383). If political economy is the attempt to grasp the relationship between territorial and capitalist logics of power, struggles over the activities of states and struggles over the process of capital accumulation, then it is not just a form of critique but also a device for effecting emancipation. The operations and objectives of global capital, as Ellen Meiksins Wood argues, are mediated by, which means that they are often *dependent* on, the financial, institutional, and frequently coercive capabilities of nation-states. But that dependency also entails great risks and opportunities.

> In particular, [nation-states] are subject to their own internal pressures and oppositional forces; and their own coercive powers can fall into the wrong hands, which may oppose the will of imperial capital. In this globalized world where the nation state is supposed to be dying, the irony is that, because the new imperialism depends more than ever on a system of multiple states to maintain global order, it matters more than ever what local forces govern them and how.[36]

The contradictions of capital certainly precipitate imperialist violence. But there is nothing inevitable about that process. Once such connections are made visible, they are also made available for scrutiny and, hopefully, for practical transformation through struggle. Now *that* is a sufficiently topical and invigorating remit for postcolonial scholarship.

Notes

1 Aijaz Ahmad, *In Theory: Nations, Classes, Literatures* (London: Verso, 1992), p. 1. I am grateful to Bashir Abu-Manneh, David Alderson, and Rena Jackson for their helpful comments on a previous draft of this chapter.
2 Giovanni Arrighi, *The Long Twentieth Century: Money, Power, and the Origins of Our Times* (London: Verso, 2010 [1994]), p. 328. Subsequent references are given in the text after *LTC*.
3 See Gérard Duménil and Dominique Lévy, *Capital Resurgent: Roots of the Neoliberal Revolution*, trans. Derek Jeffers (Cambridge, MA: Harvard University Press, 2004).
4 Giovanni Arrighi, *Adam Smith in Beijing: Lineages of the Twenty-First Century* (London: Verso, 2009), p. 8. Subsequent references are given in the text after ASB. For a discussion of the important question, on which Arrighi tends to equivocate, of what sort of political and economic alternatives are opened by the decline of US hegemony and the current prolonged political and economic crisis in world capitalism, see Richard Walker, "Karl Marx between Two Worlds: The Antinomies of Giovanni Arrighi's *Adam Smith* in Beijing," *Historical Materialism* 18 (2010), 52–73.
5 Edward W. Said, *Power, Politics, and Culture: Interviews*, ed. by Gauri Viswanathan (London: Bloomsbury, 2004), p. 161.
6 V. I. Lenin, *Imperialism: The Highest Stage of Capitalism* (London: Lawrence & Wishart, 1948 [1917]), p. 107.
7 Said, *Power, Politics and Culture*, p. 160.
8 Ahmad, *In Theory*, p. 178.
9 Benita Parry, "Edward Said and Third-World Marxism," *College Literature* 40.4 (2013), 105–126 (107).
10 R. P. Blackmur, "A Critic's Job of Work," in *Language as Gesture* (New York: Harcourt Brace, 1972), pp. 372–399, p. 372.
11 Edward W. Said, *From Oslo to Iraq and the Roadmap* (London: Bloomsbury, 2004), p. 21. Subsequent references are given in the text after *FOIRM*.
12 Edward W. Said, *Covering Islam: How the Media and the Experts Determine How We See the Rest of the World* (London: Vintage, 1997), p. 53.
13 Ibid., p. 49.
14 Edward S. Herman and Noam Chomsky, *Manufacturing Consent: The Political Economy of the Mass Media* (London: Vintage, 1994).
15 Naomi Klein et al., *No War: America's Real Business in Iraq* (London: Gibson Square Books, 2005), p. 17.
16 Ibid., p. 10.
17 Rajiv Chandrasekaran, *Imperial Life in the Emerald City: Inside Iraq's Green Zone* (New York: Vintage, 2007), p. 136.
18 Ibid., p. 143.
19 Ibid., p. 205.
20 Klein, *No War*, p. 38.

21 Edward W. Said, *Orientalism* (Harmondsworth, UK: Penguin, 1985 [1978]), pp. 284–328; *Culture and Imperialism* (London: Vintage, 1994), pp. 341–366.

22 On the increasing "financialization" of the world economy during this period, see Yanis Varoufakis, *The Global Minotaur: America, Europe and the Future of the Global Economy* (London: Zed Books, 2015); John Bellamy Foster and Fred Magdoff, *The Great Financial Crisis: Causes and Consequences* (New York: Monthly Review Press, 2009); and Costas Lapavitsas, *Profiting without Producing: How Finance Exploits Us All* (London: Verso, 2013).

23 See David Harvey, *A Brief History of Neoliberalism* (Cary, NC: Oxford University Press, 2005).

24 Wolfgang Streeck, *How Will Capitalism End? Essays on a Failing System* (London: Verso, 2016), pp. 73–94.

25 Wolfgang Streeck, "The Return of the Repressed," trans. Rodney Livingstone, *New Left Review* II.104 (March–April 2017), 5–18 (6).

26 NSC-68, which Leo Panitch and Sam Gindin describe as the US National Security Council's "master document on the strategy of containment" of 1950, declared that the "overall policy at the present time may be described as one designed to foster a world environment in which the American system can survive and flourish... a policy which we would probably pursue even if there were no Soviet threat." Quoted in Leo Panitch and Sam Gindin, *The Making of Global Capitalism: The Political Economy of American Empire* (London: Verso, 2012), p. 95. The "containment" of the "Soviet threat" thereafter became a euphemism and a pretext for the suppression of every attempt on the part of the peoples of the colonized world to redress what in 1948 George Kennan, the head of the State Department's planning staff, called the "disparity" between the United States' relatively small population and its gigantic share of the world's wealth. Quoted in Noam Chomsky, *Turning the Tide: US Intervention in Central America and the Struggle for Peace* (Boston: South End Press, 1985), p. 48.

27 Milan Rai, *Regime Unchanged: Why the War on Iraq Changed Nothing* (London: Pluto Press, 2003), p. 22.

28 See Michael Hudson, *Global Fracture: The New International Economic Order*, 2nd ed. (London: Pluto, 2005).

29 On the bombing of Serbia, intended not to halt ethnic cleansing (which it expedited) but to boost the "credibility" of NATO and further marginalize the United Nations, see Noam Chomsky, *The New Military Humanism: Lessons from Kosovo* (London: Pluto Press, 1999); and *A New Generation Draws the Line: Kosovo, East Timor and the Standards of the West* (London: Verso, 2000).

30 Vivek Chibber, "American Militarism and the US Political Establishment: The Real Lessons of the Invasion of Iraq," *The Socialist Register 2009* 45 (2009), ed. by Leo Panitch and Colin Leys, pp. 23–53, p. 30, emphasis in the original.

31 Giovanni Arrighi, "The Winding Paths of Capital: Interview by David Harvey," *New Left Review* II.56 (March–April 2009), 61–94 (83).

32 Immanuel Wallerstein, *The Decline of American Power: The US in a Chaotic World* (New York: The New Press, 2003), p. 306.

33 David Harvey, *The New Imperialism* (Oxford and New York: Oxford University Press, 2005), p. 30.

34 Thomas Piketty, *Capital in the Twenty-First Century*, trans. Arthur Goldhammer (London: Harvard University Press, 2014), p. 8.

35 Arrighi and Beverley J. Silver, quoted in *ASB*, 165.

36 Ellen Meiksins Wood, *Empire of Capital* (London: Verso, 2003), p. 155.

Further Reading

This short selection only begins to reflect the wide range of critical and scholarly research on Edward Said and after. See also the footnotes of individual chapters in this volume.

By Edward W. Said

Joseph Conrad and the Fiction of Autobiography (New York: Columbia University Press, 2008 [1966]).

Beginnings: Intention and Method (London: Granta, 2012 [1975]).

Orientalism: Western Conceptions of the Orient (London: Penguin, 1995 [1978]).

The Question of Palestine (London: Vintage, 1992 [1979]).

Covering Islam: How the Media and the Experts Determine How We See the Rest of the World (London: Vintage, 1997 [1981]).

The World, the Text, and the Critic (New York: Vintage, 1991 [1983]).

(with Jean Mohr) *After the Last Sky* (London: Faber and Faber, 1986).

(ed. with Christopher Hitchens) *Blaming the Victims: Spurious Scholarship and the Palestine Question* (London: Verso, 1988).

Musical Elaborations (London: Chatto and Windus, 1991).

Culture and Imperialism (London: Vintage, 1994 [1993]).

Peace and Its Discontents: Essays on Palestine in the Middle East Peace Process (London: Vintage, 1996 [1993]).

Representations of the Intellectual: The 1993 Reith Lectures (London: Vintage, 1994).

The Pen and the Sword: Conversations with David Barsamian (Edinburgh: AK Press, 1994).

The Politics of Dispossession: The Struggle for Palestinian Self-Determination 1969–1994 (London: Vintage, 1995).

Out of Place: A Memoir (London: Granta, 1999).

The End of the Peace Process: Oslo and After (London: Vintage, 2001).

Reflections on Exile: And Other Literary and Cultural Essays (London: Granta, 2001).

Power, Politics and Culture: Interviews with Edward W. Said, ed. Gauri Viswanathan (New York: Pantheon, 2001).

(with Daniel Barenboim) *Parallels and Paradoxes: Explorations in Music and Society* (New York: Pantheon, 2002).

Freud and the Non-European (London: Verso, 2003).

(with David Barsamian) *Culture and Resistance: Conversations with Edward W. Said* (Cambridge, MA: South End Press, 2003).

From Oslo to Iraq and the Roadmap (London: Bloomsbury, 2004).

Humanism and Democratic Criticism (New York: Columbia University Press, 2004).

On Late Style: Music and Literature against the Grain (London: Bloomsbury, 2006).

Music at the Limits: Three Decades of Essays and Articles on Music (London: Bloomsbury, 2008).

Said, Postcolonial Criticism, and Theory

Abu El-Haj, Nadia, "Edward Said and the Political Present," *American Ethnologist* 32.4 (2005), 538–555.

Ahmad, Aijaz, *In Theory: Nations, Classes, Literatures* (London: Verso, 1992).

Ansell-Pearson, Keith, Benita Parry, and Judith Squires (eds.), *Cultural Readings of Imperialism: Edward Said and the Gravity of History* (London: Lawrence and Wishart, 1997).

Aruri, Naseer, and Muhammad A. Shuraydi (eds.), *Revising Culture, Reinventing Peace: The Influence of Edward W. Said* (New York: Olive Branch Press, 2001).

Ashcroft, Bill, and Pal Ahluwalia, *Edward Said: The Paradox of Identity* (London: Routledge, 1999).

Bartolovich, Crystal, and Neil Lazarus (eds.), *Marxism, Modernity and Postcolonial Studies* (Cambridge: Cambridge University Press, 2002).

Bhabha, Homi, and W. J. T. Mitchell (eds.), *Edward Said: Continuing the Conversation* (Chicago: University of Chicago Press, 2005).

Boehmer, Elleke, *Colonial and Postcolonial Literature* (Oxford: Oxford University Press, 2005).

Bové, Paul A. (ed.), *Edward Said and the Work of the Critic: Speaking Truth to Power* (Durham, NC: Duke University Press, 2000).

Brantlinger, Patrick, *Victorian Literature and Postcolonial Studies* (Edinburgh: Edinburgh University Press, 2009).

Brennan, Timothy, "The Illusion of a Future: *Orientalism* as Travelling Theory," *Critical Inquiry* 26 (Spring 2000), 558–583.

Chibber, Vivek, *Postcolonial Theory and the Specter of Capital* (London: Verso, 2013).

Curthoys, Ned, and Debjani Ganguly (eds.), *Edward Said: The Legacy of a Public Intellectual* (Carlton: Melbourne University Press, 2007).

Ganguly, Keya, "Roads Not Taken: Notes on the Legacy of *Orientalism*," *History of the Present: A Journal of Critical History* 5.1 (2015), 65–82.

Hart, William D., *Edward Said and the Religious Effects of Culture* (Cambridge: Cambridge University Press, 2000)

Howe, Stephen, "Edward Said and Marxism: Anxieties and Influence," *Cultural Critique* 67 (Fall 2007), 50–87.

Hussein, Abdirahman A., *Edward Said: Criticism and Society* (London: Verso, 2002).

Iskandar, Adel, and Hakem Ruston (eds.), *Edward Said: A Legacy of Emancipation and Representation* (Berkeley: University of California Press, 2010).

Kennedy, Valeria, *Edward Said: A Critical Introduction* (Cambridge: Polity, 2000).

Lazarus, Neil (ed.), *The Cambridge Companion to Postcolonial Literary Studies* (Cambridge: Cambridge University Press, 2004).

Lazarus, Neil, *The Postcolonial Unconscious* (Cambridge: Cambridge University Press, 2011)

Loomba, Ania, *Colonialism/Postcolonialism* (London: Routledge, 1998).

Macfie, A. L. (ed.), *Orientalism: A Reader* (New York: New York University Press, 2000).

McCarthy, Conor, *The Cambridge Introduction to Edward Said* (Cambridge: Cambridge University Press, 2010).

"Edward Said and Irish Criticism," *Éire-Ireland* 42.1/2 (2007), 311–335.

Moore-Gilbert, Bart, "Beyond *Orientalism*? Culture, Imperialism and Humanism," *Wasafiri* 11.23 (1996), 8–13.

Postcolonial Theory: Contexts, Practices, Politics (London: Verso, 1997)

O'Hanlon, Rosalind, and David Washbrook, "After Orientalism: Culture, Criticism, and Politics in the Third World," *Comparative Studies in Society and History* 34.1 (1992), 141–167.

Parry, Benita, "Edward Said and Third-World Marxism," *College Literature* 40.4 (2013), 105–126.

Poddar, Prem, and David Johnson (eds.), *A Historical Companion to Postcolonial Literatures in English* (Edinburgh: Edinburgh University Press, 2008).

Radhakrishnan, R., *A Said Dictionary* (Oxford: Wiley-Blackwell, 2012).

San Juan, E., "Edward Said's Affiliations: Secular Humanism and Marxism," *Atlantic Studies* 3.1 (April 2006), 43–61.

Sing, Manfred, and Miriam Younes, "The Spectres of Marx in Edward Said's *Orientalism*," *Die Welt Des Islams* 53.2 (2013), 149–191.

Singh, Amritjit, and Bruce G. Johnson (eds.), *Interviews with Edward W. Said* (Jackson: University Press of Mississippi, 2004).

Ertur, Basak, and Müge Gürsoy Sökmen (eds.), *Waiting for the Barbarians: A Tribute to Edward Said* (London: Verso, 2008).

Spanos, William, *The Legacy of Edward W. Said* (Chicago: University of Illinois Press, 2009).

Sprinker, Michael (ed.), *Edward Said: A Critical Reader* (Oxford: Blackwell, 1992).

Veeser, H. Aram, *Edward Said: The Charisma of Criticism* (New York: Routledge, 2010).

Williams, Patrick (ed.), *Edward Said*, 4 vols., Sage Masters in Modern Social Thought (London: Sage Books, 2001).

New Imperial History

Burton, Antoinette, *After the Imperial Turn: Thinking with and through the Nation* (Durham, NC: Duke University Press, 2003).

Bush, Barbara, *Imperialism and Postcolonialism* (London: Routledge, 2006).

Howe, Stephen (ed.), *The New Imperial Histories Reader* (London: Routledge, 2009).

Porter, Bernard, *The Absent-Minded Imperialists: Empire, Society, and Culture in Britain* (Oxford: Oxford University Press, 2004).

MacKenzie, John M., "Edward Said and the Historians," *Nineteenth Century Contexts* 18 (1994), 9–25.

   Orientalism: History, Theory and the Arts (Manchester, UK: Manchester University Press, 1995).

Prakash, Gyan (ed.), *After Colonialism: Imperial Histories and Postcolonial Displacements* (Princeton, NJ: Princeton University Press, 1994).

Political Theory

Anderson, Kevin B., *Marx at the Margins: On Nationalism, Ethnicity, and Non-Western Societies* (Chicago: University of Chicago Press, 2010).

Benner, Erica, *Really Existing Nationalisms: A Post-Communist View from Marx and Engels* (Cambridge: Cambridge University Press, 1995).

Claeys, Gregory, *Imperial Sceptics: British Critics of Empire 1850–1920* (Cambridge: Cambridge University Press, 2010).

Flikschuh, Katrin, and Lea Ypi, *Kant and Colonialism: Historical and Critical Perspectives* (Oxford: Oxford University Press, 2014).

Muthu, Sankar, *Enlightenment against Empire* (Princeton, NJ: Princeton University, 2009).

   (ed.), *Empire and Modern Political Thought* (New York: Cambridge University Press, 2012).

Pitts, Jennifer, *A Turn to Empire: The Rise of Imperial Liberalism in Britain and France* (Princeton, NJ: Princeton University Press, 2005).

Porter, Bernard, *Critics of Empire: British Radicals and the Imperial Challenge* (London: I. B. Tauris, 2008 [1968]).

Index

Bové, Paul, 29–31, 33, 80–83
Bradioti, Rosi, 119
Brecht, Bertolt, 73–77, 84
Bremer, Paul, 197
Brennan, Timothy, 21, 33–34, 50–51
Britain, 37–39. *See also* England
  Marx on, 18–19
  Victorian literature of, 18
British, 5–16, 41–44
  Irish's war with, 60–62
Brontë, Charlotte, 98–102
bull markets, as transnational, 148–152
Burton, Richard, 73–77
Bush, George H. W., 62–67
Bush, George W., 62–67, 129–131
Bush, George W., administration, 183–188.
  See also Iraq war
Byron (Lord), 179–188

Cain, Peter, 8–14
canon, 34–35
capillary theory of power, 75–76
Capital (Marx), 8–14, 98–102
Capital in the Twenty-First Century (Piketty),
  204–205
capitalism
  empire's role in, 19
  imperialism and, 16, 97, 106
Capitalism and Slavery (Williams, E.), 8–14
capitalist counter-offensive, 197–203
Carlyle, Thomas, 98–102, 109
Casanova, Pascale, 129–133, 140–144
cash nexus, 98–102, 109
cause and effect, *Orientalism* as, 37–41
central authority, 25
Césaire, Aimé, 11–12
Chalk, Bridget, 152–154
Chandrasekaran, Rajiv, 197
Chartism (Carlyle), 100, 109
Chibber, Vivek, 15–16, 37–51, 157–159,
  200–202
China, 109, 143–144
Chomsky, Noam, 14, 194–195
CI. *See Culture and Imperialism*
citizenship, 162
civilisational survival, 29–31
Clare, John, 98–102
Clark, Robert, 109
Clarkson, Thomas, 108
clash of civilizations, 54–55, 181–188
classes, 95–97
Cleary, Joe, 15–16, 129–144
Clifford, James, 20
Clinton administration, 200–202
Coalition Provisional Authority (CPA), 196–197

Cobbett, William, 95–97
Cocks, Joan, 15–16, 162
Cold War, 4, 37–39, 129–134
  for Auerbach, 139–140
A Collection of Fiction from Abroad (Lu and
  Zhou), 143–144
Collins, Barbara Bail, 87, 91–95
colonial gaze, 48–49
colonialism. *See also* imperialism
  culture and, 44–48
  imperialism and, 95–102, 108, 151–159
  settler, 8–9
Columbia University, 62–67, 132–133
The Communist Manifesto (Marx and Engels), 1–2
comparative literature, 131–134, 139–144
Congressional Institute, 187–188
Conrad, Joseph, 12–14, 90–91, 148–151.
  *See also Joseph Conrad and the Fiction
  of Autobiography*
  "A Glance at Two Books" by, 22
containment, of Soviet threat, 208
contradictory unity, 156–158
contrapuntal criticism, 11–12, 53, 73–84,
  118–125
  of Darwish, 112–113, 124–125
  rereading of, 88–105
cosmopolitanism, 162–176
counterpoint, 117–124, 184–186
The Country and The City (Williams, R.), 7–11,
  95–102, 108
Covering Islam (Said), 56–57, 194–195
Cowper, William, 98–102
CPA. *See* Coalition Provisional Authority
Crawford, Rachel, 105, 109
critic
  birth of, 20–35
  early, 41–44
  Said as, 20–35, 52
critical consciousness, 69–70
critique, disposition toward, 112–113
Cromer (Lord), 25, 84
culture
  administration and, 73–84
  colonialism and, 44–48
  as imperial, 5–16
  in *Orientalism*, 84
Culture and Imperialism (Said) (*CI*), 3, 5–16,
  23–25, 34–35
  on contrapuntal rereading, 88–91
  Deane on, 53–67
  *Mimesis: The Representations of Reality in Western
  Literature* echoed by, 53–67, 132–134
  Orientalism compared with, 54–57
  overview of, 53–67
  parataxis appearing in, 77–78